THE CARRIER CORPS

The War Memorial, Kenyatta Avenue, Nairobi: (left) Carrier, (center) King's African Rifleman, (right) Arab Rifleman
The Author

Inscription

Swahili	English
Haya ni makumbusho ya askari wa nti za huko Africa waliopigana katika vita pamoja na watukuzi waliokuwa ni miguu ni mikono ya hao askari na watu wote wengine waliotumika wakufa	This is to the memory of the native African troops who fought, to the Carriers who were the feet and hands of the army, and to all other men who served and died.
Mutakapo pigana kwa nti zenu hatta mukifa vijana vyenu watakumbuka majina yenu	If you fight for your country even if you die, your sons will remember your name.

THE CARRIER CORPS

Military Labor in the East African Campaign, 1914–1918

Geoffrey Hodges
Introduction by Elspeth Huxley

Contributions in Comparative Colonial Studies, Number 18

Greenwood Press
New York • Westport, Connecticut • London

Library of Congress Cataloging in Publication Data

Hodges, Geoffrey.
  The Carrier Corps : military labor in the East
African campaign, 1914-1918.

  (Contributions in comparative colonial studies,
ISSN 0163-3813 ; no. 18)
  Bibliography: p.
  Includes index.
  1. Great Britain. Army. East African Forces.
Carrier Corps—History. 2. World War, 1914-1918—
Regimental histories—Great Britain. 3. World War,
1939-1945—Campaigns—German East Africa. I. Title.
II. Series.
D547.C33H63 1986   940.54'12'41   84-22557
ISBN 0-313-24418-9 (lib. bdg.)

Library of Congress Catalog Card Number: 84-22557
ISBN: 0-313-24418-9
ISSN: 0163-3813

First published in 1986

Greenwood Press, Inc.
88 Post Road West, Westport, Connecticut 06881

Printed in the United States of America

The paper used in this book complies with the
Permanent Paper Standard issued by the National
Information Standards Organization (Z39.48-1984).

10 9 8 7 6 5 4 3 2 1

To Gillian, Nicola, Joanna and Beth

Contents

Illustrations

Tables and Maps

(Maps by Lesley Hopkins)

Series Foreword

There was a time when military history was one of the poles around which colonial and imperial studies revolved. The other was constitutional history. Today both fields have taken a seat far to the rear of social and economic history, to the point that overcompensation by neglect should soon create its own reaction. Of course, the military side of imperial history is always tacitly present, for empire, while "about" many things, is certainly about conquest among a few things. Military history as a broad field has been transformed by the work of such scholars as John Keegan, Norman Dixon, or Glenn Gray. Matters strategic and logistical, psychological and ethical, have been closely explored, with much fine new work blurring the traditional lines between military and political history. But this, in turn, has meant that the close study of single units - except in those frequently boring, always celebratory regimental histories produced, more often than not, by individuals committed in advance to the conclusions they argue - seems to have languished doubly over, being neither fashionable nor generally able to embrace larger issues.

I am happy, therefore, to have a short, intriguing, and lively history of the Carrier Corps added to this series. This is not, strictly speaking, military history, although it is about the military. It is labor history, with many overtones of social history, and it contributes new insights to the always romantic story of the conquest of German East Africa. But I like it most because it tells a plain, unadorned story, in sprightly, unadorned prose, and because it tells us of the life and work of the Carrier Corps in homely, rich detail, not omitting to carry the story to the period after the war. The research is broad, the judgments come from an experienced hand, and the insights into colonialism broadly and the people of Kenya specifically are intriguing. This is a happy addition to a series that is now well established and diverse.

Robin W. Winks

Acknowledgments

Research on the Carrier Corps began in 1968; an unwieldy first draft was completed in 1973, but further work was impossible until 1978. A new draft was finished in 1979, and finally accepted by Greenwood Press in 1983; I am most grateful to Robin W. Winks and to James T. Sabin for kindly including it in their Comparative Colonial Studies series: to Lynn Sedlak Flint for all her patience, help and advice as production editor: to Trudy Martin and Karen Powell of SuperService, Ross-on-Wye, for the skilful and expert work which they have put into the camera-ready copy. My warm thanks also go to Lesley Hopkins for her exquisitely drawn maps, and to Wendy Duggan for so successfully typing the first draft.

Researching and writing such a book, and getting it published, would have been totally impossible without the willing and generous help of many other people, which one realises all the more when it is about to be published. First, I am deeply indebted to Mrs. June Knowles for lending me the personal papers of her father, Lieutenant-Colonel O.F. Watkins, C.B.E., D.S.O., who ran the Carrier Corps, and for details of his career. I am very grateful indeed to Mrs. Elspeth Huxley for reading part of the first draft, for valuable suggestions, and for very generously contributing the Introduction. Miss Margaret Elkington very kindly gave me copies of two relevant books, formerly belonging to her father, a pioneer settler.

In Kenya I am especially indebted, first, to Mr. David Sperling, Principal of Strathmore College, Nairobi, under whom I taught for six years, for much initial good advice, and latterly for help with various missing details; to Professor Alan Ogot, who as Head of the History Department at the University of Nairobi helped me with essential advice on sources and official procedures; to Dr. Brian McIntosh for his vital collection of Carrier documents in the Research Project Archives in the University Library; to Dr. Clive Irvine for so generously allowing me a free choice of his superb campaign photographs, which so much enhance this book; to Dr. Ralph Scott, for personal reminiscences, friendly interest and the use of his library. I am very grateful also for the help and interest of Professor

Godfrey Muriuki, Professor Gideon Were, Dr. Kenneth King, Dr. Ben Kipkorir, Dr. Terry Ryan, Dr. Gordon Mungeam and Dr. John Kieran. I am greatly indebted for their kindness and helpfulness to the following: Mr. N.W. Fedha and his staff at the Kenya National Archives, and the librarians and their staffs at the McMillan Library, the University Library, the Wellcombe Library, the East African Standard and the Presbyterian Church of East Africa. I am also grateful for the help and advice of Archbishop Leonard Beecher, Mr. Edward Rodwell, Mr. John Nottingham and Mr. Keith Hardyman.

I owe an immeasurable debt of gratitude to all those friends who helped so willingly with field research, either as eyewitnesses – especially Mr. Jonathan Okwirri, Mr. Josiah Njonjo and Mr. James Beauttah – or as companions, guides, interpreters, translators of tapes and contributors of notes; their names are recorded in the Bibliography and Sources, and without their kindly assistance this book would have been very much the poorer.

In Britain, I am deeply grateful to Dr. John Lonsdale for his guidance both with research, and with writing up the results; to Dr. A.T. Matson, Dr. Anthony Clayton, Dr. Richard Cashmore and Mr. S.H. Fazan for reading several chapters of the first draft, and for helping me freely with their wide knowledge and experience of Kenya and her history; to Mr. H.B. Thomas for some very valuable information and documentary sources, especially the Military Labour Bureau Handbook (after I had despaired of ever finding a copy); to Dr. Andrew Agnew, who read much of the first draft, and helped me to reduce its bulk; to Dr. J. Forbes Munro for some valuable help with sources; to Mr. Charles Richards, for reading the second draft and making some important suggestions; to Professor Terry Ranger for useful comments in the early stages; to Professor George Shepperson for encouraging me to produce a new draft in 1978; to Professor Richard Gray and Dr. Andrew Roberts for welcoming me to a Conference on Africa and the First World War, at the School of Oriental and African Studies, and for their advice; to Professor Roland Oliver for vital help in finding a publisher; to Mr. Rex Collings; to Mr. Jeffery Ede (formerly Keeper of Manuscripts) and his staff at the Public Record Office, who helped me track down much essential material; to Mr. Donald Simpson, Librarian of the Royal Commonwealth Society, and his staff – his advice on sources and books has been immensely valuable; also to the librarians and staffs at Rhodes House (Oxford), Edinburgh University Library, the Church Missionary Society and Central Africa House, both in London (the latter was then the headquarters of the former Universities' Mission to Central Africa, with whom the author worked for five years in Zambia).

Thanks are also due to the archivist at the Tanzania National Archives, and to the librarian at the University of Malawi. I would also like to thank two friends who long ago tutored me in elementary Luganda, and laid the foundations of an enduring interest in Africa: Mr. Ronald Snoxall and Mr. Ernest Sempebwa.

Last but not least, affection and gratitude are due to my wife and daughters for constant quiet encouragement, and for their tolerance towards the unsociable behaviour which authorship seems bound to involve.

Aymestrey, Herefordshire. May, 1986.   Geoffrey Hodges

Introduction

by Elspeth Huxley

Today the bronze statue of three larger-than-life African men
that stands in the heart of Nairobi can easily be overlooked, dwarfed
as it is by the high-rise buildings that sprout like a cluster of pale
and glittering termite-castles all around it. Nairobi encapsulates the
modern Kenya, humming with life, polyglot, looking to the future as
the capital of a proudly independent African state. The statue
commemorates events that happened even before Kenya became a
colony, but was still called the East Africa Protectorate. Two of the
three bronze figures are askaris, one of the King's African Rifles, the
other of the Arab Rifles. The third represents members of the
Carrier Corps which, while non-combatant, suffered heavier casualties
than all other units put together in the East African campaign of the
Great War of 1914-1918. Dysentery, malaria, pneumonia, hookworm
and other ailments carried off many more men than the bullets of
the enemy in that long, gruelling, cruel and costly thrust of British
forces through the whole of German East Africa, as it was then,
from the Kenyan border to that of Northern Rhodesia, where the
elusive German forces did not finally surrender until after the
Armistice in November 1918.

The soldiers carried guns, the carriers everything the soldiers
needed to survive and fight - food, ammunition, medical supplies,
equipment of every kind as well as the carriers' own food and bare
necessities. The men carried all these things on their heads, trudging
through thick bush and wading across swamps and rivers under a
remorseless tropical sun, sleeping in the open, drenched by ferocious
rainstorms, suffering hunger and thirst under the weight of loads
officially limited to fifty pounds, often considerably more. Without
their endurance and achievement, scarcely a shot could have been
fired. It is surprising that the full story of the Carrier Corps has not
hitherto been told. Now Mr. Geoffrey Hodges has amply, painstakingly
and with fervor filled this gap in East African history.

Every military campaign is, I suppose, unique in some way or
another, and this must surely have been unique in its total
dependence on porters carrying loads on their heads, on the numbers
of such porters and on the distances they marched; nearly 180,000

long-serving carriers were recruited from Kenya alone, of whom about 40,000 died. The main reason for this dependence was the tsetse fly. Ever since Hannibal used elephants to march on Rome, and perhaps before, armies normally relied on animals for the bulk of their transport - on horses, mules, donkeys, oxen or camels. In the early days of the East African campaign, animals as well as men were recruited; the first of the volunteer bodies was the East African Mounted Rifles. Horses, oxen and mules made their way south but, when they reached the tsetse belt that stretches across what has become Tanzania, they perished. In one of the thumb-nail sketches which now and then enlivens Mr. Hodges' narrative, there is a grim description of a road - a few military roads had been made by then - thick with dust and made hideous by the foetid stink of innumerable corpses of oxen and mules rotting by the wayside. So there was no alternative to head-porterage.

The formation of the Carrier Corps was a remarkable feat of improvisation. Nothing existed on which it could be based. It was brought into being by officials of the Protectorate's administration (which became the Colonial Service), at their head a District Commissioner named Oscar Watkins. He first came to East Africa in 1908, a classics graduate from Oxford. He had interrupted his university career to fight in the Boer War and had returned to South Africa, serving first in the Mounted Police, then as a clerk in the newly established Municipal Council of Pretoria. It was here that he was greatly impressed by the introduction of finger-printing as a means of giving individual identity to hordes of illiterate tribesmen. He was later to introduce this same system into the Military Labour Corps, saying that it was this alone which made it possible to administer hundreds of thousands of men, of whom only a small fraction of one percent could even sign their names. On his first home leave from East Africa, in 1912, Oscar Watkins returned to Oxford, where he obtained a distinction in the Diploma of Anthropology. This led him to contribute various articles to anthropological journals, and it was these, coupled with his exceptional grasp of Kiswahili, which led him to be seconded to the Carrier Corps.

During the war, nearly half a million men still living in their tribal areas untouched by the influences of the outside world, were recruited through the network of district officers, chiefs and headmen. As commandant of the Carrier Corps, Oscar Watkins arranged for their medical inspection, the provision of equipment and rations, their pay and their deployment along ever lengthening lines of communication in unfamiliar territory far from families and homes which many were never to see again. It was an outstanding achievement.

In the course of Oscar Watkins' duties he, and those under his authority, waged a battle of their own against the military who, in their view, made excessive demands upon the Carriers and, by bleeding their homelands of manpower, weakened the economic structure of the East Africa Protectorate to a dangerous degree. It was to strengthen his position in this battle that towards the end of the war Watkins persuaded his erstwhile boss, Provincial Commissioner John Ainsworth, to join the Carriers with a rank senior to Watkins' own. After the war Ainsworth was to become Chief Native

Commissioner and Watkins his deputy and right-hand man. On Ainsworth's retirement, Watkins became acting Chief Native Commissioner but to his intense disappointment was never confirmed in this post. The "pro-native" reputation which he had gained during the war made him unacceptable in the changed climate of peace.

There is nothing new in this conflict between the civil and the military powers in time of war, and doubtless the military had strong arguments on their side. There was a war to be won. Mr. Hodges is partisan, and his book may be all the better for it. He takes the side of the carriers, who endured so much for so meagre a reward. Throughout the long campaign, despite so much disease, so many deaths, exhausting marches through harsh terrain often on stomachs half-filled with half-cooked food, cheerfulness kept breaking in. A unit raised and commanded by the missionary Bishop of Zanzibar, Frank Weston, faced the task of getting military rations urgently from Bagamoyo to Dar es Salaam. Short of porters, he commandeered all the carts in the town, to be drawn by men, not oxen. For two days and two nights, with a total of two-and-a-half hours sleep, they dragged the laden carts or carried seventy-five pound loads, for the last part of the journey trundling a naval three-pounder gun into the bargain. "It was a very cheerful and grateful crowd that entered Dar es Salaam at the double, with the gun rattling over the road," wrote the Bishop. "The very rattle was welcome, telling of sand and mud left behind."

Perhaps I should intrude an explanation of how I came to write this Introduction. In 1937 I lived for a while in a part of the Kikuyu country, and invited members of the older generation to recall the past before the coming of the European, and their impressions of the impact of that traumatic coming upon their personal fortunes. At that time, men who had been circumcised before Europeans had even been heard of were still in late middle age. I carried my enquiry through to what was then the present, so as to gain a picture - insofar as anyone of an alien culture could hope to do so - of the daily lives of three generations of Kikuyu people, and of how their fortunes had been shaped by the colonial experience. The result was a documentary novel called Red Strangers. Among the events recalled by my informants was the conscription of a number of their young men for service in the Carrier Corps in 1917. Some years later, Mr. Hodges' interest was aroused by reading about this episode, and he resolved to unravel the full story of the Corps. The outcome was this book, in whose conception I am honored to have played a minor and unconscious part.

As with all wars, some elements of progress came out of the muddle and mess. Because white officers and black soldiers and carriers shared the same dangers and hardships, slept side by side on the same hard ground, often ate the same food, the rigid barriers that then divided the races were, for the time being, at least partially dissolved. Sir Philip Mitchell, future Governor of Kenya, noted that his wartime service gave him an insight into African ways and customs, and a respect for those who, as non-commissioned officers, "taught us our business tactfully and sensibly," that influenced him for the rest of his life. On many Africans, wartime experiences had an opposite effect. White men were seen to be vulnerable, fallible and on occasion less brave and inured to hardship than the men they commanded. Europeans who had condemned tribal wars among Africans were seen to be conducting a much more bloody tribal war among themselves. In other words, the war dispelled illusions entertained on both sides, and so perhaps enabled the two races to arrive at a less distorted view of each other's qualities.

After the askaris and carriers returned to their homes, political activities began to foment. Political bodies which were to play a crucial part in future developments were formed, notably in the districts of Kiambu and central Nyanza. But it was not, as Mr. Hodges shows, in the main the returned soldiers and carriers who formed and organised these associations, though they may have given them passive support. A new generation of literate young men (as yet few, if any, young women) had begun to emerge from the schools. Their newfound skills were too useful, and too rare, to be wasted in the bush, and most of them spent the war as clerks and the like in Kenya's still embryonic towns. Harry Thuku, for instance, a founding father of African nationalism, was a printer on the staff of a Nairobi newspaper. So returned combatants and carriers did not form the spearhead of political advance. Nevertheless the campaign, like the war to come but to a much lesser extent, did loosen the tribal bonds, take men to distant unknown regions, teach them new things, arouse new questions in their minds and so begin, or at any rate accelerate, the germination of political ideas among the African people. But the motivation behind the political movements that followed the war was fear - fear, among the Kikuyu especially, that European settlers would take away their land.

"Happy is the nation," it had been said, "that has no history." East African historians would not agree. Every nation, of course, has its history, but much of the interior of East Africa's history has not been recorded. Since independence, a search for a historical identity has been greatly intensified; books, theses, academic studies have proliferated and will continue to do so. Mr. Hodges has quarried in a hitherto neglected deposit, and students of East African history will be grateful to him for his thorough, scholarly and compassionate book.

Abbreviations

AIM	Africa Inland Mission
AR	Annual Report
BEA	British East Africa (unofficial title of EAP)
CAB	Cabinet Office Papers
"Carbels"	Belgian Congo Carrier Corps (recruited in Uganda)
CCS	Central Committee of Supply
CDO	Carrier Depot Officer
CGL	Central Government Library, Nairobi
Ch. S.	Church of Scotland
Ch. Sec.	Chief Secretary
Cmd.	Command (Parliamentary) Paper
CMS	Church Missionary Society
CNC	Chief Native Commissioner
CO	Colonial Office
DAAQMG	Deputy Adjutant and Quartermaster General
DADT	Deputy Assistant Director of Transport
DC, ADC	District Commissioner, Assistant DC
DML	Direct of Military Labour
DMS	Director of Medical Services
DST	Director of Supply and Transport
EACC	East Africa Carrier Corps
EAP	East Africa Protectorate
EAS	East African Standard

EATC, CS	East Africa Transport Corps, Carrier Section
EUL	Edinburgh University Library
GEA	German East Africa
GMS	Gospel Missionary Society
HMG	His Majesty's Government
JAH	Journal of African History
KAR	King's African Rifles
KMJ	Kenya Medical Journal
KMV	Kikuyu Mission Volunteers
KNA	Kenya National Archives
Leader	The Leader of British East Africa
MCL	Military Commissioner for Labour
MLB	Military Labour Bureau
MLC	Military Labour Corps
MO, SMO	Medical Officer, Senior MO
NAU/SMP	National Archives of Uganda, Secretariat Minute Paper
NCO	Non-Commissioned Officer
NFD	Northern Frontier District
NFRO	Native Followers Recruitment Ordinance, 1915
NLC	Native Labour Commission, 1912-1913
OG	Official Gazette
Ords. and Regs.	Ordinances and Regulations (EAP)
PC	Provincial Commissioner
PEA	Portuguese East Africa
PRB	Political Record Book
PRO	Public Record Office (London)
PWD	Public Works Department
RCSL	Royal Commonwealth Society Library (London)
RPA	Research Project Archives (Department of History, University of Nairobi)
Sec. Circ.	Secretariat Circular
SSC	Secretary of State for the Colonies
TNA	Tanzania National Archives
TNR	Tanganyika Notes and Records
UMCA	Universities' Mission to Central Africa
UTC, CS	Uganda Transport Corps, Carrier Section

WO	War Office
WP	Watkins Papers
WR	Watkins Report
ZMCC	Zanzibar Mission Carrier Corps

THE CARRIER CORPS

Chapter 1
The Historical Problems

"Watukuzi waliokuwa ni miguu ni mikono ya hao
askari."
"The Carriers who were the feet and hands of the
army."
> (Rudyard Kipling, the Nairobi War Memorial)

Most people in East Africa have relations, or know old men, who
served in the Carrier Corps, raised for the conquest of German East
Africa. Suburbs of Nairobi, Mombasa and Dar es Salaam are called
"Kariakor" or "Kariakoo," named after the Carrier Depots which
stood on those sites. The War Memorials are familiar, with their
bronze inscription composed by Rudyard Kipling, in English, Swahili
and Arabic, commemorating the King's African Rifles, the Carrier
Corps and the Arab Rifles. (1)
   Shortly before leaving Kenya, I met a Carrier veteran, sitting by
the War Memorial on Kenyatta Avenue, Nairobi, named Juma Kihara.
No doubt he was there accidentally, but to me his presence there
was significant and moving. He came from Nyeri, and seemed to
have served as a Carrier for a long time; his wooden leg was the
result not of a war wound, but of an accident some years later.
There he sat, survivor of a terrible experience which had involved so
many of his generation. The saga of the Carrier Corps is the story
of hundreds of thousands of humble men, of their fortitude and
suffering in a cause which was not their concern; of the agony of
their families when they were taken away, one in ten never to
return, and many who did, broken in health and spirit, only to
succumb to their sufferings.
   Several questions require answers. First, did the political unrest
in Kenya in the early 1920s result directly from the war, or not?
This demands a brief summary of affairs before, during and after
the war. Secondly, what effects did war experience have on
individuals, politics and race relations after the war? Thirdly, why
was this war fought at all? Fourthly, what part was played by
Christian missions and their adherents, and with what results?
Finally, what did the civil and military authorities learn from it?
   Though a vast amount can be found out, there is remarkably
little about the Carrier Corps in the copious literature on the
campaign. Typical of the attitude to the Carriers is that of the
historian of the Nigerian Brigade, who tells us more than most other
authors, and gives interesting accounts of the appalling transport

problems as well as of the murderous fighting in which the Nigerians were involved. But in an appendix listing the units which participated in the campaign he omits one which was bigger than all the rest put together, and without which the campaign could never have taken place - the Military Labour Corps. (2) But a semi-official history of the imperial war effort as a whole, which came out in 1924, retails official statistics and accounts of military labor in all the territories which provided carriers. (3)

The only well-known book published between the wars which says much about the Carriers is based upon oral evidence. Mrs. Elspeth Huxley's Red Strangers is a novel about Kikuyu life with a deeply sympathetic approach, which was in fact my own original introduction to the story of the Carrier Corps. (4)

The first volume of the official history of the campaign came out in 1941, and says much about transport and carriers, though as it ends in 1916, it has little on statistics. (5) The second volume was never published, but the materials for it are essential reading for all aspects of the campaign. (6) Little use seems to have been made of these papers so far; they may not have been available for two short histories of the campaign which came out in 1963, but the author of a third popular account, published in 1974, had not this excuse; he says hardly anything about the Carriers, and then only about half way through. (7) The story of the Carriers is inseparable from that of the African troops whom they served, and whose importance grew steadily with the retirement of the Indians and South Africans; by the beginning of 1917 it was clear that African soldiers could stand the climate much better than any others. Here the student is greatly helped by an official history of the King's African Rifles, a mine of information about East African askari in two world wars, and many minor ones as well. (8)

Official unpublished sources have lately become available, with the assembling of provincial, district and secretariat archives in the East African capitals, though the Kenya Secretariat archives up to 1938 were destroyed in a fire that year. One document, the "Watkins Report" on military labor, has become familiar to history students at the University of Nairobi, and can also be seen in London. (9) There have as a result been several articles on aspects of Carrier history. (10) A major work has also appeared on labor in Kenya, with a chapter on the Carriers' war. (11)

A full account of the Carrier Corps is imperative; the copious material available has made it possible, and the subject is important, with the growth of interest in African history as a whole, and in the effects of the two world wars on Africa in particular. This book is not a regimental history, but an attempt to set the Carrier story against its human and political background, with special reference to Kenya where most of the work was done. Further books from the points of view of other territories are now doubtless on the way. This one owes much to the veterans of Great War, who were alive and willing to tell their stories fifteen years ago.

NOTES

1. TNA, Secr. W1/A/23428, "Askari Statue, Dar es Salaam" (RPA, War F/1/3 1).

2. W.D. Downes, With the Nigerians in German East Africa (London: Methuen, 1919), Appendix B.

3. Charles Lucas, The Empire at War (London: OUP, 1924), vol. IV.

4. Elspeth Huxley, Red Strangers (London: Chatto and Windus, 1939), Ch.7.

5. Charles Hordern, History of the Great War: Military Operations, East Africa (London: His Majesty's Stationary Office, 1941), vol. I, 1914 to 1916.

6. PRO, CAB 44/3-10, and CAB 45/6-74.

7. Leonard Mosley, Duel for Kilimanjaro (London: Weidenfeld and Nicholson, 1963); Charles Miller, Battle for the Bundu (London: Macdonald, 1974), 256-8; Brian Gardner, German East (London: Cassel, 1963).

8. H. Moyse-Bartlett, The King's African Rifles (Aldershot: Gale and Polden, 1956).

9. "Report by Lieutenant-Colonel O.F. Watkins, C.B.E., D.S.O., Director of Military Labour" (typescript, Nairobi, 1919) - short title.

10. Donald C. Savage and J. Forbes Munro, "Carrier Corps Recruitment in the British East Africa Protectorate 1914-1918," JAH, 7, 2 (1966), 313-342; the following from JAH, 19, 1 (1978), a special number on "Word War I and Africa," following a conference on that subject in March 1977 at the School of Oriental and African Studies: David Killingray, "Repercussions of World War I in the Gold Coast," 39-59; Melvin E. Page, "The War of thangata: Nyasaland and the East African Campaign, 1914-1918," 87-100; G.W.T. Hodges, "African Manpower Statistics for the British Forces in East Africa, 1914-1918," 101-116.

11. Clayton, Anthony, and Donald C. Savage, Government and Labour in Kenya, 1895-1963 (London: Frank Cass, 1974).

Chapter 2
Politics in the East Africa Protectorate

> "Your feet are set on strange paths; they travel away from the knowledge that has been handed down to us from our ancestors."
>
> (Irumu to his sons) [1]
>
> "I went away during the famine of the maize bags ... I started building the railway from Mombasa up to Uganda."
>
> (Mwanyula Bikatana, Giriama, 1970) [2]

African politics in post-war Kenya can be traced back even before the colonial era. The British conscripted over 200,000 men for the war in the East Africa Protectorate alone, and bought compulsorily vast numbers of livestock, with virtually no African resistance, which would have been impossible without the aid of African headmen. Four questions need answering: first, how were African politics developing when the Europeans arrived? Secondly, how did this affect the setting-up of British rule? Thirdly, how did European demands for labor and land affect the Africans? Fourthly, what effects did the missions have? [3]

AFRICAN POLITICAL INITIATIVES

The European settlement was not relevant to tribal movements which were already in progress. The Maasai were still ranging over much of the steppe lands of modern Kenya and northern Tanzania; the agricultural highlands were held by the Kikuyu, Kamba, Nandi and others. But the Maasai were already in decline, owing to cholera, smallpox, rinderpest, clan feuds, and the vigour of their opponents; in 1986 the pioneer administrator John Ainsworth thought that the Maasai were losing their ability to resist their neighbours. [4]

Since about 1820 the Kamba had been moving nearer to the coast, because their trade was increasingly connected with that of the coast, and because their rather dry country was prone to famine. Though the Kamba trade was bypassed by the main Swahili caravan route, the stations which the Swahili established from Taveta to north Nyanza led inevitably to political developments among the people concerned. The British road and railway were based upon African trade routes. [5]

The southward movement of the Kikuyu into Kiambu was the most momentous of these developments, preceding the coming of the Europeans. It led not only to war with the Maasai, but also to trade and intermarriage. The Mathenge or Gatherimu clan became related to the Maasai oloiboni Mbatian and his son Lenana. (6) The Kikuyu now controlled the future hub of Kenya, on the British route to Uganda. On the lower edge of Kiambu, with its abundant food supplies, the British built their future capital of Nairobi. Consequently the local Kikuyu had earlier access than most other highland people to European and Asian trade and industry, with opportunities to learn, either as labor or at mission schools. They took full advantage of this although they had suffered severely from the disastrous famine and smallpox epidemic of 1898 and 1899, having to abandon much newly gained land (which the Europeans consequently thought was vacant). The Kikuyu soon recovered, thanks to their resilience and their system of mixed agriculture. (7)

These upheavals altered the political systems of many tribes. Though there were no hereditary chieftainships camparable to those in Uganda, by 1900 men were undoubtedly appearing whose personalities placed them above the traditional councils of elders. There were religious experts and diviners, like the Luo jobilo, the Maasai oloiboni and the Nandi orkoiyot. Others arose for more worldly reasons: military skill, a flair for trade, or linguistic ability, any of which gave them an advantage in dealing with other tribes, the Swahili or the Europeans. Several such men arose among the Kikuyu, though their power must not be exaggerated. Wangombe of Nyeri, recognised as Paramount Chief by the British, was half Maasai, speaking that language fluently. In north Nyanza, Mumia built up his power with the aid of Maasai mercenaries. (8) Others who were to be equally helpful to the British were Karuri in Fort Hall (now called Muranga), and Kutu in Embu. (9)

Other clan groups were producing more centralised systems of government. Though the status of the orkoiik among the Nandi was no more a true chieftainship than was the Maasai oloiboni, from which it was derived, the Nandi orkoiyot had great prestige among their people. (10) Near the coast, the Digo had been developing a limited chieftainship for some centuries under Muslim influence; their neighbours the Giriama and Duruma had, however, kept their traditional kambis, councils which were much weakened by the famine of 1899 – the famine of the maize bags. (11)

The Europeans had nothing to do with these changes, which may be roughly compared with events among the Nguni clans in Natal before the rise of Chaka. But the British were to make use of the new men, who in their turn benefited by cooperating with the colonial government.

AFRICAN POLITICS AND BRITISH ADMINISTRATION

The British had to find agents through whom to govern, though they knew little of tribal politics. To some extent they imposed chiefs where formerly there had been none. Authority was held by three types of men. Some used their power and authority against the British, like Koitalel of Nandi, or Waiyaki of Dagoretti. Some who already held power helped the British, like Mumia, Lenana or Wangombe. But some owed their rise entirely to the British, like Kinyanjui wa Gatherimu, called wa Nugu by his detractors, meaning son of the baboon. "A youth absolutely without property," he made himself indispensable as interpreter and transport organiser, and was paramount chief of Dagoretti until his death after the war. (12)

In Machakos District, officers were very puzzled by the absence of anyone with real authority. Petty headmen abounded, who "owed their position solely to their success in imposing on our ignorance." (13) In 1893, John Ainsworth conducted a punitive expedition into the Kilungu Hills, until he realised that he had been deceived by a Machakos interpreter who had accused the Kilungu people of disobedience. (14) An upcountry man who knew some Swahili could put his people in touch with the white man, and so gain political power. Probably a headman's most important duty from the days of the Uganda road to the post-war years was to supply labor. The Carrier Corps represented the climax of this period.

In Nyanza, for example, Ogada Ondiek supplied labor when Port Victoria was the anticipated terminus of the Uganda Railway, because he spoke some Swahili, thus usurping the place of the real chief, Opiyo. In 1915, however, he was imprisoned for embezzling fines imposed on the relatives of runaway carrier recruits. (15) Another self-made man who forced his way to the top was Mwirigo wa Irimu of Nyeri, the original of Muthengi in Red Strangers who accepted British rule after being defeated. In 1914 he was deputy paramount chief of Nyeri; "powerful, cunning and relentless as an enemy," he acquired many wives and goats, and the land of others, including his own brother's. (16) By contrast Kutu, his neighbour in Embu, served the British but was deposed in 1917 for causing the District Commissioner to quarrel with a labor recruiter. (17)

The first generation of headmen, being illiterate, could not collect taxes. To fulfil labor quotas, they used their relations as tribal retainers or "spearmen." Compulsory labor was used on roads and bridges within the locations, or registered for work outside the district. Chiefs soon became unpopular, because moral or physical coercion was really inevitable, though in theory labor was only "encouraged" to come out. Both headmen and ordinary witnesses told the Native Labour Commission (NLC) that livestock and other property would be confiscated if orders to work were disobeyed. In Nyanza the "paternal curse" was used, it being impious to disobey one's father. Ainsworth, however, believed that compulsion would finally become unnecessary. (18) Meanwhile chiefs had no alternative but to use various forms of moral suasion. They included men of real ability who took the only realistic course open to them, even if it has been fashionable to refer to them pejoratively as "loyalists." Examples abound of the way British administration depended on headmen, especially for the recruiting of labor, which was to reach such grim proportions in wartime.

AFRICAN POPULATION MOVEMENTS AND LABOR DEMANDS

European and Asian demands for labor caused many Africans to leave their homes and go far away, some to settle permanently at their new places of work. First came the demand for porters, who before 1891 were mostly Swahili and Zanzibari, until the Sultan forbade his subjects to work outside his dominions, which included Seyidie, the ten-mile-wide coastal strip of the East Africa

Protectorate. (19) Upcountry men now had to be recruited for the vital Uganda caravans. Next, the building of the railway, and the problems caused by the Sudanese mutiny, led to increased labor demands between 1986 and 1899, the very years when famine and smallpox were to cause such distress.

These calamities probably drove many out to seek a new life, as the story of Mwanyula Bikatana shows. He lived at Kaloleni in Giriama, and was about twenty at the time of the "famine of the maize bags." He left home and worked on the railway. When it reached Kisumu, he and others went into German territory for work; he settled in Unyamwezi, famous for its caravan porters. He was conscripted, and served as an ammunition carrier with von Lettow till he was taken prisoner by the British in Portuguese East Africa (PEA). Finally he returned home after the war. (20) The implications of this odyssey, if the details are substantially correct, are fascinating. If a member of a tribe so home-loving as the Giriama developed such a desire to break loose and see the world, very many others must have done the same, as much through the human desire for adventure as from the direct or indirect pressure of the Europeans.

Labor was not available in Seyidie to satisfy the growing demands after 1900. The climate is hot and enervating, the population small and, having enough food for its needs, normally had no incentive to work for the Europeans. (21) Up to 70 percent of the labor came from outside the province; by 1914 large numbers of Kikuyu, Luo, Luyia and immigrants from German territory were working on the railway, the plantations, the waterworks, the Kilindini Docks, in government and domestic service. Many went unwillingly; railway ballast-breaking, the waterworks and sisal plantations (where the spines cause septic wounds), all had a bad reputation.(22) But though many immigrants settled permanently, this did not solve the labor problem; by 1912 the shortage was serious, and in 1914 the District Commissioner of Malindi was gloomy about the prospects. The Giriama did not want to work, and the "famine of the maize bags" had reduced the authority of the kambi.(23) Pressure was tried to induce the Giriama to work, and also to stop their expansion north of the Sabaki River. The uprising which followed in August 1914 was sparked off by attempts at carrier recruiting; the tribe was subsequently forced to pay a fine of military porters.(24)

There is, however, no doubt that many men went to work voluntarily, especially from the more prosperous areas, as trade increased consumer demands. From Nyeri, members of the Njaange riika (circumcision group or age-grade of 1901, meaning "Roam") went to Nairobi to work, as the railway construction proceeded towards the Rift Valley. They returned with calico cloth which became fashionable at dances. Elijah Kaara, of the Mbauni riika ("Pound") of 1914, also wanted this cloth, so worked in Nairobi as a kitchen boy. He was a clerk at the Nairobi Carrier Depot, and after the war became a political organiser.(25) Josphat Njoroge worked on a farm in Kiambu, but left because the European only gave him Rs.3, whereas the others were getting Rs.4. He then worked as an assistant cook for another European for six months, then went home to be circumcised. In 1917 he served with the Kikuyu Mission

Volunteers as a carrier.(26) This agrees with what one of Kinyanjui's retainers told the Native Labour Commission, that though men disliked going in large gangs to unknown employers, they would make individual bargains with farmers.(27)

The desire of the Giriama to expand conflicted with European labor needs, but the movement of the Kikuyu onto farms in Kiambu and the Rift Valley did the opposite. They provided resident labor as tenants-at-will (ahoi) or as squatters. They also posed a serious problem for government, as "a large, landless population which will not obey the tribal law and will become a menace to the good order of the country."(28) Wartime carrier recruiting was further to encourage this movement away from tribal control, both into the Rift Valley and to a lesser extent into Ukambani. There was every reason both before and during the war to escape from the headmen and their bullying retainers into the Rift Valley, where there was no tribal control, but more grazing and firewood than in Kiambu, and plenty of cheap goats and sheep to be bought from the Maasai.(29) But European settlement, on occupied or empty land, caused real hardship and grievance to the Kikuyu, Nandi, Kipsigis and above all to the Maasai, who lost more land than any other tribe. In the long run, European settlement has helped to extend the lands of the Kikuyu very greatly, since they now hold land which was formerly not theirs, and on which they squatted when the white men had taken it over. But loss of land was causing deep resentment in Kiambu before the war.(30) Fear of further losses was felt, not only in Kiambu but also in Muranga (Fort Hall) and Nyanza. News of alienation in Nandi, for instance, caused some alarm in Uyoma location; in 1912 Sergeant Asino of the East Africa Protectorate Police warned his brother Jonathan Okwirri and other relations about it.(31) But neither here, nor in any part of Muranga except the lower fringes, can the land in fact have been in serious danger; nevertheless men like James Beauttah, who like Okwirri was of the first literate generation, were able to take note of settler intentions openly declared in the press.(32)

Compulsory labor was disliked, and the methods used were resented, but the advantages of wages were apparent. But if people feared for their land, they would try to protect it. Here were powerful grounds for political action which were in no way due to the war.

THE MISSIONS, POLITICS AND WELFARE

By 1914 there was a generation of young men, mission-educated, who could understand the implications of settler demands. The churches brought new political as well as religious ideas. They preached the doctrine of hard work. They competed with traditional authorities and beliefs. They offered intelligent men new prospects. They also kept the European conscience, and were the main critics of injustice. They pioneered the educational and medical services. In many ways they agreed with district officers about the feeding, treatment and housing of labor. The Protestant churches were making an experiment called the Kikuyu Movement, because conferences were usually held at the Church of Scotland Mission at

Kikuyu, or Thogoto. During the mass levy in 1917, they were to raise their own force, the Kikuyu Mission Volunteers.

The mission schools provided even greater incentives for young men to break away from home and tradition than did European colonisation. In 1912, at a baraza (assembly) of headmen in Dagoretti, the Assistant District Commissioner Mervyn Beech, was told that young men not only ran away from homes to farms, but also to missions, thus shirking tribal obligations. While still expecting their fathers to pay dowries for wives, they ceased to bring them money, thinking only of themselves.(33) Though elders frequently deplore the fecklessness of youth, there can be no doubt that the missions helped, through their teaching and provision of a range of new skills, to reduce the dependence of the young men on their traditional societies; they trained a generation who were to protest against European rule in general, and against its African agents in particular.

But Africans also reacted against mission teaching before there was any organised political protest. On the one hand, there were traditionalist cults like that of Siotune in Ukambani, or like Mumboism in South Nyanza.(34) On the other hand, there was the Nomia Luo Mission Church, begun by John Owalo in 1910, which in a few years had 10,000 adherents.(35) Africans resorted to their own spiritual resources "because their concepts of peace, good government and life were rudely shattered by colonial rule."(36) The war must have strengthened this feeling, but never to the extent of armed resistance, as in Nyasaland with John Chilembwe's uprising in 1915.(37) The step from religious to political protest is never a long one.

Among the Kikuyu, Jomo Kenyatta is naturally the best known of the first mission educated generation. He was baptised in 1914 at the Scottish mission, Kikuyu, where he had been educated since 1907.(38) James Beauttah left home in 1904, first for Freretown, the Church Missionary Society (CMS) school near Mombasa, and then to the school for telegraphists near Rabai. Harry Thuku went to the Gospel Missionary Society (GMS) school at Kambui, and later became a compositor for The Leader; a colleague there, educated by the CMS at Kabete, was Josiah Njonjo.(39)

Central Nyanza was ahead of these other areas, partly because the Luo chiefs valued good relations with the missions more highly than did Mumia or Wangombe. The CMS schools at Maseno and Kaimosi produced educated converts called jangwana, a Luo variant of the Swahili wangwana (freeman). Consequently, the first mission-educated chief in the East Africa Protectorate was oppointed in this area in 1913; Mathayo Onduso had led a strike at Maseno as early as 1906, yesterday's rebel becoming today's ruler. Though not successful as a chief, he was a pioneer in literate African advancement; three of his classmates also became chiefs, as did a fourth, Jonathan Okwirri, many years later.(40)

The missions fully agreed with most officials and some settlers about the need for better medical and welfare conditions for labor. Dr. H. R. A. Philp, who founded the Church of Scotland mission at Tumutumu, near Nyeri, told the Native Labour Commission that 40 percent of the people north of the Tana River were unfit for labor; government's failure to drain the swamps on the Fort Hall-Nairobi road meant that many immigrant workers caught malaria and died by the way. (41) Norman Leys, a government doctor, agreed with Philp about the diseased state of the people, and with Ainsworth about the need for a free flow of labor. (42) Closely linked with health and hygiene were dietary and social matters, about which officials like Ainsworth and O.F. Watkins, and missionaries like A.R. Barlow, were much better informed than most settlers. African menfolk, said Barlow, were not idle, but did the heavy work like clearing bush, building huts and herding cattle. (43) However, one of the more enlightened settlers quoted Ainsworth:

> So long as there continues an idea that any wretched hut and a minimum amount of mealie and matama meal is good enough for a native and where, as is the case in the Highlands, a black man from hot Kavirondo [Nyanza] is turned out into the early morning and worked nearly all day and then has to sleep in a leaky or wind-exposed hut with possibly one thin blanket to cover him, with no one to cook his food or bring him food or water after the day's toil is done, and with no one to take an interest in him, then the labour must naturally suffer. (44)

In other words, there was, before the war, much blind ignorance of African needs, which could only have been amended by an authoritative Native Affairs Department, which Ainsworth, other officials and the more enlightened settlers recommended. (45) Ainsworth thought that the white public needed education in African life and welfare. (46) When the war began, there was no civil authority to lay down ration scales, or rules for the management of labor; ironically, the first body to do this was the Military Labour Bureau, set up in 1916 to administer the growing army of military followers. This drew extensively on South African experience, in view of the prevailing ignorance in the East Africa Protectorate. The last word may be left with Ainsworth: the only way of getting "the more ignorant white" to treat labor decently was to see that he got none until he had learned to do so. (47)

This brief political survey suggests two conclusions. First, the seeds of African opposition to European dominance were already beginning to germinate. Secondly, there was no foundation on which to build the Carrier Corps when the war came, in the absence of any government department with authority to lay down standards of African welfare. Nor was there any military basis, as will be shown, though fortunately there was the necessary professionalism among the civil authorities in East Africa to make up for military deficiencies. But the officers who ran the Carrier Corps were to have a terrific uphill struggle to establish the standards which they knew to be essential.

NOTES

1. Huxley, Red Strangers, 231.

2. Interview at Kaloleni, Giriama, 24 Jan. 1970.

3. Bethwell A. Ogot, ed., Hadith 3 (Nairobi: EAPH, 1971), 82-102: G. W. T. Hodges, "African Responses to European Rule in Kenya (to 1914)," the basis of this chapter.

4. V. Harlow, E.M. Chilver and A. Smith, eds., History of East Africa (Oxford: Oxford University Press, 1965), vol. II, chapter 1: D. A. Low, "British East Africa: the Establishment of British Rule, 1985-1912," 1-5.

5. KNA, 8/157, Rabai AR 1912-1913, on Kamba settlement nearer the coast after a famine "50 years ago."

6. Harry Thuku, ed., K. J. King, Autobiography (Nairobi: Oxford University Press, 1970), 4, 58; the Njonjo family also have Maasai blood. Talk with Mr. Josiah Njonjo, 15 Dec. 1970.

7. KNA, 75/47, "Ukamba Inward" 1898-1899; DC/MKS/4/11, 25 percent died in Machakos and Kitui, 15 percent in Kiambu.

8. J. Kenyatta, My People of Kikuyu (Nairobi: new ed., OUP, 1966), 33-50; KNA, DC/NYI/6/1, Nyeri PRB: for Mumia, Gideon S. Were, A History of the Abaluyia of Western Kenya (Nairobi: EAPH, 1967), 125-126.

9. KNA, DC/FH/4/3, for Karuri (Fort Hall headmen 1912-1920); PC/CPI/5/1, Embu PRB, for Kutu.

10. A. T. Matson, Nandi Resistance to British Rule 1890-1906 (Nairobi: EAPH, 1972), 28-32.

11. KNA, DC/MSA/8/2, Mombasa PRB, note on Digo; 46/1074, "Opposition of Duruma to Recruiting 1917."

12. KNA, DC/KBU/3/25, Kiambu PRB, part 2.

13. KNA, DC/MKS/4/1, Machakos PRB 1, part 1, notes by K.R. Dundas.

14. Notes on Mulovi and Mbwika Kivandi kindly given by Ezekiel Musau, who assisted at an interview with his grandfather Mbwika, 3 Oct. 1970, Kilungu, Machakos.

15. KNA, DC/CN7/1, Central Nyanza PRB: J. M. Lonsdale, draft political history of Western Kenya, 210. I am grateful to the author for a view of this.

16. Huxley, Red Strangers, 158-180, 250-252, 378-384; also letter from Mrs. Huxley to the author 2 Aug. 1971. Also KNA, DC/NYI/6/1, Nyeri PRB.

17. PRO, CO 533/184/49986, describing the affair as "a storm in a tea-cup."

18. NLC, 1912-1913: Karuri, 214-215. Kutu, 215. Nyanza witnesses, 129-131. Ainsworth, 135-138.

19. Matson, Nandi Resistance, 192.

20. See n.2. above; oral evidence, whether by direct interview or notes, is given in full, with acknowledgments, under Bibliography and Sources. Witnesses are also listed.

21. KNA, 16/49 vol. 2, Seyidie AR 1914-1915, and 8/157, AR 1912-13, also 38/582-6 for labor in Seyidie.

22. KNA, 8/157 on Kikuyu and Nyanza workers.

23. KNA, DC/MAL/1/1, Malindi quarterly report 1910-1911; 16/49 1, Seyidie AR 1913-1914 and 46/1074, "Opposition by Duruma....," Hemsted to Hobley 18 July 1917.

24. KNA, 5/336, The Giriama Rising.

25. Interview at Mihoti, South Tetu, 7 Nov. 1970.

26. Notes kindly given by Danson Kimani, 23 Dec. 1969.

27. NLC, 234-235: Mbatia wa Gicheru and Kamau wa Kabiana.

28. KNA, PC/CP1/4/1, Kikuyu PRB, 1 (1908): notes by Charles Dundas, 40, 112-113.

29. KNA, DC/KBU/1/9, Dagoretti AR 1915-1916, and DC/KBU/1/11, AR 1917-1918.

30. KNA, PC/CP1/4/2, Kikuyu PRB 3, M. W. H. Beech on "The Kikuyu Point of View," 12 Dec. 1912.

31. Interview, 5 July 1970, assisted by Aloysius Ongutu, his grandson.

32. Interviews, 28 Feb. 1970: (a) with James Beauttah at Maragwa, (b) with Wangoto and Kihara, ex-carriers, at Kirogo.

33. See n. 30.

34. KNA, DC/MKS/10B/8/1, "The deportation of Mukeki wa Ngwili and Muthui wa Ndani for inciting mania in Ukambani," 1911; for Mumbo, DC/KSI/3/2, "History and Customs of Kisii and Luo," and B. A. Ogot and Wiiliam Ochieng', "Mumboism - an

anti-colonial movement," presented to the University of East Africa Social Sciences Conference, Dec. 1969, and available by courtesy of Professor Ogot.

35.   Bethwell A. Ogot, "British Administration in the Central Nyanza District of Kenya, 1900-60," JAH, 4, 2 (1963), 256-257.

36.   Ogot and Ochieng', "Mumboism," 17.

37.   George Shepperson and Thomas Price, Independent African (Edinburgh: Edinburgh University Press, 1958).

38.   Anthony Howarth, Kenyatta - A Photographic Biography (Nairobi: EAPH, 1967), 20, 27.

39.   Thuku, Autobiography, 6-10, 14-16.

40.   Lonsdale, "Western Kenya," 165, 181-187, 223-225; KNA, DC/CN7/1, Central Nyanza PRB, DC Kisumu to PC Nyanza, 25 Dec. 1915.

41.   NLC, 203-207; letter from James Elkington to The Leader, 21 Aug. 1911; KNA, PC/CP1/4/1, Kikuyu PRB 1, 141-143.

42.   KNA, PC/NZA/2/3, Ainsworth's Miscellaneous Record Book, Leys to Ainsworth, 5 Dec. 1910.

43.   NLC, 207-210.

44.   Ibid., 171, E. D. Drought's evidence.

45.   KNA, PC/NZA/2/3, Ainsworth's "Memorandum on Native Affairs," 11 April. 1914; see also European witnesses to NLC, 111-112, 124-125, 171, 225-226, 264-265.

46.   KNA, PC/NZA/2/3, Ainsworth to Ch. Sec., 9 Oct. 1912.

47.   Ibid., Ainsworth to Leys, 5 Feb. 1910.

Chapter 3
The Origins of the East African Campaign

Gutiri undu utari kihumo - There is nothing without
a cause.

(Kikuyu proverb)[1]

"The real decision in any Anglo-German war will be
arrived at in Europe and not in Africa."

(Richard Meinertzhagen, 1906)[2]

The British were unready for the major campaign which began in
East Africa in 1914; they had no transport organisation, though there
had already been several disasters related to ill-organised carrier
forces, especially after the Uganda Mutiny.(3) If German East Africa
was to be invaded, the idea was to use Indian troops rather than
African; by 1914 the King's African Rifles were well developed, but
intended to quell internal disorder, rather than fight a major
campaign.

THE SUDANESE MUTINY AND MILITARY PORTERAGE

In early days, British East Africa depended on India, both for
manpower and for skill to build the Uganda Railway, and for troops
in emergencies like the Sudanese Mutiny of 1897. There ensued a
severe object lesson in the problems of military transport in East
Africa, which was ignored by the War Office. In November 1897, 400
Sikhs and Punjabis were sent to enforce the Uganda Rifles after the
mutiny of its Sudanese members; they were followed by the 27th
(Baluchi) Light Infantry (BLI), with twelve European officers and 737
troops.(4) The resources of the Uganda road were thus appallingly
overstretched on the eve of the great famine; the demand for
porters was all the greater because all the food for the sepoys had
to be imported, and carried upcountry from railhead.

In 1899 the 27th BLI returned in the wake of the famine; the
vast extra demands imposed an added burden, especially in Kikuyu
and Ukambani. An enormous caravan of 3,700 Soga and Ganda
porters under William Grant, a Uganda Protectorate officer, brought
the BLI to railhead. Few Nyanza men could be used, as being
unclothed they tended to die of cold on the 9,000 foot elevations of
the Mau Escarpment. The caravan reached Eldama Ravine in a bad
way.(5) Private caravans still continued, with further deaths resulting
from the callousness of some employers, who included Indians. "I am
happy to say," wrote Major Austin, "that John Ainsworth dropped on
these murderous contractors. . .in a manner that left little to be
desired."(6)

As the main caravan approached Kiu, on the eastern edge of the Kapiti Plains, which was railhead, and then returned to Fort Smith, hundreds fell out and died from dysentery and exhaustion. Unconsciously foretelling the fate of carriers in the East African campaign, Ainsworth commented:

> "In all this I do not think Mr Grant is at all to blame. The main cause for the mortality I consider to be the entire change from their native food to rice, which they do not understand how to cook properly....Men having to march daily on improperly cooked food soon get into bad condition."

He and Francis Hall did what they could to help; he felt that Ganda and Soga porters should not go beyond Ravine, but Uganda at that time stretched as far as Naivasha, another eighty miles.(7)

This terrible affair showed what could happen if military operations demanded exceptional numbers of porters. Similar horrors on a smaller scale could have happened on various minor expeditions up to 1914; "the finish of the Uganda Mutiny and the Nandi campaign are remembered by senior officers as terrible illustrations of the effects of an epidemic of dysentery among carriers."(8) No doubt it was never anticipated that, after the completion of the railway, porters would ever again be needed in large numbers.

STRATEGIC PLANNING BEFORE THE WAR

> The outbread of hostilities in B.E.A. caught the country entirely unprepared....Army Field Manuals....were practically silent on that speciality of African warfare, Carrier Transport on a large scale. Local defensive arrangements had apparently never envisaged the possibility of a long line of communications by Carriers, or of operations on any scale larger than a few companies.(9)

This was true. In 1897 the War Office and Indian Army had made plans for the invasion of German colonies in the event of war because of German naval expansion and support for the Transvaal. But neither then nor later was serious thought given to what an invasion of German East Africa would involve.

The plan drawn up by the Director of Intelligence, Indian Army, recommended an offensive to the south of Kilimanjaro; the simultaneous capture of the ports of Tanga, Bagamoyo and Dar es Salaam would ensure the conquest of the northeast of German East Africa. The waterless country to the south of the Uganda Railway would guard it against German raids. The main attack would be made at Taveta by two battalions of "good native infantry" and a mountain battery, with a porter column and a mixed Indian-Sudanese force in reserve. The seaborne attacks and diversions from Uganda should prevent the Germans from concentrating, and would encourage native risings against German rule. The War Office wanted to conquer the whole of German East Africa, which the naval blockade would make relatively easy. For transport, mules would be used, carriers from Nyasaland, and even camels, whose bellies could be protected against the wet grass at night by tarpaulins. Mules would be best; carriers were "the worst form of military transport," although it was not foreseen that they would prove to be the only really practical form, or that the campaign might be so protracted that long lines of communication worked by carriers would have to be set up.(10)

There were four false assumptions in this plan. First, the waterless terrain did not prevent the Germans from raiding the railway very effectively. Secondly, the Germans were to have no trouble from native risings; the Maji-Maji revolt lay in the future, but there was little resistance after its devastating suppression. Thirdly, reliance on Indian troops ignored the potentialities of African soldiers, whom the Germans were to use so successfully to defend their territory. Finally, and most fatal of all, was the belief that German East Africa would be easy to conquer. The thinking behind these delusions was to persist, and does much to explain the disasters of the East African campaign. Underestimating the enemy led to the failure to take transport more seriously. It was ironical that the British should be counting on risings against the Germans, the very year of the Uganda Mutiny; an added irony was that the lesson provided by the disaster to the Uganda porters was to pass unheeded, and no military transport organisation set up. Worst of all was the persistence in underestimating the African troops, both British and German, until 1916, when harsh realities compelled a change of attitude.

Nevertheless, the Simla-Whitehall plan established the fact that the natural route for an invasion of German East Africa was by Taveta and Moshi. During the 1900s the Colonial Defence Committee considered the possibilities of German attacks; though this fear had been derided, "allusions to such a contingency," wrote the Deputy Commissioner for Uganda, "though very discreetly made, are sufficiently distinct."(11) Various civil and military officers made enquiries, but otherwise there is no evidence of any real intelligence service before 1914.(12) East Africa was too low an Imperial priority to receive much attention from an infant General Staff, distracted by the problems which a war in Europe would pose. Apart from linking their colonies to Berlin by wireless, the Germans seem to have done nothing very effective either.(13)

THE KING'S AFRICAN RIFLES

Apart from the intelligence work, nothing seems to have been done to bring the 1897 plan up to date. "The details indicate clearly the absence of any uniformity or continuity of policy." Internal security was the only consideration. No preparations were made, it being assumed that Indian troops would be available.(14) The three African regiments in East and Central Africa had been formed into the King's African Rifles (KAR), in 1902, under officers seconded from the British and Indian armies. "The old policy of strengthening local defence by calling on troops from India had proved very expensive, and was increasingly unpopular with the Government of India."(15) Long before 1914 officers with African experience had seen that Indians were less suitable than Africans for operations in

Africa. Colonel Rigby, commanding troops in Uganda, wrote in 1907 that an Indian soldier cost nearly half as much again as an African, and needed four times as much baggage, "excluding transport necessary for rations, which are not carried as a rule by African troops who can generally live off the country." It was, however, admitted that the as yet raw African troops could not equal Indian military tradition.(16)   But not only were sepoys more costly man for man than askari; they needed far more baggage than any African soldiers. No doubt since the Indian Mutiny endless trouble had been taken over sepoys' food.   But though Indians had been needed to quell the Uganda Mutiny, this had led to vast problems with transport. African soldiers would not need nearly so many carriers as Indians. The 27th BLI had used six carriers per sepoy, and during the war there was a report that sepoys had five each in Uganda.(17)

In 1902 the KAR were composed as follows: the 1st and 2nd (Central Africa) Battalions comprised fourteen companies. The 3rd (East Africa) had eight companies, one of which was camel-mounted for the use in the Northern frontier and Juba provinces. The 4th and 5th (Uganda) Battalions totalled thirteen companies, and the 6th (Somaliland) had three infantry companies and a camel corps. Both the 5th and 6th still had Indian companies, but both were disbanded by 1914, as was the 2nd.(18)   The latter was the most serious loss, many of the askari leaving Nyasaland to join the German garrison at Neu Langenburg; "so many ex-K.A.R. askaris were serving there that English bugle calls and words of command were in regular use."(19)

It was not surprising that in 1913 Colonel Thesiger, Inspector-General of the KAR, made an adverse report on the strength of the regiment, in which he was supported by Lieutenant-Colonel Graham, commanding the 3rd KAR. Graham may have been over-pessimistic in doubting if the KAR could control even an internal rising; but his opinion that it would depend on local forces to stop the East Africa Protectorate being overrun hardly merited a minute by H. J. Read, a Colonial Office official, "Rubbish - who is going to overrun E.A.?"(20)   This is an illuminating remark; it simply was not the business of the Colonial Office, even though it was responsible for the KAR, to think of strategic issues. The KAR was to them a sort of military police force, for use in semi-pacified areas. Defence was a matter for the War Office, and for the Indian Government which would provide troops in case of need.

The German attitude was similar. Like Sir Henry Conway Belfield, Governor of the East Africa Protectorate, his German opposite number, Dr. Schnee, thought it impossible for European powers in Africa to be at war with each other, with great native populations to rule, and economic development in progress. Most officials, and not a few settlers, tended to agree; the Berlin Act of 1884 was there to prevent such a calamity.(21) But since the War Office and Simla had not really considered what to do if war broke out, they had no plan for external defence; nor had the Germans, whose General Staff had been told that the colonies would be abandoned.(22)

The disbanding of the three KAR battalions had been due partly to settler pressure in the East Africa Protectorate and Nyasaland,

A K.A.R. Column crossing a river, 1917
by courtesy of Dr. Clive Irvine

also to enable the Imperial Government to reduce grants-in-aid. Belfield's predecessor, Sir Percy Girouard, who though a soldier was accessible to settler pressures, was anxious to reduce military costs in the northern areas, which had resulted from his own military activities there, and which had much increased both the duties of the KAR and the strain on protectorate finances.(23) It is therefore strange that Thesiger's emphatic warnings should have been heeded, not by a Governor who had been a soldier, but by Belfield who was very much the reverse.   Up to 1914 the KAR were gradually strengthened, and the tendency to scatter it about in half-companies all over the northern provinces was reversed. Thesiger's successor, Colonel A. R. Hoskins, planned a reorganisation, the main point of which was that there should be a new Nyasaland battalion, of four companies to be stationed in East Africa, together with two flying columns of 250 rifles each.(24)

In 1914 the KAR was in no condition for war, which overtook the realisation of Hoskins' scheme; there was no transport corps, no fresh strategy.   The lessons of the Uganda Mutiny were ignored, except by those officers who had been involved. But in one respect the KAR were better off than their German opponents; they had been armed since 1902 with Enfield .303" magazine rifles, replacing the obsolete single-shot .450" Martini-Henry. From a transport point of view, ammunition for the latter was far heavier.(25) Twelve years later, Lieutenant-Colonel Paul von Lettow-Vorbeck took over Schutztruppe still armed mainly with 1871 pattern .450" single shot rifles, which had the added disadvantage of using black powder cartridges whose smoke when fired gave away the rifleman's position.(26)   So East Africa stood no higher with the German government than with the British, on the list of priorities; there was some reason for the British to think that the Germans would not defend their colony, which would be totally cut off by sea.

Other comparisons were less favourable to the KAR, whose companies varied between 75 and 130 rifles, with two or three European officers, no European NCOs, and no permanent carriers, who were provided as and when required by civil officials. Furthermore, companies were often split up and scattered about.(27) But a Schutztruppe company had up to 160 rifles, 250 permanent carriers, and up to twenty white officers and NCOs. Such companies were self-contained flying columns, used to fending for themselves; the carriers were uniformed and disciplined, showing how much better the Germans understood the whole problem. Their troops had learned self-reliance in such operations as Maji-Maji.(28)

The lack of serious strategic planning by the British had much to do with the fact that, if war came in East Africa, the Colonial, India and War Offices, and the Admiralty would all be involved; when war broke out, there was little effort to coordinate measures.

TANGA

The most northerly port in German East Africa was the scene of a decisive and humiliating British defeat; though a very minor engagement by Great War standards, it gave the German commander, von Lettow, an initiative which he never really lost, and the moral authority to carry on the war in defiance of the wishes of the governor, Heinrich Schnee, and of the neutrality principles of the Berlin Act. Lieutenant-Colonel Paul von Lettow-Vorbeck saw his duty clearly:

> I knew that the fate of the colonies....would be decided only on the battlefields of Europe....The question was whether it was possible for us in our subsidiary theatre of war to...prevent considerable numbers of the enemy from intervening in Europe ....or inflict on our enemies any loss of personnel or war material worth mentioning? I answered this question in the affirmative.(29)

He succeeded in imposing his will on the civilian authorities in Dar es Salaam, just as the General Staff did in Berlin. But though his will was decisive, he could command a well-organised colony, with a strong economy, able civil servants and an excellent medical service. Although the British naval blockade was almost entirely effective, the Germans maintained their war effort by prodigies of improvisation.(30)

The Indian government, accepting its traditional responsibility for the Indian Ocean area, prepared three expeditionary forces in August 1914: "A" was for Mesopotamia, "B" and "C" for East Africa. The latter, under Brigadier-General Stewart, took up position in the East Africa Protectorate in accordance with the 1897 plan. The former, under Brigadier-General Aitken, finally tried to take Tanga. Captain Richard Meinertzhagen, in charge of intelligence, had advised concentrating both forces inland, since his intelligence reports said that the Germans were doing precisely this in the Moshi area.(31) Having been with the KAR in the 1900s, he was one of the very few officers with East African experience.

Aitken showed the general view of the KAR by not using the 3rd Battalion when it was offered; but though some of his units were poor, he had enough good troops. But he was totally defeated with the loss of eight machine guns, 455 rifles and about 600,000 rounds of ammunition, enough to rearm two German companies with modern weapons. Aitken was not entirely to blame, but made a convenient scapegoat. Von Lettow, with 300 whites, 900 askari and no artillery, had defeated 8,000 Anglo-Indian troops, supported by a mountain battery (which Aitken had inexcusably failed to land), and a 6" gun cruiser; von Lettow lost 69 killed, but the British 360, to say nothing of a shattering loss of morale and prestige.(32) The British also had 2,000 Zanzibari porters, whose appalling sufferings in open lighters are described by Lieutenant (later Sir Gordon) Covell of the Indian Medical Service; his ship towed some of these unhappy carriers, who had been re-embarked "and had remained drifting around for two days in the full heat of the sun without food and with very little water."(33) Such callousness towards followers on the part of the military was unfortunately to be typical.

The Tanga catastrophe was due to decades of unrealistic thinking, to ignorance of East African conditions by Indian Army staff officers, and their frequent refusal to listen to advice; finally to their total underestimation of the Germans and their efficiency, and determination to defend their colony. Even before Tanga, Meinertzhagen had observed that "we have handed over the initiative to the Germans, placed ourselves on the defensive and are now awaiting their attack."(34)   This posture resulted both from Tanga and from another defeat, also in early November 1914, at Longido, between Nairobi and Arusha. The British now remained on the defensive until Smuts' arrival early in 1916. The lessons ignored before the war had now to be painfully learned. One of these was the importance of carrier transport and its problems, which were now to contribute to the growing friction between the military and civil authorities.

NOTES

1. G. Barra, 1,000 Kikuyu Proverbs (London: Macmillan, 2d ed., 1960), no. 123.

2. Richard Meinertzhagen, Kenya Diary (Edinburgh: Oliver and Boyd, 1957), 307.

3. A previous one had been during the first Nandi campaign: PRO, Foreign Office Confidential Print 6805/50, Berkeley to FO, 30 May 1895, for a copy of which I am indebted to Dr. A. T. Matson.

4. Moyse-Bartlett, KAR, 73-74; Matson, Nandi Resistance, 303-304.

5. Matson, Nandi Resistance, 303-313, 359-372.

6. H. H. Austin, With Macdonald to Uganda (London: Edward Arnold, 1903), 271-272.

7. KNA, 75/47, Ukamba Inward, Ainsworth to Crauford, 16 May 1899: in Kenya from Chartered Company to Crown Colony (London: 2d ed., Cass, 1970), 104, C. W. Hobley says that 75 percent died.

8. WP, Watkins to DMS, Nairobi, 9 Dec. 1914.

9. WR. para. 50.

10. PRO, WO 106/46, "Scheme for Operations against German East Africa 1897."

11. Moyse-Bartlett, KAR, 142-143.

12. Meinertzhagen, Kenya Diary, 304-325: for an intelligence mission in 1906; KNA, DC/TTA/3/2, Reminiscences of S.H. La Fontaine, ADC Taveta in 1914, whose agents correctly forecast the German attack on Taveta.

13. Detail by courtesy of Dr. A. T. Matson.

14. Hordern, Operations in EA, 559.

15. Moyse-Bartlett, KAR, 123.

16. PRO, CO 534/5/29393, Rigby (OC Troops Uganda) to Deputy Commissioner (Uganda), 14 June 1907 - George Wilson, whose comment on defence is referred to in n. 11 above.

17. Matson, Nandi Resistance, 359; 3,700 porters carried for 600 sepoys; R. Meinertzhagen, Army Diary (Edinburgh: Oliver and Boyd, 1960), 126, refers to the 13th Rajputs.

18. Moyse-Bartlett, KAR, 129.

19. Ibid., 265 and footnote.

20. Ibid., 153-159; see also PRO, CO 534/16/7783, Belfield to Harcourt, 4 Feb. 1913.

21. Hordern, Operations in EA, Appendix 2.

22. John Iliffe, Tanganyika under German Rule (Cambridge: Cambridge University Press, 1969), 57.

23. G. H. Mungeam, British Rule in Kenya, 1895-1912 (Oxford: Clarenden Press, 1966), 229-238.

24. Moyse-Bartlett, KAR, 158-159.

25. Ibid., 135.

26. Ibid., 261; but while the Germans had two to four machine guns per company, the KAR had only one. See also Paul von Lettow-Vorbeck, My Reminiscences of East Africa (London, 1920), 8.

27. Moyse-Bartlett, KAR, gives various instances, 147-159.

28. Ibid., 261; von Lettow, Reminiscences, 8-9 and 22.

29. Von Lettow, Reminiscences, 3-4 and 29.

30. Harlow et al., East Africa, Chapter 3, W. O. Henderson, "German East Africa, 1884-1918," 159-161; see also D. F. Clyde, History of the Medical Services of Tanganyika (Dar es Salaam: Government Press, 1962), 49-98.

31. Meinertzhagen, Army Diary, 83-84.

32. Ibid., 85-106; Hordern, Operations in EA, 97-100 and 107, n. 1; CAB 45/6 and 45/31c for general comments, also Army Diary, 86, for Aitken's refusal of KAR assistance.

33. Clyde, Medical Services, 56.

34. Meinertzhagen, Army Diary, 84-88.

Chapter 4
A Defensive Strategy

Ngeretha na Terumani niithui mwaruagira?

English and Germans, are you fighting over us?
(Kikuyu song)[1]

After Tanga, the Germans invaded Seyidie Province, and raided the Uganda Railway. Carriers were raised in Seyidie, Ukamba, Kenia and Nyanza provinces.(2) Transport problems were at first slight, lines of communication short. The development of the Carrier Corps, and of roads, railways and bridges made the 1916 offensive possible.

THE MILITARY SITUATION AND LABOR DEMANDS

Fighting began south of the Uganda Railway, and at the head of Lake Malawi, where the loss of African life at Karonga led to John Chilembwe's uprising, the only articulate African protest against involvement in the war.(3) In the south two long lines of communication went north to the German border along Lake Malawi, and from the Rhodesian railway near Broken Hill.(4) The Uganda Railway was in danger for nearly half its length; though the Germans tried to attack the railway viaducts near Kisumu, their attempt was repulsed at Kisii, only half way.(5) At Gazi they were only thirty miles from Mombasa, which was virtually safe from attack on its island. But the Germans held the initiative in their damaging raids on the railway, and usually also in the grim patrol warfare. Though von Lettow could not take any major town, his strategy of involving superior British forces worked.

There were four sectors in the East Africa Protectorate with carriers working on lines of communication. The most important was the old Voi-Taveta caravan route, noted in 1897 as the route for a British offensive. A branch route ran from Tsavo station via Mzima Springs to join the main road. Secondly, there was the road from Mombasa to the border at Vanga, less important after the initial six months of heavy fighting. Thirdly, there was nearly 100 miles of road from Athi River (fifteen miles from Nairobi) to the border at Namanga. Finally, and of minor importance after the Kisii raid, came the route from Kisumu to the border. The first three covered the vulnerable stretch of the railway from Maji

Chumvi (Mile 48 from Mombasa) to Kiu (Mile 250), on the edge of the Kapiti Plains. In over a year fifty-six attacks were made, ten being between July and November 1915, and within Voi District alone.(6) The British put pressure on local people to give information, while the Germans frightened them into keeping quiet; inevitably, some people helped the Germans, and the British actually deported some communities as reprisals.(7)

The commanders-in-chief, Major-Generals Wapshare and Tighe, persisted in failing to concentrate, leaving isolated posts exposed to the enemy, and having no adequate reserve. Discipline was undoubtedly bad; both generals tended to accept advice which was wrong or biased from officers of dubious ability and from some settlers.(8) But there were three extenuating facts: first, whereas von Lettow had a cohesive force with internal communications, Wapshare and Tighe and polyglot troops of uneven quality, many suffering from the moral effects of Tanga.(9)   All the German troops were good at patrol work, but of the British only the KAR were reliable. Secondly, using large military labor forces, the British did achieve roads from Mombasa to Msambweni, and from Tsavo past Mzima, and above all the railway from Voi to Maktau. Thirdly, they had little help from the War Office, fully preoccupied with Europe; Lord Kitchener sternly forbade further offensive operations, after the recapture by the Germans in January 1915 of Jasin, a fort on the coast just inside German East Africa.(10) This did not of course rule out patrol activity, which is vital for maintaining morale and watching the enemy; the KAR were notably successful at it around Lake Victoria.(11) Jasin, and Kitchener's reaction, caused some despondency, but on the other hand it was in an area both unhealthy and hard to supply except by sea.

Kitchener, as Secretary for War, had an office suited only for a small regular army; he was also responsible for a vast recruiting drive, for mobilizing industry and for strategy. The Imperial General Staff and its Chief had little to do; Kitchener was his own Chief of Staff, despite his professed belief in staff work. His legendary reputation faltered after the Dardanelles defeat, which was partly due to the lack of an effective General Staff. Kitchener was consistently opposed to the waste of resources on such a side-show as East Africa.(12)

Later offensive operations had an unhappy tendency to miscarry. The idea of the first was to cover the withdrawal of posts in the Voi-Tsavo area, the main column trying to force the Germans out of the position covering the Taveta road at Mbuyuni and Salaita. One column consisted of 158 sepoys and askari, ninety-eight donkeys and 158 carriers; the main column of 300 men used sixteen cars, one towing a twelve-pounder gun, which was bogged down by rain, and the machine gun carriers panicked when the enemy attacked. It was an object lesson in front-line transport problems, and "another disaster due to rotten soldiering," in the opinion of Meinertzhagen.(13)   In July 1915 another attack on Salaita also failed, though as the German carriers panicked first, an alert British commander would have had a good chance of success.(14) Finally, Tighe was defeated at Salaita in February 1916.

At sea, British ships twice failed to complete the destruction of enemy vessels, with disastrous results for the land forces. The

Rubens or Kronborg, a merchant ship, was scuttled by her crew in
shallow water under fire, but the British committed what von
Lettow called their greatest mistake of all by allowing the
Germans to recover most of her cargo of rifles, ammunition and
mountain guns, enabling them to fight on.(15)   All twelve guns
were recovered from the light cruiser Konigsberg after she was
sunk in the Rufiji delta, which gave von Lettow a temporary
advantage in field artillery, and her crew also served under him as
infantry.(16)

In 1915 Kitchener began to consider Wapshare's plan to have
two more KAR battalions. It was by now clear that the African
soldier excelled at bush warfare, except to blinkered officials who
rejected an increase of only 600, despite reports of growing
German strength.   Colonel Sheppard, formerly of "B" Force, wrote:

> "The KAR....hardly ever lose a rifle....The conclusion is the
> same that every thinking soldier....has arrived at after a year
> in British East Africa, namely that only the best and most
> highly trained troops....are....a match for the trained Africans
> of a fighting tribe in the bush."(17)

At the end of 1915 two new appointments promised more
effective leadership. Brigadier-General Edward Northey was to
command the southern force in Nyasaland and Rhodesia. Sir Horace
Smith-Dorrien, a distinguished officer whose experience went back
to the Zulu War of 1879, would command in East Africa. He would
stop the rot all right, wrote Meinertzhagen exultantly, but was
wrong if he thought he could bring von Lettow to terms; the cost
in casualties and money would be high.(18)   Forty years later
Moyse-Bartlett voiced the same doubts: "the whole situation was
thought out in terms of guns, aeroplanes and lorries, instead of
bushcraft, carriers and quinine."(19)   Smuts and his South Africans
thought that the East African bush was like their veld; they did not
consider malaria, tsetse fly, nor the vital importance of the carrier.

THE EARLY HISTORY OF MILITARY LABOR

From time immemorial, the East African caravan trade had been
mainly carrier borne, because of tsetse fly; the bush made wagons
impracticable. Some porters might have been slaves, but the Swahili
and Nyamwezi in particular were professionals. Here the Germans
had an advantage, because their country contained more men used
to porterage as well as soldiering. In the East Africa Protectorate,
more upcountry people had served government or private safaris as
porters since the 1890s, as part of the trend towards wage earning.

Porterage offered a chance of adventure and seeing the world. A
shooting safari tempted a young man with plenty of meat, even if
load-carrying was women's work in his tribe. A good mnyapara
(headman) was essential for the morale and efficiency of the
safari; unless there was strict supervision, the weakest tended to
get the heaviest loads.(20)   The savannah bushlands of East and
Central Africa, over which Livingstone and many others used to
trudge, are intersected by paths made by walkers or game, and are

passable to porters, though usually not to oxcarts or mules with panniers. Tracks must be widened, levelled and cleared of stumps for any wheeled vehicle. The rains turn wide expanses into morasses, especially on black cotton soil, where even four-wheel-drive vehicles will bog down. Eighty years ago the only means of transport which could always get through was the carrier, provided that he was properly fed and cared for.

War brought a demand for all kinds of labor. Oscar Ferris Watkins, a District Commissioner by the East Africa Protectorate government to start the Carrier Corps, had joined the administration in 1908 after military and police experience in South Africa, and had served mainly in Nyanza and Seyidie.(21)   He and J. M. Pearson, an Assistant District Commissioner, were to work as civilian officers with "B" Force in its operations in German East Africa, for which many carriers would be needed. Late in August they received at Mombasa a torrent of porters from Uganda and from the other three East Africa Protectorate provinces which, besides Seyidie, were to be recruiting grounds: Nyanza, Ukamba (which included Kiambu), and Kenia (which meant Fort Hall, Nyeri, Embu and Meru districts). Many of these men deserted in Nairobi, or joined friends in "C" Force, and vice versa. So from the start the rolls sent with the recruits by their District Commissioners were at fault, causing endless trouble in the future. The harassed civil officers knew nothing of the whereabouts of "B" Force; they were joined on 27 August by two Assistant District Commissioners from Uganda with another 1,000 men. One of them, E. L. Scott, had gained considerable experience in the rationing of labor during the Busoga Railway construction, and became one of Watkins' most valued advisers in this vital matter.(22)

There were now five units of about 1,000 men each, individually called Carrier Corps (CC); each had two administrative officers, one medical officer and a Corps headman, and was divided into ten companies with two or three headmen each. But it could hardly remain a civil organisation; government could not spare enough officers, and only a military officer could be sure of the honors of war if he were captured. Watkins was made a captain, and the others lieutenants. Since, unlike the Germans, British units had no permanent front-line carriers, officers tended to take over carriers without reference to Carriers headquarters. Though this was eventually stopped, combatant officers were always liable to ignore regulations about carriers, and the fact that Watkins never rose above the rank of Lieutenant-Colonel meant that battalion commanders, or even lesser officers, felt free to treat carriers as they liked.(23)

This problem of control led to the early resignation of Pearson. In October 1914 a British force at Gazi, on the coast, was joined by Pearson with CC No. 1; he moved from Mazeras, fifteen miles from Mombasa on the railway. He had been ordered to do this by Major Hawthorne, commanding at Mombasa and Gazi, and acted without Watkins' authority. A coast planter named Kerslake Thomas, who had joined as a carrier officer and was later discharged as unsuitable, was also somehow involved; he crops up several times in the records, always in some equivocal situation.

Lieutenant-Colonel O. F. Watkins, C.B.E., D.S.O., Director of Military Labour
by courtesy of Mrs. E. J. F. Knowles

Watkins accused Pearson of disloyally seeking the support of a post commandant in a matter concerning the internal working of the CC, and threatened to return him to civil duty, for which Pearson duly applied. This shows the teething problems of an organisation expected to work first in a civil role, and then in a military capacity for which its officers were not trained. A few of these carriers were unlucky enough to go to Tanga with "B" Force, "and the survivors were eventually disembarked at Mombasa on November 8th after considerable suffering in open lighters."(24)

After Tanga the carriers of "B" and "C" were merged; the latter were mostly syces and mule drivers, who had already been allocated to units. This all further confused the rolls and encouraged desertions. Watkins was now Deputy Assistant Director of Transport, Carrier Section, East Africa Transport Corps, in charge of all carriers between Lake Victoria and the coast. Carrier Depots were opened at Mombasa, Nairobi, Kisumu, and at the end of 1915 at Voi.(25)

The carriers worked from bases at Mombasa, Voi, Kajiado on the Namanga Road, and Karungu on the Lake. Until about April 1915 the coast was the most active area, the British having been driven back from Jasin to Gazi. Carriers waiting for the arrival of "B" Force were used for the Giriama operations. The Germans were not yet ready to begin their raids on the railway. In April 1915, work began on the military railway from Voi to Maktau, which concentrated attention on this key corridor linking British and German territory; this was the main theatre of war till Smuts drove the Germans south a year later.

The aim in Gazi District was to build the road from Mombasa to Msambweni. The hinterland is dominated by the Shimba Hills, which touch the innermost creeks of Port Reitz, an extension of Kilindini, the southern harbour at Mombasa. The coastal belt was malarious, and unhealthy both for Europeans and upcountry Africans. Scott suffered in health there, but was then returned to Uganda to start the new Carrier Section (CS) there. Early in 1915 the surviving Uganda carriers had been repatriated after suffering frightful losses from disease.(26)

The Taita people provided most of the military labor between Voi and Maktau, converting the track linking these places into a cart road. Then they were used on the railway after April 1915, and on the water pipe-line from the Taita Hills to the forward troops. The Provincial Commissioner of Seyidie, C. W. Hobley, was asked to provide labor for these in February 1915, when 1,000 Taita were already working on the road. Two Indian railway experts, Sir William Johns and Colonel Sutherland, had come with "B" Force, and Sutherland now took charge of completing the railway work, for which 2,000 men were needed.(27) Labor was to be recruited by two men with local knowledge. S. H. La Fontaine was the Assistant District Commissioner who had narrowly escaped when the Germans took Taveta in 1914. The Rev. V. V. Verbi was a Bulgarian-born missionary with the CMS. Both also joined the intelligence department, with which military labor had a tendency to overlap at this time.(28) The labor force also included Indian Sappers and Miners and 300 railway coolies.(29)

Military railways were a separate department during the campaign, with their own labor. Nor were the men on the Maktau road or the pipe-line (essential for the coming offensive across the waterless Serengeti) under Watkins, but with the East Africa Pioneers, who also built the road from Mzima to Tsavo. The District Commissioner of Voi, W. A. Platts, heard of desertions and bad treatment from a Taita headman, who was beaten on his return, or so he said, "presumably for his impertinence in reporting the state of affairs to me." A Royal Engineers officer blamed the Pioneers (who had by then left), and attributed much desertion to men being kept on for more than the three months for which, they believed, they had contracted.(30) Desertion was also more likely when a man was near his home, but with so many labor units, a man might go to whichever seemed to have the best conditions, or might join friends in another unit. Another group independent of the Carrier Section was the 1,500 strong African Labour Corps, and mutual desertion between the two caused much difficulty.(31)

Carriers, construction workers, drivers, syces and dockers were all military labor, who were all taken over in 1916 by the Military Labour Bureau, except for railwaymen. Watkins explains how construction work and active operations affected each other.

> A Carrier Corps might be a flying column one day, and split into small gangs along a section of railway line on the next. Control became very difficult, as an enemy attack on a post usually meant the dispersal into the bush of every unarmed African, who often seized this moment to desert,.....to join friends at some other post or offer himself as a personal servant to some officer or NCO passing on column.(32)

This was one of the ways in which the wages system got so confused early in the campaign.

Owing to the high sickness and death rates, it was better to employ local men if possible, especially if they could be fed at home; they were also used to the climate. In Rhodesia and Nyasaland much of the labor worked locally. The war drove home the lesson that African labor needed time to adapt to an unfamiliar environment. But even in Voi and Gazi, where local labor was available, far more were needed.(33)

Watkins thought that local labor had worked well in Voi, and wanted to use it on the Msambweni Road in Gazi. The officer commanding there, having heard that the military in Voi had disliked the system, opposed its introduction in Gazi. The military, medical and political problems experienced on the Msambweni Road show how the various facets of the Carrier story are interwoven like a multi-coloured electric cable. Carrier Section men might be better controlled and less likely to desert, but they were more likely to die in unfamiliar climes. Watkins, still a civil officer in outlook, felt that political considerations must carry weight.(34) This clash of wills can be seen on the other side; relations between von Lettow and Schnee were also frigid. Watkins' superior officer, Brigadier-General Fendall, admired his work, but wrote: "Being a Protectorate man he has tried too much to run with the hare and hunt with the hounds, and when the two contrasts were inclined to clash he was inclined to take the civil view because he had his future to think of." Fendall later tempered this unjust view: "the government held him responsible for the good treatment of the men, [the officers] to whom the men were handed over, flouted his authority and objected to his interference."(35)   The strain of the campaign caused much ill-feeling, not least between officers of different professions, but it proved increasingly to be true that neglecting the health of followers was not only inhumane, but also bad for the efficiency of fighting troops.

The flouting of Carrier Section authority was very blatant on the Msambweni Road: "the tendency of military officers to adopt carriers....as their own, and to resent their removal," as Watkins put it. In February 1915 he had sent CC No. 6 to Msambweni, 1,004 men followed by another 238. By mid-March the labor shortage in Mombasa compelled him to ask for the return of the 238. The Royal Engineers officer in charge objected; he only needed them for another week, and they knew the work. This was not unreasonable, but what annoyed Watkins was the officer appealing to the General Officer Commanding, who agreed that the men could be retained at Msambweni without asking Watkins.   He complained that carrier requirements could not easily be met if this sort of obstruction by individual officers was allowed; he asked that the convenience of transport officers who had to keep track of the constant movements of carriers not be subordinated to the employers of the carriers, without any enquiry. He consulted a colleague in Mombasa about "the outpourings of my wrath," saying that it was not an isolated, but merely a flagrant case.(36) It clearly shows the difficulty of keeping the Carrier Section together when the officer in charge was only a captain; nor is it surprising that, as Fendall admitted, officers of equal or higher rank flouted his authority.

Activity died down on the Gazi front when von Lettow concentrated his forces inland to begin his attacks on the railway. By August, sickness and death among the carriers on the coast were causing alarm. As the disturbances among the Digo tribe caused by the German invasion were subsiding, it made good political sense to use them as local labor; they would be under their elders and exempt from recruitment, as in Taita. Watkins expressed to Hobley his concern at the heavy mortality among Kikuyu porters at Gazi; dysentery among them could so easily cause an epidemic among the coast people and increase their trials. Charles Dundas (District Commissioner of Mombasa) pointed to the need for an agreement with the elders, enforced "against every member of the community." Osborne (District Commissioner of Gazi) thought that the elders would agree if there was exemption from other service. But the Officer Commanding Msambweni would only agree if 350 Carriers were retained. Finally, 350 donkeys were included with the local labor, but they were not available as they were "recuperating at Machakos," perhaps after the rigors of the Namanga Road.(37) Farce often goes hand in hand with tragedy in the Carrier saga. One can only hope that the Kikuyu were sent to some healthier area.

Animal transport was used wherever possible, even in tsetse country, until the beasts died: mules, horses, oxen, donkeys and even

A K.A.R. *askari* with a Vickers heavy machine gun
by courtesy of Dr. Clive Irvine

camels, in roughly that order of usefulness. By December 1914
tsetse had killed many animals in Voi District, including camels,
the only mention of them, though they were in the 1897 plan.(38)
Wapshare described the problems:

> Porters are very expensive and are never dependable, whilst
> water precludes their use for large bodies of troops. The
> supply of oxen is not plentiful, and it will damage the country
> considerably if large numbers are taken for military purposes.
> It would greatly increase our chances of success if India could
> earmark a mule corps for use in B.E.A., when the general
> offensive is resumed after the completion of the railway.(39)

Three points need comment. First, it was realised that
commandeering large numbers of trained transport oxen was
undesirable; they were scarcer and more valuable than ordinary
cattle.(40) Secondly, the aim of conquering the Kilimanjaro area is
plainly referred to, after the completion of the railway, whose
construction had been envisaged before the war. Thirdly, all these
animals needed syces and drivers, who later came under the MLB,
and enjoyed a higher status than general labor. Some were
uniformed, and thought of themselves as askari, like Nguku Mulwa,
who rose from stretcher bearer to mule driver.(41)   The warrior
tribes in Nyanza, the Nandi and Kipsigis were recruited for the
Carrier Corps only as drivers and in small numbers.(42)
  Wapshare complained about the shortage of mules, and
unreliability of donkeys, though they were easier to get. "Donkeys
are only a makeshift; they are noisy and hard to control and carry
only half the weight of a mule."(43) Although they might do on a
line of communication, they were highly unsuited to active
operations; the "sickening cry" of G.K. Chesterton's "tattered
outlaw of the earth" might betray a patrol to the enemy, as
happened at least once in the Tsavo area.(44)
  A possible way of overcoming the danger of tsetse to mules
used to carry machine guns was to march them through the tsetse
belt, between Bura and Maktau, at a time of day when the fly was
inactive; this would only be possible when the railway reached Bura,
and mules could be taken by train.   Maktau was thought to be
relatively clear of fly. One mule could save three or four porters,
as it could carry the barrel, tripod and ammunition for one Vickers
gun.(45)   Tsetse is found mainly in bush, so that the open
Serengeti plain is relatively free, though fly may occur in patches
of bush anywhere in that area. The coastal strip is also a tsetse
belt, but the Namanga Road goes through country which is high
enough to be clear of fly.(46) This was good for oxcarts; Marius
N'gang'a Karatu had begun his varied career with oxcarts on this
road, contributed by the Roman Catholic Bishop. The Germans
surrounded Karatu's detachment and burned their wagons, but
Karatu, a resourceful man, had brought a bicycle on his wagon and
with it, he said, made his way back to Nairobi.(47)
  Even on such short lines of communication there were not
enough porters, which was perhaps partly due to "the grave tension
then existing between the Indian H.Q. and the local inhabitants,

TABLE 1

TRANSPORT FOR AMMUNITION AND MACHINE GUNS, 1915

Notes from Standing Orders and Regulations for the Forces in B.E.A.
1915; there were more animals than in 1916, after Smuts' advance.

Scale of Ammunition in the field.
(Figures are numbers of rounds of ammunition)

	.303 ammunition	.450 ammunition
1 porter	500 rounds	450 rounds
1 ox or donkey	1,500 "	900 "
1 mule, probably	2,000 "	1,200 "

		3 mules	7 Porters	Column	Advanced Base
Normal	.303"	6,000	3,500	9,800[@]	20,000
Transport	.450"	3,600	2,450	8,600+	10,000

Packing
(@ packed for porters.   + 2,800 only packed for porters)

		4 oxen or donkeys	6 porters
Porter	.303"	6,000	3,000
Transport	.450"	3,600	2,700

Donkeys or Oxen and Porters for Machine Guns.

.303" MG	Weight	Porters	Donkeys
Kit of Gun Teams (20 lbs)	120 lbs	-	1 (or ox)
Gun	62 "	1	-
Tripod	56 "	1	-
Shield, spares, etc.	60" "	1	-
9,000 rounds ammunition:			
1. 3,000 in 2-belt boxes	360 "	6	-
2. 6,000 in 3-belt boxes	360 "	-	4
Spare porters		1	
Headman (1 per section if short of porters)		1	
Porters' kit and water		3	
Totals		14	5 + 1 boy

The .450" MG needed 2 donkeys for extra ammunition, and another boy
for the 7 animals; the MG weighed only 1 lb. more.

(Source: H.B. Thomas Paper, RCSL)

black and white." But there was no compulsive legislation before the
passing of the Native Followers Recruitment Ordinance (NFRO) in
September 1915.(48) Other causes were wastage from disease,
imperfect administration, ease of desertion, and poor distribution of
porters which the attitude of military officers did not help; Indian
troops needed too many. No flying column at Voi would have had
1,250 carriers to 250 men, the proportion reported with the 13th
Rajputs in Uganda.(49)   In the populous southwest of Uganda, large
numbers of "job" porters were raised for the Belgians.(50)   But
besides all these military demands, there were private and government
needs, including those for operations in the Turkana and Marsabit
areas.(51)

Watkins also had difficulty obtaining European staff, and to his
great irritation was often given unsuitable men without prior
consultation: "I can only use two kinds of Europeans, the young and
active men who can march with a transport column, and the trained
office man for depot work ... I cannot carry on if my staff are
chosen for me from the point of view of their needs rather than
mine."   A knowledge of Swahili was fundamental, but too often
lacking. A Hindustani-speaking officer who had been transferred
elsewhere when the Carrier Section was formed was later returned, to
Watkins' annoyance. Then there was an unseemly quarrel between an
Indian medical officer and a Carrier corporal, in private life a
plantation manager, who resigned as a result. It was an example of a
problem no doubt common; probably the medical officer had been
officious towards a European with a strong racial sense. Watkins did
not condone the corporal's behaviour, but told the senior medical
officer that "the indiscretion of one of your officers had added to
my   difficulties,   which   in   the   matter   of   staff   are   already
considerable." Various applicants for commissions were suitable, but
others were not. A sergeant, in civil life a Cape Town barrister,
applied for a commission "which he appeared to consider due to
himself practically as a right," a view which was not shared. Another
was "one of the class of man who appears always to be at work, and
at the end of the day has nothing to show for [it]"; one carrier
officer complained to a colleague of his "coolness" in fobbing off this
man on him: "I most strongly object to have the good man sent here
... to bring my grey hairs in sorrow to the grave."(52)

Watkins might have echoed this feeling; the sense of strain was
showing. For example, he complained bitterly about a District
Commissioner's remarks on the subject of the pay sheets which
returning   carriers   were   supposed   to   give   to   their   District
Commissioners, so that they could be promptly paid off. The District
Commissioner's reply was so temperate that Watkins may have been
over-reacting.(53) This incident shows that in February 1915 carriers
were only serving for up to six months, and raises the unanswerable
question as to how far statistics are falsified by plural recruitments.
The payment of discharged carriers was to be a constant source of
trouble, owing to the initial confusion of registers with the old
Carrier Corps and Carrier Section of 1914-1916. Improvisation has
been inevitable at the start, with the need to evolve a system of
nominal rolls and identification, so that men could be paid.(54)

An Indian Army staff had been thrown at short notice into an African territory, and expected to work with its government, settlers and people. One of the forces under it had been shamefully defeated at Tanga. The lack of proper planning by the War, Colonial and India Offices before the war could hardly induce respect, or fail to cause friction. The political officers in East Africa could be pardoned for feeling that they were expected to fill a breach left open mainly by the War Office and Simla.

POLITICAL UNDERCURRENTS AND THE IMPACT OF WAR

Before the war, white settler power had grown rapidly; when war came, settler pressures on government were at first reduced. Settlers and officials forgot their differences in their mutual dislike of the Indian Army staff who, for their part, deplored what they saw as a lack of partriotic feeling. The governor let his officials take normal leave, but would not let them join the armed forces. Home leave was finally stopped, except on medical grounds, in September 1915, which is surprising, a year after the war had begun.(55)

The original enthusiasm to join the East Africa Mounted Rifles and other impromptu units was dashed by the defeats at Longido and Tanga, by the lack of concerted leadership from the governor and generals, and by the lack of support from the War and Colonial Offices. Officials and settlers on both sides had believed that the Berlin Act of 1885 would save the Anglo-German territories from any involvement in the war. It was feared that war would upset their control over their African subjects, and after all "nothing that this or the neighbouring protectorate might do could permanently affect the course of events."(56) The mass meeting of settlers on 8 September 1915 caused a revolution in attitude.

As for officials, there were four reasons why staff could not be reduced by officers joining the forces. First, there must be enough officers to maintain contact with the tribes. Secondly, they had to meet the great pressure brought by carrier recruiting. Thirdly, the interests of settlers must be safeguarded, where they had gone off to fight, leaving their womenfolk in charge of their farms. Finally, even more administrative officers would be needed if the German territory was occupied. Many officers were, in fact, serving with intelligence, as political advisers with the forces, with the Carrier Corps or even the KAR.(57)

It was therefore not true that the administration was doing nothing towards the war effort, any more than the settlers. They also had to cooperate over the control of foodstuffs and other vital commodities, which were put under the Central Committee of Supply (CCS) in Nairobi, with subordinate committees in the other main towns. The President, Secretary and Senior Indent Officer of the CCS were officials; other members were businessmen and farmers.(58) It was therefore a base from which settler influence could extend. Quite early in their career the CCS was trying to lay down the law to the Carrier Corps about the quality of meal issued to the men.(59)

A letter from Watkins to H. R. McClure (District Commissioner of Nyeri) shows his problems, the feeling against the military and another side of this triangle of contention:

> Labour has been thrown out to military officers, who can't
> understand what it says and don't know what it eats or where
> to get its food. In India, they say, a native can always feed
> himself....They continue to distribute the porters in details of
> 50 to 100 and expect us to supervise them all. The men you
> mention were not mine, but thanks for the information. It may
> make a lever for moving the Indian Army.(60)

The settlers gained many points in 1915. Against Colonial Office
opposition, the Crown Lands Ordinance gave them 999-year leases,
virtually entrenching the Elgin Pledge of 1906 against Indians owning
land in the Highlands.(61) The Registration Ordinance brought in the
kipande, an identity document in a metal cylinder hung on a string
round an African's neck; in the Carrier Corps this was the only
possible means of keeping track of a man for pay purposes. Officials
and settlers had been roughly in agreement in recommending this to
the Native Labour Commission.(62) Again, the Native Followers
Recruitment Ordinance went considerably further in extending
compulsory labor, as settlers had so often demanded.(63) They
became totally committed to the war effort, as a result of the
meeting organised by E. S. Grogan at the Theatre Royal on 8
September.(64) The resolution on compulsory service, carried with
immense enthusiasm, led to ordinances for the registration and
compulsory service of Europeans and Asians. Most significant of all,
however, was the War Council, which gave the settlers a share in
the executive power, though its functions were in theory advisory. It
soon made the government lower the wages of carriers from Rs.10
to Rs.5 a month. In evidence to the Council, Watkins agreed, so
long as the pay of men already engaged was not affected, or that
of the various front-line carriers. In this way it was felt that "the
permanent public interest in the labour supply should be fully
protected." The announcement of these reductions a few days later
a Defence Force dinner was greeted with cheers.(65)
   Of the four provinces where porters were recruited, only Seyidie
was a theatre of war. The Arabs were still influential on the coast,
and their cooperation was vital to ensure the support of the
Africans, Muslim or otherwise, so that carrier recruiting and
intelligence work could proceed. Disaffected Arabs might incite
African resistance, as was supposed to have happened in Giriama,
where German agents were reported to have been concerned with
the uprising in August 1914.(66) Though the Sultan of Zanzibar
supported the British, and was obeyed by most of his subjects in
Seyidie, the Mazrui clan kept up their traditional resistance. Their
leader Mbaruk had led the uprising against the British in 1895, and
had died in Dar es Salaam about 1910. His sons were the agents
said to have incited the Giriama; they were denounced by the Sultan
as rebels, and were arrested in Gazi District, where the local Arabs
now disclaimed the Mazrui.(67)   British fears may have been
exaggerated, but in November 1914 the Sultan of Turkey had
proclaimed a Holy War against them; concern was also felt about Lij
Yasu, Negus of Abyssinia, who was suspected of being a Muslim, but

lost his throne in 1916. The Ottoman Sultan was a puppet of the Young Turks, whose pan-Turkish doctrine of Yeni-Turan was inherently hostile to the Arabs. The revolt of the Sherif of Mecca, the leading prince of Arabia, led to the Arab alliance with the British, who now regained the initiative, if they had ever lost it, in bidding with the Germans for Muslim support.(68)   Finally, there were some very able European officers in Seyidie: Hobley as Province Commissioner, for example, Ainsworth Dickson, who joined Intelligence, and Wavell, a brilliant soldier who formed the Arab Rifles and fell leading them in battle. Hobley wrote of Dickson: "He was present at the disastrous engagement when Major Wavell was unfortunately killed, and made a valiant attempt to recover the body," with the help of some of Wavell's men. The loyalty of able Arab leaders like Ali bin Salim (Liwali of Mombasa) and Abubakari bin Ali (Sheikh of Gazi) was also vital.(69)

Seyidie bore the heaviest burden during the first phase of the war, with its trials by German invasion as well as military recruiting. Elsewhere there was little but patrol activity along the border.(70) But the early days of the Carrier Corps can already be seen as a constant struggle by the staff to establish and maintain standards, before the 1916 offensive sent numbers soaring almost out of control.

NOTES

1. Interview with Leah Nyamuiru Karuga, Nov. 1969, assisted by her grandson, Ngureh Mwaniki.

2. See Appendix 1 below.

3. Shepperson and Price, Independent African, 234-235.

4. PRO, CAB 45/14, "Transport Difficulties in East Africa during the Great War," by Sir Lawrence Wallace, Administrator of North-East Rhodesia.

5. KNA, DC/KSI/3/7, "The Battle of Kisii

6. KNA, DC/TTA/3/2, Voi District War Diary, appendix; M. F. Hill, Permanent Way vol. I (Nairobi: East African Railways and Harbours, 2d ed., 1961), 347-348, 361-362.

7. KNA, 44/972 1 & 2, "Removal of Natives from Kasigau."

8. C. P. Fendall, The East African Force, 1915-1919 (London: Witherby, 1921), 58-59; Meinertzhagen, Army Diary 122-123, 137-139, 160, 200-205.

9. Meinertzhagen, Army Diary, 106-109, 112, 116-117.

10. Moyse-Bartlett, KAR, 282-284; Meinertzhagen, Army Diary, 112-113; Hordern, Operations in EA, 127, 129 n.1.

11. Moyse-Bartlett, KAR, 284-286; Meinertzhagen, Army Diary, 118, 129-131.

12. Philip Magnus, Kitchener: Portrait of an Imperialist (London: Murray, 1958), 283-288, 380.

13. Hordern, Operations in EA, 143-144; Meinertzhagen, Army Diary, 122.

14. Hordern, Operations in EA, 155-158; Moyse-Bartlett, KAR, 291-292; Meinertzhagen, Army Diary, 137-139.

15. Von Lettow, Reminiscences, 67-68; Meinertzhagen, Army Diary, 140-145; Moyse-Bartlett, KAR, 290 n. 1.

16. Edwin P. Hoyt, Jr., The Germans Who Never Lost (London: Leslie Frewin, 1968), passim.

17. Moyse-Bartlett, KAR, 257, 290-291; Hordern, Operations in EA, 132-134.

18. Meinertzhagen, Army Diary, 160.

19. Moyse-Bartlett, KAR, 294.

20. Hobley, Kenya, Ch. 14; C.W.L. Bulpett, ed., John Boyes King of the Wa-Kikuyu (London: Methuen, 1911), 38-41.

21. Savage and Munro, JAH, 7, 2 (1966), 314, n.6.

22. WR, paras. 3-9; KNA, 12/223, civil status of Watkins and Pearson; Scott was later Ch. Sec., Uganda. Hill, Permanent Way, 340-341 for the Busoga Railway.

23. WR, paras. 10, 11 and 55; OG, 1914, 1124 for CC staff list; KNA 44/971, "Patrols south of the Railway," for risks run by civil officers, who were given military rank after Hobley's protests - 45/994.

24. WP, exchange of letters Watkins-Pearson, 7 and 10 Nov. 1914; KNA 12/265, Pearson's return to civil duty. WR, para. 24 on Tanga porters; see Chapter 3 above, n. 33.

25. WR, paras. 18, 19, 58, 59; KNA, 38/604, Voi Carrier Depot, Watkins to Ch. Sec., 23 Nov. 1915.

26. WR, para. 20; WP, Watkins to ADT, 3 & 11 March 1915; Chapter 8 below, "Uganda Casualties."

27. KNA, 43/921, Voi Military Railway; DC/TTA/3/2, Taita PRB 1.

28. Meinertzhagen, Army Diary, 171; KNA, DC/TTA/3/2.

29. KNA, DC/TTA/3/2; Hordern, Operations in EA, 129-130.

30. KNA, 38/599, "Treatment of WaTaita Natives 1915"; Hordern, Operations in EA, 130, 154-155.

31. Hordern, Operations in EA, 130, 141.

32. WR, para. 22.

33. NLC, 171; Chapter 8 below.

34. KNA, 37/577, vol. 2, "Porters for the Military," Watkins to Hobley, 14 Aug. 1915, and Officer Commanding Gazi to Osborne (District Commissioner of Gazi) 21 Aug. 1915.

35. PRO, CAB 45/44, Fendall's Diary; Fendall, EAF, 204.

36. WP, letters on movement of carriers, 11 & 12 March 1915: Watkins to ADT, not sent on advice of Colonel Orr.

37. KNA, 37/577, vol. 2, correspondence August and September 1915.

38. KNA, DC/K/TTA/3/2, Taita War Diary.

39. PRO, CAB 45/31, Wapshare to WO, 10 March 1915; Hordern, Operations in EA, 139-141.

40. Karen Blixen, Out of Africa (London: Putnam, 1937), 252-254 for a description of working oxen.

41. Interview at Muthetheni, Machakos, 14 June 1969.

42. KNA, DC/KER/46 Lumbwa; DC/NDI/1/2 Nandi; moran (young warriors) from these tribes went mostly to the KAR or Nandi Scouts, a small special force.

43. PRO, CAB 45/31, Wapshare to WO, 10 March 1915.

44. Hordern, Operations in EA, 147, n. 4.

45. KNA, 37/577, vol. 1, Malleson to DAAQMG, 19 May 1915, on desertions of machine gun carriers; Hobley to Watkins, 31 May 1915 on tsetse; see Table 1 on transport for machine guns.

46. Dr. Andrew Agnew has kindly drawn my attention to John Ford, The Role of Trypanosomiasis in African Ecology (Oxford, 1971), especially chapter 8.

47. Interviews near Limuru, June and November 1969.

48. PRO, CAB 45/31C, Wapshare's complaint about the difficulty of raising porters "an amazing statement in view of the fact that over 200,000 porters were subsequently raised." - anon. comment.

49. See Chapter 3 above, nos. 16 and 17.

50. NAU/SMP 4290 (RPA, War F/1/2), ADT to Ch. Sec. Uganda, 12 March 1917; see Table 3.

51. KNA, PC/NZA/1/10, Nyanza AR 1914-1915, records 4,000 to Turkana; DC/MRU/1/1, Meru ARs 1914-1919, and PC/CP1/9/1, Meru PRB 1908-1921, for carriers to Marsabit.

52. WP, staff correspondence and confidential file.

53. Ibid., Watkins to Talbot Smith (DC Kisumu), 3 Feb. 1915 and reply 12 Feb. 1915.

54. See Chapter 6 below.

55. Sec. Circs. Nos. 61-63, 6 to 10 Aug. 1914, No. 59, 16 Sept. 1915, and No. 61, 20 Sept. 1915; Meinertzhagen, Army Diary, 106, 118-120.

56. EAS, Editorial, 8 Aug. 1914; "Discretion or Valour?" 22 Aug. 1914.

57. Sec. Circ. No. 71 of 25 Oct. 1915.

58. OG 1914, 823-826, 865-866 (banning sales of vital supplies under martial law); 889-905 (duties, membership).

59. WP, Ration Correspondence, R3-17.

60. Ibid., Watkins to McClure, 29 Dec. 1914.

61. EAP, Ords. & Regs., No. 10 of 1915.

62. EAP, Ords. & Regs., No. 104 of 1915; see also EAS, 9 and 23 Jan. 1915, and NLC, 331.

63. EA Ords. & Regs., No. 95 of 1915; OG, 1915, 737; EAS, 20 Aug. 1915, and editorial in Leader, 20 Aug. 1915.

64. EAS, 11 Sept. 1915.

65. Ibid., 6 Nov. 1915, War Council meetings, 20 and 21 Sept. 1915; Defence Force dinner report, 24 Sept. 1915.

66. KNA, 5/336 1, Beech to Hemsted, 28 Aug. 1914.

67. KNA, 43/914. "Military Situation in Vanga District" (Gazi); 45/1010, "Native Prisoners of War."

68. KNA, 45/1056, "Holy War against the British"; see also T.E. Lawrence, Seven Pillars of Wisdom (London: J. Cape, 1935), 46, 49-54.

69. KNA, 2/267, "War Service of Government Officers", including testimonials by Hobley on the Liwali, the Sheikh, Platts, Hemsted, Osborne and Dickson; two Arab Riflemen were killed trying to recover Wavell's body.

70. Lord Delamere raised some Maasai scouts: Elspeth Huxley, White Man's Country (London: Chatto and Windus, 2d. ed., 1953), vol. 2, 16-17; Angus Buchanan, Three Years of War in East Africa (London: Murray, 1920), Chapter 3.

Chapter 5
The Conquest of German East Africa

"We said if God kept us we would go home, for we knew that one does not die, unless by the will of God."

(Nguku Mulwa, syce)

"We were working - cutting bush and carrying bullets, taking them to the river called Rufiji."

(Kinyanjui wa Mukura, carrier)[1]

The offensive against German East Africa in 1916 was made possible by the engineering works accomplished in 1915; the plan to attack was adopted by the Cabinet despite Kitchener's protests. Many more white and Indian troops would be needed, more followers, arms and equipment, in the very year when the new volunteer armies were to be used in France. No doubt Kitchener's advice was rejected because of the pressures of home and Imperial politics; a rapid conquest would look good.(2)   After their comparatively easy overrunning of German South-West Africa, the South Africans were ready and eager to do the same in a territory which they thought they might be able to keep after the war. General Smith-Dorrien reached Cape Town too ill to continue, and was replaced by General Smuts, who was faced by bitter Nationalist opposition. The traditional Boer method of manoeuvre therefore had an added appeal for Smuts, if costly infighting was to be avoided.(3)

SMUTS, HOSKINS AND VAN DEVENTER

During the remainder of the campaign, operations depended more and more on the carrier as time went on. Before Smuts arrived, the first engagement in which the South Africans participated, at Salaita Hill on 12 February 1916, gave them a salutary lesson in the problems of bush warfare, and the superiority of the German African troops, and indeed of crack Indian units like the Baluchis whom they also despised. Smuts, too, had much to learn, Meinertzhagen discovered:

Smuts....underrates the fighting qualities of the German native soldier. I warned him that in the bush he would find them as good as his South Africans....We spoke also about malaria and the dense bush which von Lettow likes for his manoeuvres. Smuts dislikes bush; he will like it less in a year's time.(4)

But because of the abundance of South African troops, the expansion of the KAR was again put off.

Smuts showed much greater energy and dynamism than any earlier commander. Following Tighe's plan, he ended the first phase of the campaign with the occupation of Kahe, on the Tanga-Moshi railway, on 21 March 1916. The Kilimanjaro area was now conquered, but Smuts had not destroyed von Lettow, which alone could have ended the campaign. Smuts was unwilling, for political reasons, to risk heavy casualties in battle, but the truth of Meinertzhagen's comment was to be fully borne out, that "every man killed in battle means ten invalided with disease."(5) So von Lettow was manoeuvred out of one position after another, suffering relatively light casualties, and still as strong as ever.

The second phase of Smuts' campaign was similar: two sweeping movements were made west and east of the huge steppe south of Kilimanjaro, meeting eventually along the line of the Central Railway from Dar es Salaam to Lake Tanganyika. Smuts now at last decided to expand the KAR, and made them fully Imperial troops. After the fall of Kahe, Major General van Deventer led the 2nd Division to the west of the steppe, leaving Arusha on 1 April. But the rains had now begun with a vengeance, and their paralysing effect had not been foreseen. The road from Arusha included "wet black cotton soil poached to a morass." Men could only do two miles an hour, and a telegraph lorry was seen moving only by using its winch; it was an exceptional season.(6) It was therefore an undoubted feat by van Deventer and his South Africans to have taken Kondoa, near the Central Railway, and held it against a counter-attack led by von Lettow himself, who was for once taken aback by this dynamic performance.(7)

The rains prevented Smuts from resuming his advance on Tanga until later in May; but after occupying Usambara and Korogwe, he went south to Handeni, which was linked to Mombo (on the Usambara Railway) by a light tramway, a vital future part of the British line of communication. This advance, which ended at Morogoro on the Central Railway, was accomplished with much fighting and great hardship to troops and followers, fulfilling von Lettow's aim of making his withdrawal as damaging as possible to the enemy.(8) Smuts reached Morogoro on 26 August, van Deventer having taken Dodoma on the Central Railway a month earlier; thus the second phase of Smuts' offensive was over. But the Germans had done much damage to both the Usambara and the Central Railway. Lines of communication stretched back tenuously for hundreds of miles to the north. Van Deventer's gloomy report, on 3 June, on the state of his division, its equipment and transport was followed by another at the end of August, from Kilosa west of Morogoro, on "the extreme exhaustion of my animals and men."(9)

Another advance under Smuts' direct control was along the coast, with naval support, as a result of which all the main ports were occupied during July and August: Tanga, Pangani, Bagamoyo, Dar es Salaam, Mikindani, Kilwa and Lindi. Two further offensives were not under Smuts' control. First, Northey's force advanced from the head of Lake Malawi to Iringa, in the southern highlands of German East Africa, which fell on 29 August. Secondly, the British and Belgians advanced from the northwest, from Uganda and Ruanda respectively,

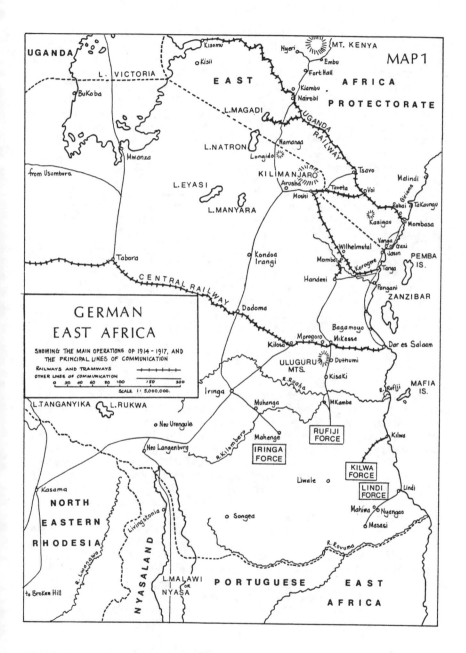

Map 1

occupying German territory as far as Tabora, which the Belgians entered on 14 September.(10)

A second German merchant ship, the Marie, now succeeded in penetrating the British blockage and reached Sudi Bay, near Lindi. She brought four 105mm howitzers, two 75mm mountain guns, some machine guns, ammunition and other stores, including a supply of well-deserved Iron Crosses; there was also a detachment of trained gunners. As with the Rubens, this probably meant to von Lettow the difference between being able to carry on or not. General Headquarters heard nothing of the affair for a month, and the acid comment of the Official Military Historian is that "the affair is not referred to in NAVAL OPERATIONS." The light howitzers were excellent in the bush, much better than the flat-trajectory mountain guns.(11)

Smuts "had allowed his duel with von Lettow to become something of an obsession." His impatience with supply problems drove both him and his exhausted army on: "Hunger! Thirst! There are no such things when the success of a great operation hangs in the balance."(12) But this third phase of his offensive also failed to destroy the enemy; thirst may not have stopped it, but torrential rains, hunder and disease did so just as effectively in the reeking swamps of the Rufiji. The enemy refused to fight at Morogoro, as Smuts had hoped. "To me this idea was never altogether intelligible," wrote von Lettow. "Being so very much the weaker party, it was surely madness to await at this place the junction of the hostile columns."(13)

As von Lettow had expected, Smuts again made flanking movements, this time on each side of the Uluguru Mountains; pushing straight on from Morogoro, his two columns fought their way south, suffering from hunger, exhaustion and disease, until they met in appalling weather at Kisaki on 15 September. Deneys Reitz wrote a lurid account of the road: rain, tsetse, dying horses, rotting carcasses, hunger; "with the heavy rains the carriers failed, and where we had been on short commons before, we went on shorter now."(14) Smuts was undeniably unlucky with the weather during his year of command; both rainy seasons were exceptional, that of 1917 being two months early. Having made Dar es Salaam his base, he would have done better to rest on the Central Railway.The troops, especially the South Africans, were fever-stricken and exhausted; the hospitals were overflowing. Smuts now made a futile attempt to bluff von Lettow into surrender.(15) In September he began a final drive, with a diversionary flanking move based on the newly captured port of Kilwa Kisiwani. In October and November Hoskins advanced with a division of fresh Indian troops and new KAR units. West African troops also were now in action; the Nigerian Brigade took part in the crossing of the Rufiji River on New Year's Day and in heavy rain. The Germans withdrew to the south bank as the floods rose.

"Already, as one of the main lessons of the campaign, it was indisputable that for warfare in tropical Africa troops other than native Africans had proved in general unsuited."(16) Operations at last halted; all the remaining South Africans left. The Rhodesians and the Loyal North Lancashire (the only regular British battalion, who had been at Tanga) had already gone. At the end of January 1917 Smuts handed over command to Hoskins, and went to London for the Imperial Defence Conference; he then joined the Imperial War Cabinet. The belief that he had defeated von Lettow still lingers, originating in the propaganda statements which he made in South Africa and London: "The campaign in East Africa may be said to be over," though the rains in March in April might delay the end. The Germans might then invade Portuguese East Africa, but "it is merely the remnant of any army that is left, and not a formidable fighting force." The white troops had been unequal to the climate, but the excellent native infantry had already done well; "in May they can move, and the thing will be finished."(17)

General Hoskins now asked the War Office for troops, guns, motor lorries, railway equipment; 160,000 carriers would be needed for his plans, which hardly bore out Smuts' sanguine statements. The posting of Hoskins to France in 1914, when he was Inspector-General of the KAR, has been well described as "one of the greatest blunders of the war," consistent with the use of officers with East African experience there instead of forming new KAR battalions, which they should have been doing, under Hoskins. In January 1917 Hoskins "had taken over from General Smuts an instrument - however good its material - blunted and useless for any offensive action. A force tired in mind and body."(18)   His offensive was planned to begin in May; his requests greatly embarrassed the War Cabinet, which Smuts joined in June 1917. Smuts had made blatantly false statements about his supposed defeat on von Lettow, but was in a position to cover up by advising the replacement of Hoskins by van Deventer; Hoskins had supposedly "lost grip of the operations and perhaps had become tired." His cynical aim was achieved in May, and was much resented as an act of political expediency. Nor was Smuts' claim to have trained the new KAR units appreciated either; there was reason for Meinertzhagen to conclude that Smuts was "a brilliant statesman and politician, but no soldier."(19)

Having totally misread von Lettow's military aims, Smuts had helped him to achieve these, and greatly increased the misery of the East African people. Far from ending, the war now intensified. Van Deventer began the offensive in June 1917. Four columns, based on Iringa, the Rufiji, Kilwa and Lindi, tried to trap the German forces, and a series of fierce engagements was fought, culminating in the ferocious battle of Mahiwa or Nyangao, from 16 to 19 October. The British casualties were about 2,500 men, over half the force engaged; the Lindi column in particular was so shattered as to be out of action until after the Germans had escaped southward. The German casualties of over 500 out of 1,500 were in a sense more severe, as von Lettow could not make good such losses, though he could claim a tactical victory.(20)   These very severe operations bear out the impression that Smuts' campaign had mainly been a brilliant piece of political showmanship, avoiding serious fighting if possible, and designed for public consumption in the Union; it also suited the British government politically to connive at the deception. But Mahiwa really broke von Lettow's offensive power, though he kept his force in being for another year. Would Smuts or Van Deventer have involved South African troops in such a battle?

The Germans now kept going by invading Portuguese East Africa, meeting no resistance worthy of the name; a hard core of 300 Europeans, 1,700 askari, and 3,000 followers lived off the land. The British tried to stop them, with columns operating from coastal bases at Port Amelia, Lumbo and Quelimane. The Germans went down to the Zambezi, back to the east of Lake Malawi, and into North-East Rhodesia, where they took the provincial headquarters at Kasama, and fought the last engagement of the Great War the day after the Armistice. Von Lettow had entirely succeeded in his war aims, and made the British waste vast human and material resources. Kitchener and others were undoubtedly right in thinking that it would have been enough to occupy the Kilimanjaro area and the ports, for which quite small forces would have sufficed.(21)

THE PORTERS' WAR BEGINS

During 1916 the army relied more and more on military labor. The Carrier Section had consisted of corps which were too big for most tasks, and when they were split up, the men were often out of their officers' control. The capture of the post at Kasigau Mountain in December 1915 by the Germans increased the threat to the railway, along which carriers became so spread out that the system of large corps collapsed. Instead there was a more flexible system of gangs of about twenty-five men, each under a headman and if possible of one tribe, but even gangs tended to get split up, with loss of control.(22)

The Carrier Section was by now concerned not only with transport, but with all kinds of labor: roads, bridges, the pipe-line, the Voi Military Railway. So in February 1916 the Military Labour Bureau, under Watkins, took over all followers except railway labor; in April it equipped, and in July paid, all non-combatant personnel.(23)   Units in the field could no longer adopt followers indiscriminately, as they had to have authority to pay them, ending "the competitive scramble of earlier days."(24)   Labor officers with advancing divisions would recruit men as required, either paying labor out of divisional funds, or registering it permanently with the MLB. On lines of communication, labor officers dealt with men at the various posts; who either carried goods between the posts, or did maintenance work. Finally, Advanced Depot Officers kept records and set up sub-depots for recruiting or repatriating labor as they advanced.(25)   As the British occupied German territory, they recruited from people who had already met heavy German demands for labor and stock.

It is hard to say how many men the MLB took over. By March 1916 the East Africa Protectorate had produced nearly 72,000 men, of whom perhaps a third went to the MLB: in April Smuts had 30,000 carriers. Until his advance began, carriers were relieved every six or nine months; but it now became very hard to do this promptly, and men recruited during 1916 either had to wait for release, or were kept to reinforce the mass levy of 1917. It is clear, however, that the discharge process was continuous, even if delayed.(26)

Carriers were less prominent in Smuts' first drive than they became later; the 25th Royal Fusiliers, for instance, advanced from Longido to Moshi, then down the Usambara Railway and through

Handeni to Morogoro, using mules, oxen and horses.(27) The same
column, advancing down the left bank of the Pangani River, had
horses and bullocks, most of which were lost from horse sickness
and tsetse as had been expected. Brett Young, a medical officer,
had under him stretcher bearers and orderlies who were "Kavirondo,"
the old name for Nyanza, which tended to be applied to East Africa
Protectorate porters in general, as half of them in fact came from
Nyanza. He refers to the squalor and dysentery among carriers left
behind by the Germans at Endarema, near Handeni, where the light
trolley line ended. The Germans had apparently given up all sanitary
precautions in the haste of their retreat.(28) Van Deventer's column
suffered heavy losses in animals which, with lorries, were his main
means of transport.(29)   It must have been impossible to replace
such vast losses of transport animals; carriers largely took their
place after the crossing of the Central Railway.

African reminiscences of this advance are scarcer than those of
later advances, when numbers rose so much. Marius Karatu went as
far as Moshi; he then deserted because of the bloodshed he
witnessed, especially at seeing a European's body in two halves on
each side of a stream. He said it had been sawn in half by the
Germans, though it was more likely a gruesome result of shell fire.
There is no record of such an atrocity, though Europeans were
certainly afraid of falling alive into the hands of German askari.(30)
Jonathan Okwirri was a superior headman with carriers during the
Moshi offensive, and spent the rest of the war at Tanga and at the
Mombasa Carrier Depot. A Meru askari, Muthanya wa Muiri, served
in the Moshi area as well as later in the Kilwa-Lindi hinterland; he
took part in one of the attacks on Maktau. The war work of the
majority of his age-grade is shown by its name of Kaaria.(31) Nguka
Nyoake from South Nyanza was first a carrier, then a stretcher
bearer with the KAR; he spoke of a long, hard march apparently
ending at Dar es Salaam.(32)   If he was transferred to the
stretcher bearers, he cannot have been trained at the special depot
near Ngong called Kwa Maleve, which was initially for gun carriers,
then for all first-line porters. Another stretcher bearer, William
Kwinga Nthenge, was trained there: "from here I went to Voi and
Mwatate,....We fought our way to Mbuyuni and from here to Dar es
Salaam, whence we were shipped to Mombasa when the war
ended."(33)

After the British had crossed the Central Railway, Watkins wrote,

> The lines of communication back to the Tanga-Moshi railway
> were now of unprecedented length, and the first step was to
> convert the Central Railway....into the base line of the Force...
> as rapidly as possible, the situation being much ameliorated if
> not saved from absolute disaster, by the fitting of trolley
> wheels to transport vehicles of various kinds....The first however
> only got to Dodoma on October 6th....The interval was one of
> short rations and considerable sufferings....and, where the
> troops suffer the condition of the followers is apt to be
> pitiable.(34)

The Germans had extensively damaged all the railways, but Indian
Army Sapper units restored them remarkably fast and thoroughly.
The Central Railway was therefore open to steam trains by

December 1916; but the enemy had "failed to take the one step we feared....of pulling up track and throwing miles of fastenings into the bush." The sappers had restored 300 miles of line in three months.(35)   Meanwhile the force was having a very bad time: the 1st Division at Kilwa, the 2nd at Dodoma, and the 3rd around the Uluguru Mountains. The latter were given an "appalling report" by their chief medical officer, which augured ill for Smuts' southward thrust.(36)

Three developments need mention here. First, Bishop Frank Weston and his Zanzibar Mission Carrier Corps took part in the drive on Dar es Salaam.(37)   Next, Tabora had been taken in August 1916 by Anglo-Belgian forces whose carriers were mainly from Uganda; the Belgians, whose administration dated only from 1908, were unable to recruit enough of their own. Also, thinking of the future of the conquered territory, the British may not have wanted to be too indebted to the Belgians, who seem to have been disinclined to exert themselves in conquests where the British would get the lion's share. Uganda accordingly provided the so-called Belgian Congo Carrier Corps (Carbels) of 8,429 men, and about 120,000 "job" porters. Carbels and the Uganda Transport Corps (UTC) Carrier Section were disbanded at the end of 1916.(38)

The third development was the expansion of the KAR in April 1916; the 2nd and 6th regiments were revived, the former being Nyasa, the latter ex-German askari. All six regiments had two battalions each; the 7th KAR was formed out of the Zanzibar Rifles and Mafia Constabulary, with one battalion. Finally there were twenty-two battalions, which took over the entire campaign at the end of 1917.(39)   This affected the Carrier Corps because of competition for recruits. Smuts suggested picking 3,000 men for the first three new battalions from the 30,000 carriers available in April 1916.(40)   On the other hand, the Administrator of North-East Rhodesia was reluctant to deplete his carrier forces by allowing the recruitment of Bemba for the new 2nd KAR.(41)

"I got a gun at Kilwa," said Kimumo Kitui, who had done a long haul as a stretcher bearer throughout 1916. "I became a soldier, KAR, Company D of Captain Ngomoli." He then served in Portuguese East Africa; he was under fire many times, and had a bullet through the leg. The list of the places he went to - including Moshi, Morogoro, Kilwa, Lindi, Port Amelia - suggests that he missed little and was lucky to have survived.(42)   As well as enhancing the status of the carrier, the superiority of the African soldier was clearly established. In justice to the departed Indians, South Africans and others, it was not their fault that they had been unable to win this terrible war, in which the climate was a greater enemy than the Germans.

After the exhausted collapse of Smuts' offensive in September round the Uluguru Mountains, an even more gruesome phase was the advance on the Rufiji River.

> The practice of relieving carriers every six or nine months....
> which had obtained throughout 1915, had proved impossible
> during the advance. By September 1916, when they were
> suddenly called upon for a supreme effort on short rations, the
> men were already debilitated and overworked. As a final

torture the rains broke early, and converted large areas into swamp, throwing still more work on the Carrier, who....on the Dodoma-Iringa road had to carry nine miles mostly waist-deep in water, much of it on raised duck walks made of undressed poles laid side by side....The sufferings and casualties of this period from September 1916 to March 1917 will never be fully known.(43)

In his final despatch, Hoskins described the plight of the forces he had taken over from Smuts. Near Kilwa, tsetse killed animals; motors stuck in mud. Boats supplied troops on the Matandu and Rufiji rivers, and porters carried further inland. The Dodoma-Iringa line had to be supported by another from Kilosa, to supply Northey's force, involving "heavy casualties among porters and donkeys" as well as whites. Troops were often on half rations, and the Dodoma line was not usable again until May.(44)

Iringa and the Southern Highlands could be supplied from Dodoma and Kilosa on the Central Railway, but the Great Ruaha River, a tributary almost as big as the Rufiji itself, divides the Highlands. The other line, from Mikesse on the Railway to the Rufiji, crossed the eastern skirts of the Uluguru Mountains, with their ridges and valleys. In such country, when roads are of earth, with few if any bridges, prolonged heavy rain transforms dry watercourses into raging torrents, which may flow for weeks if the rain is continuous, as it was in early 1917. A line upon which part of an army depended for supplies was exposed to rains which were more copious in such mountainous country than on the plains. The Rufiji itself was 300 yards wide, and ten Nigerian soldiers were once drowned trying to cross it. The Mgeta River was crossed by an overhead wire and trolley, while further north the road was under water for two miles, and crocodiles from the river sometimes killed carriers:

> Dead mules and donkeys and even dead carriers littered the road on each side in various stages of putrefaction. [In the twelve miles from Duthumi to Tulo] the road ran through the worst sort of stinking black mud....The state of the road explained for itself the shortage of rations on the Rufiji.... In order to feed 3,000 native troops, Europeans and various departmental units, an army of at least 12,000 men had to be employed.(45)

Motor transport drivers fell sick almost at once; even the light Ford, which could negotiate black cotton soil, was little use.

The plight of the porter, with his load of over fifty pounds, passes imagination. Cold, wet, hungry, sick with dysentery, pneumonia or both, their only food half cooked porridge made of mealie meal which was fermenting from being soaked, many staggered off the road to die in the reeking mud. Soldiers and followers must have shared a common level of misery.

THE MASS LEVY OF 1917

Meanwhile, Smuts was assuring everyone in the outer world that it was all over, and the Germans were incapable of serious resistance. His successor, in charge of the mopping-up operations, soon put out plans whose contents Smuts knew perfectly well; before he left, Colonel Dobbs gave him a sombre briefing on the seriousness of the motor transport situation, in view of which "I honestly cannot see how we are going to feed the troops." He advised reducing the size of the forward units.(46)

Smuts was therefore well aware of the scale of the operations which would follow his departure. As for carriers, on 31 December 1916 there were only 62,334 effectives left, 150,000 having been recruited by then in the East Africa Protectorate and German East Africa. Hoskins can only have had 40,000 when he stated that he would need 160,000 carriers. He also protested at the withdrawal of troops, artillery and aircraft to Egypt; there was no margin of either personnel or material for his strategic railways. He also asked for 500 Reo American light lorries, and the War Office, taken aback by all these demands for a campaign which was supposed to be over, promised 200 for mid-May. Carriers would be needed from Portuguese East Africa, as well as the new West African porters, but "this involved questions of diplomacy not easily to be resolved," at least until von Lettow did so by crossing the Rovuma. Hoskins also asked for 15,000 extra carriers a month, to replace wastage expected to be at 15 percent.(47)

This meant three times as many carriers as Smuts had had the previous December, when recruitment had been hard enough. "The D.M.L. is doing his best, but as far as I can see (unless we get Belgian help) we will have to rely on local carriers, and the most we can get is 5,000."(48) The bid for Belgian help had failed at a high level, as a telegram from the War Office made clear: "You will have learnt from Byatt that the protracted negotiations with Belgians was due entirely to the attitude adopted by them. Negotiations for their further military co-operation will be dropped definitely. Foreign Office has been requested to make immediate representations to ensure your supply of porters from Tabora."(49) Little hope seems to have been felt for porters from the Belgians; they had no formulae on which to calculate porter requirements, reported their British liaison officer:

> They have neither the tradition of nor the qualities essential to porter organisation, [nor] European personnel for this purpose... Porters are merely dumped in bulk into a combatant unit and have to take their chance.... In all matters concerning porters their Hibernian propensity to interpret "hopes" as facts is ineradicable.... [Thus] the wastage of such raw material as they collect is terrible, and....even if they do manage to mobilise their theoretical complement, [soon] their forces may become relatively immobile.

The soldiers' numerous women needed an extra 20 percent of food, "the price which must be paid for the general morale of their force." They needed about 18,000 porters for their own force, of whom they had about 10,000. Half were German East Africa men already handed over to the MLB; another 3,000 were from Katanga and had "established some organic relationship with the troops to whom they are attached." (50) Having occupied the centre of the country, the Belgians were to advance from Kilosa to Mahenge.

Horace Byatt had become Administrator of Occupied Territory (north of the Central Railway), on 11 December. First, of course, he had to supply military labor, which the military themselves did south of the Railway; they would have been much less concerned with political repercussions than Byatt, or the authorities in the East Africa Protectorate or Uganda.(51) General Staff plans to finish the campaign were now to exact from the civil governments their supreme effort in labor recruiting.

This meant the "mass levy." Hoskins' first aim was to make the Rufiji the northern base line, though the notorious road from Mikesse through Duthumi and "Summit" had to be kept up.(52) There was a preliminary survey of transport problems. There were an estimated 7,000 German troops (forty companies), half of whom were south and east of the Rufiji, a quarter in the mountains between Neu Langenburg (Tukuyu) and Songea, and the rest divided between the Mahenge Plateau and the Lindi hinterland. They could either hold the whole area or concentrate on a rich inland area like Songea, but "whichever course the enemy takes, his eventual retirement into Portuguese East Africa is possible." Van Deventer already had four columns. First, a brigade under Colonel Taylor was to advance on Mahenge from Iringa. Secondly, the Nigerian Brigade was to meet it in the same area, basing itself on the Rufiji. Thirdly, the two Kilwa brigades under Brigadier-General Hannyngton were to strike inland towards Liwale, using the sixty miles of tramway built mainly with Taita labor from Voi District. Finally, there was the Lindi force under Brigadier-General O'Grady. The backbone of the force was now African; the Gold Coast Regiment was part of "Hanforce." All would depend on motor transport where possible, but ultimately on porters.(53)

The lorries were vital to Hoskins' plans; if his minimum requirements of 400 lorries with 800 drivers were not met by the end of April, he would need another 12,000 porters, thirty of whom would do the work of one lorry.(54) But it would be the end of May before the country was dry enough for the troops to move and the new carrier levies were available. Hoskins warned the War Office: "[Smuts' statements] may be conveying a wrong impression as to the probability of this campaign being brought to a speedy conclusion. Enemy's force is in being and well controlled." It could be even more prolonged if von Lettow dispersed over a wide area or crossed the Rovuma; "if contrary to above is believed, misunderstanding and disappointment will arise." The decision to replace Hoskins had already been taken.(55)

Watkins explained in detail why the new plans would need so many carriers. The new campaign would be in a country without modern communications, and with little white settlement. The enemy would leave few supplies or able-bodied men, and could wage a guerilla war, using no fixed centre; the aim was to surround him. It was estimated that 160,000 carriers would be needed, with 16,000 replacements a month. The East Africa Protectorate produced 67,799 and Uganda 10,934 up to 31 July 1917, when there were about 120,000 on MLB books, "besides personal servants and casual labour. Owing to the difficulties of shipping such large numbers, this number was the nearest approach ever made to estimated requirements."(56)

These demands led to tremendous efforts and to bitter controversy; we are concerned here only with the effects on governments and General Staff. In the British territories, Nyanza excelled as a source of labor, because it was the most closely administered, its population not being larger than that of some other areas. Its Provincial Commissioner since 1907 had been John Ainsworth; his work in carrier recruiting had already been praised by General Ewart: "Watkins and I were saying only yesterday that if it hadn't been for you and your efforts we should have been in a bad way.... The porters you have sent are simply invaluable, and it is solely due to your having had them in the past 3 weeks that the force below the Rufigi [sic] has been able to move at all." He ends with a significant admission: "It was disappointing that the push on 1st Jan. didn't succeed in this but the country is so impossible that they invariably break through any net the General may spread for them."(57)   One suspects that staff officers can have had little faith in plans to encircle the enemy in this dense bush country, when Smuts had signally failed to do so in the relatively open Kilimanjaro area.

At the end of February, Hoskins formally asked the governor of the East Africa Protectorate for Ainsworth's services, "to arrange for the maximum number of men from BEA with a minimum of hardship to the settlers and the natives themselves." He was plainly "the only man suitable for such a position." He would have the title of Military Commissioner for Labour and the rank of Colonel.(58) Only five days earlier Provincial Commissioners had been told of the need to recruit porters from the "non-native" areas of the Protectorate, meaning the "White Highlands" - the Rift Valley, Uasin Gishu and Laikipia. The labor in the reserves was said to be nearly exhausted, a significant admission on the even of the mass levy. The orders were directed specifically at natives squatting on unalienated Crown Land.(59)   Three days after his appointment, Ainsworth announced his plans; there were reckoned to be over 195,000 men between the ages of eighteen and thirty in Nyanza, Kenia, Ukamba and Seyidie provinces. By the end of April a "capital draft" of 30,000 was to be produced, with reinforcing drafts of 13,000 a month for June and July. Ainsworth explained that motor and animal transport had become virtually impossible in the theatre of operations; "in other words it has become a porters' war." It was hoped that the campaign could be finished off in a few months by the massive effort proposed, in the interests of the Protectorate and all its inhabitants. Probably men who had already served as carriers might again be called on if they had been home for three months, but conditions had improved very greatly in the Carrier Corps.(60)

The problem of "plural enlistment" arises here, but in fact unexpectedly large numbers were found unfit, which must often have been due to the effects of previous service. Though it was now hoped to eliminate the German forces by the end of July, Ainsworth admitted that carriers might be in for longer "if hostilities go on." In fact the Rift Valley or Naivasha Province was left out of the levy, though some men may have been caught and returned to their districts of origin to be written on.

The East Africa Protectorate at once set out to meet the demands. Ainsworth was also responsible for the Uganda levy, where matters were very delicate. In the first year of the war, casualties had been very high: there had been a death rate of 23 percent among the 3,576 men who had joined the old East Africa Carrier Corps in August 1914. Indeed, H. R. Wallis (Chief Secretary) had put it at 32 percent, counting those who had died after going home. On 7 April 1917 the Governor, Sir Frederick Jackson, retired; Wallis took over as Acting Governor. Both men had felt very strongly about the deaths among the Ganda and their neighbours, who were "green food" eaters, their staple diet being matoke (plantain) or cooking banana fresh off the tree. The disasters of 1899 and of the present war suggested very forcibly that these men could not be taken far from home and fed with grain food to which they were not used, without heavy mortality ensuing.(61)

Hoskins was also trying to get porters from the Portuguese authorities and from the South African Chamber of Mines. He also sent Colonel Dobbs (AQMG) to Nairobi and Entebbe, with Ainsworth and Watkins. After a meeting with Jackson and Wallis on 28 March, they agreed only to recruit from the Eastern Province of Uganda, where the people were grain eaters. Jackson still thought it highly risky to send men from such an arid area to the swampy parts of German East Africa. Also, carrier recruiting there might conflict with both the needs of the KAR and of cotton-growing, which was an Imperial priority, being used in high explosives as well as for clothing and equipment. Wallis suggested recruiting in Mwanza and Bukoba, where there were 200,000 suitable men according to the German census, grain eaters and used to porterage. It was decided to abide by the decision of General Hoskins, and that Mjanji Port was to be the depot if Uganda recruiting proceeded. A further consideration was that, as the MLB was short of European staff also, compulsion might be needed here too.(62)

Ainsworth decided to supplement the East Africa Protectorate levy from the German Lake areas, because the Kikuyu or Kamba were less suited climatically to the lowlands of German East Africa than were the Coast or Lake people. But the Seyidie and Tanaland provinces were small in population, and had too little control as yet "to allow of any large proportion of men being got out of their districts." But political difficulties with settlers were plainly in his mind: "any interference with the normal industries of B.E.A. will be avoided. A certain number of men can....be obtained from off the farms in B.E.A. If, however, we can get the whole of the men from the Native Districts so much the better."(63)

Dobbs mentioned a private agreement about the need for porters between Ainsworth and Spire, Provincial Commissioner of Eastern Province, which was unknown to Wallis. The census suggested that the Province could produce 15,000 men on "capital account" and a monthly draft of 1,500, which Wallis could not refute, though "the question of cotton growing was the trump card put down on the table in front of us."   Dobbs thought that recruiting in the insufficiently controlled Mwanza area would take too long, and that KAR needs were an inadequate objection.(64) Finally, Wallis agreed to start recruiting, providing Ainsworth dealt lightly with the cotton areas; the Colonial Office would be kept informed as it would certainly query the effects on the next cotton crop. But in fact their view was that it would not matter if some cotton growers went as porters, since it was so difficult to ship the crop.(65)

At the end of June, Wallis reported that about 6,750 had been passed fit out of over 24,000; of one draft at Mjanji, 730 out of about 960 were unfit, which is confirmed by H. B. Thomas, assistant Carrier Officer there at the time. The administered areas had now been covered, and unrest was feared if recruitment was not now confined to the KAR.(66) Ainsworth was sceptical about the effort involved; 8,000 recruits were less than 9 percent of the number he had thought were available. Nyanza had 86,759 available compared with the 92,372 of the Eastern Province, yet had produced over 60 percent since the outbreak of war. Men were still available for the KAR, and the willing cooperation of the East Africa Protectorate authorities, he thought, showed up the grudging attitude of those in Uganda. There might be less control than in the East Africa Protectorate, but there had been no difficulty in collecting labor before the war. Possible unrest had been an excuse for having nothing comparable to the NFRO, which had led to no trouble in the East Africa Protectorate. Uganda was 7,350 men short on its drafts, but Ainsworth admitted that the levy was unsettling people in the East Africa Protectorate, the physical standard as falling and the wastage high; he doubted if the drafts could be kept up for July.(67) This despatch was used against Wallis by van Deventer, but Ainsworth had privately voiced his misgivings to Watkins a month earlier: the poor physique of the recruits "has been a revelation to me....the supply of the class of men required is nearly exhausted." Moreover, many of the East Africa Protectorate and Uganda men were climatically unsuited to the present theatre of war.(68)

Since so many men were unfit in the East Africa Protectorate as well as Uganda, it is surely most unlikely that men who had been home for only three months from the Carrier Corps would have been fit for the mass levy, as Ainsworth had originally hoped. Evidence is strongly against such men having been re-enlisted.

Watkins had been doubtful too about carrier quotas being reached, just as the furore against Wallis was starting. The numbers available had been affected by shortage of shipping, wastage in the field, and the poor physique of "the labour available in the British Protectorates after nearly three years of war." Also, the growth of the KAR and its labor requirement, and the fact that "an indefinite obligation has been taken to supply the Belgian forces with transport," all led Watkins to his previously stated opinion "that labour....will not be available to carry out the original plans of General Staff." Since the plan had come out, all needs had risen: lines of communication, wharf labor, building labor, hospital staff. "I can only repeat, in the most emphatic manner, that labour for

operations on the scale proposed will not be forthcoming." There
was no suggestion here that the Uganda government was even partly
to blame for the results in overambitious military planning.(69)

The Uganda recruiting figures did, however, compare unfavour-
ably with those of the East Africa Protectorate and the German
Lake areas. At the end of May C. C. Bowring (Acting Governor of
the East Africa Protectorate) gave the totals as 3,250, 33,483, and
5,011 respectively; Ainsworth had achieved this in only three
months, when 50 percent had been found unfit, and the normal
labor requirements of the East Africa Protectorate had had to be
met.(70) Uganda lacked the pressure exerted by the East Africa
Protectorate settlers, who welcomed carrier recruiting for its
disciplinary effects, as long as they had enough themselves. But the
East Africa Protectorate government did not have to worry about
good relations with any treaty states like Buganda.

Van Deventer alleged that "local civil officers fail to recognise
extreme urgency of our military requirements of porters and the
chiefs are withholding able bodied men from medical examination,"
a statement Wallis called "both unjust and uncalled for." Van
Deventer gave the history of the dispute to the War Office, who
forwarded it to the Colonial Office, who told Wallis that his failure
to provide the porters was regrettable, that his suggestion about
the priority of cotton was resented, and that he must explain the
rejection rate of 88 percent, as opposed to 45 percent in the East
Africa Protectorate.(71)

Wallis pointed out that 42,000 had been called up, out of
102,000 aged between sixteen and sixty. The local medical officers,
acting on standard instructions, rejected 27,000. Another 6,000 were
rejected at Mjanji, and 1,500 more at East Africa Protectorate
Depots. In view of this high rate he had dropped his objections over
cotton growing. But he was still told that, unless he could explain
the high number of rejections, he stood convicted of bad faith, and
of "attitude of passive resistance."(72)   He was retired on 10
February 1918.   "H.R.W. was hard-bitten and forthright with long
experience of Africa. He had every reason to stand up to the
military....[who] broke him in the end," wrote H. B. Thomas, who
paid tribute, in an obituary on Wallis in 1946, to his competent
handling of the unprecedented emergency as Acting Governor at the
outbreak of war, but "it will be no service to the memory of a
high-minded and selfless public servant to suppress the fact that
Mr. H.R. Wallis retired and died a disappointed man." He thought
the military demands on Uganda's limited manpower were ill-
considered, the calls on it for a far-away campaign insatiable, and
the losses from illness fearful. He was not afraid to say so. "He
was branded by the Military authorities as non-cooperative, and no
further civil promotion was offered to him." He was, in fact,
refused a knighthood.(73)

Jackson had been even firmer than Wallis in rejecting Smuts'
requests for porters the previous December; apart from the risk of
carrying plague, meningitis and smallpox, "it would in my opinion
be little short of wholesale homicide" to send men from arid to
swampy areas, a view which had the support of the doctors. But as
Jackson retired in April 1917, Wallis had to deal with the levy.

Jackson was a legendary character, who had led the first caravan of the Imperial BEA Company into Uganda in 1889; he had exceptional charm of manner, but there is no reason to think that he would have taken a different line than Wallis over the levy.(74) Wallis was less well known, and less diplomatic; he made the ideal scapegoat when the military expectations for porters proved to be so unrealistic, as the Director of Military Labour himself had pointed out. Here too, as with the replacement of Hoskins by van Deventer, one senses the desire to appease the South Africans.

The levy was suddenly called off in August 1917, though the war was far from over. Ainsworth was "absolutely certain that the B.E.A. officials have done their best to put up all available men.... but we have undoubtedly come to the end of our resources in this connection."(75) Officials were nervous about possible unrest, if not in the East Africa Protectorate, certainly in the occupied German districts. There were no more men, and the attempt to defeat von Lettow by the mass levy had failed like other expedients.(76)

When the Rufiji became the base line, casual labor was increasingly used behind it, by contracts with local chiefs. On the Mikesse line, "the local native at least undertook almost the whole burden of communication, supplying his own requirements besides a surplus of food for transport to other areas."(77) Carriers from the East Africa Protectorate highlands worked on the Dodoma to Iringa line, as the climate suited them; they included the Kikuyu Mission Volunteers (KMV). They supported the Belgian advance from Kilosa to Mahenge, which fell on 9 October 1917.

"During this period the part played by labour began to assume a character it subsequently retained." Bases were established, with wharfs, warehouses and water supplies. The Kilwa Railway and many roads were built as the troops advanced; motor transport took over from carriers, except where swamps or rain ruled out other forms of transport. Then "the Carrier took its place, while his brother the labourer fought the depredations of the rain on the causeways and bridges of the roads."(78) It all shows why so many men were needed, and the same system continued during operations in Portuguese East Africa. Here, MLB officers like Major F.M.S. Stokes acted as political officers in recruiting labor. Stokes had been worried by the gaps between Force and Line, which occurred when the former moved faster. So he organised his own link section and recruiting organisation, as he thought that the senior political officer was too inclined to meet Portuguese wishes. One way in which this was highly detrimental to recruiting was when Portuguese askari used force to collect taxes, seizing women in default, so that men naturally refused to leave their families unprotected.(79)

A final change in organisation resulted from having long lines manned by carriers; the large Corps or labor battalions had given way to the Gang System, which with the shape taken by operations in 1917 was now replaced by the Individual System, under which each man was separately paid.(80)

RETROSPECT

There were many eyewitnesses for the later stages of the war. Besides Lindi and Iringa, some served in Portuguese East Africa, and even visited Nyasaland, including two Machakos men, Nguku Mulwa and Musembi Kiindu, an ammunition carrier. At Kabati, near Muranga, Ng'ethe Kamau and Gitombo Muri knew of several who had been there.(81)

Odandayo Mukhenye Agweli, an askari in Bunyala, west Central Nyanza, had been to Morogoro, Mahenge and Iringa:

> At Lindi we had some battles. Indian troops joined us in this place to fight the enemy. The actual area was called Kampi ya Ndege (Aeroplane Camp)..... We had serious fights. Using mortars we levelled the whole place before attacking.... To this day I still do not know why we fought the Germans and how the war began. Though we admired the European ways of fighting, we were still left wondering why so many people had to die. In our tribal wars the number of the dead was never very big.(82)

Agweli and a neighbour, Asembo Odera, were with the 4th (Uganda) KAR. Odera's number was 1097, and he lost a leg. He greatly admired German courage and strength in battle. So many were fighting on the British side that sometimes they shot at each other unwittingly; he also claimed to be able to distinguish the sounds of British and German gunfire. Perhaps when alone in the bush, "I once encountered a German soldier. He did not shoot me, but just warned me that if I moved, that would be my end. 'Wewe bibi. Leo ni leo. Utakufa tu. Songa karibu, utaona,' said the German soldier to me. ('You are a woman. Today is today. You will die. Come nearer and you'll see.') The Germans used to fight from the tops of trees like monkeys." Why, he wondered, did Europeans force Africans into their wars? Agweli said that there were many songs, the best known being a victory song: "Keya dibuoro nindo gichuma oko! oko!" This means roughly that in the KAR a person spends his time away from home in battle, or has been killed away from home; the Luo word dibuoro means light skinned or even European, nindo means sleeping out, and chuma, meaning iron, implies a weapon of some kind. The repetition of oko, suggesting death far from home, gives added poignancy to the song. Both men said that the famine which followed the war was called Keya by the Nyala.(83)

Lazaro Maende was an ammunition carrier, so was often under fire; "I was present when Risasi (Bullet Camp) was shelled. I escaped injury though many died. Once I was shot at and unfortunately lost my finger from a bullet wound." Ngugi, a Kiambu machine gun carrier, was shot through the arm when carrying a load; front-line carriers could not take cover as fast as soldiers.(84)

"What they fought each other for I could not well make out," says Kaspar in Southey's poem After Blenheim. Africans felt the same, though those with mission education had an advantage. "We knew that the war had started in Europe," said a KMV man. "We thought that the Germans and British were fighting for power, and seeking to be greater and have a larger territory than the other."(85)

Anglo-German relations seemed ambiguous. "We naturally wondered why white men hated each other," said M'Inoti wa Tirikamu, a Meru carrier who had worked on the Namanga road. "They looked so much like brothers. We asked: do they fight for land, or for the power to rule, or is it because they are all white, or why?"(86)   On the other hand, when not fighting with each other, British and Germans seemed so friendly: "German officers would come to the British camp and we would see them talking, not as enemies would do. This often surprised us," said Muasya Maitha and Umoa Mbatha. But truces were not unusual in African wars; at any rate, they now knew that there was more than one white tribe.(87)

Another song was remembered by the Meru soldier Muthanya; "after killing Germans we would sing as follows":

Ui U Nkiuraga Njirimani	When I killed a German
Munene Wakwa Naiji	My leader knew about it.
Ui U Maitha ni Nkiritu	Enemies are dangerous!

The famous KAR marching song was (with variations):

Funga sa-fa-ri!	Pack up for the journey!
Funga sa-fa-ri	
Amri ya nani?	Whose order?
Amri, amri ya Kapteni!	The Captain's order!
Amri ya KAR!	The KAR's order!

They might also move upward through the ranks: Amri ya bwana Kapteni, and so on.(88)

Experiences must have given endless food for thought and discussion, but immediately after their return, the reaction of Nduini's son may well have been common: "You must not ask me of such things, for I will not speak of them so long as I live."(89) Though time can heal much of the pain and horror, people tend to suppress their worst memories.

Ultimately the campaign depended on the courage and cheerfulness of the African troops and followers; it was not their fault that the strategy failed. The verdict of General Northey was: "I would award the palm of merit to the Tenga-Tenga," as the carrier was called in Nyasaland.(90) Meinertzhagen had the greatest admiration for KAR and carriers: "with scant discipline [the porters] have proved themselves....to be stout-hearted fellows, and cheerful in adversity. On three occasions they have stood their ground when South African and Indian troops have moved back. And what some of these gallant porters have suffered will never be known."(91)

NOTES

1.   Interview near Limuru, 8 Nov. 1969.

2.   Hordern, Operations in EA, 212-213.

3.   W. K. Hancock, Smuts: The Sanguine Years, 1870-1919 (Cambridge: Cambridge University Press, 1962), 408; H. C. Armstrong, Grey Steel: J. C. Smuts, A Study in Arrogance (London: Barker-Methuen, 1937), 217-218; Meinertzhagen, Army Diary, 164, 186.

4.   PRO, CAB 45/31, note by Lieutenant-Colonel L. M. Davies on Salaita, 17 Oct. 1934; Army Diary, 165.

5.   Army Diary, 166, 176-200.

6.   Hordern, Operations in EA, 277-278.

7.   Meinertzhagen, Army Diary, 179-186.

8.   Francis Brett Young, Marching on Tanga (London: Collins, 1917), is the classic account of this march.

9.   Hordern, Operations in EA, 324, n. 1, 354, n. 1.

10. PRO, CAB 45/31B, J. J. Drought to F. S. Joelson, 17 Nov. 1938, how his irregular "Skin Corps" reached Mwanza, on Lake Victoria, before a South African force.

11. Hordern, Operations in EA, 287-288; PRO, CAB 45/34, comment by Lieutenant-Colonel Haskard, Royal Artillery.

12. Hancock, Smuts, 421; Armstrong, Smuts, 216.

13. Von Lettow, Reminiscences, 149.

14. D. Reitz, Trekking On (London: Faber, 1933), 145.

15. Von Lettow, Reminiscences, 140, 158; Mosley, Duel for Kilimanjaro, 150-153, text of surrender document.

16. Hordern, Operations in EA, 393; PRO, CAB 45/31C, Lieutenant-Colonel Crofton, and CAB 45/30, Major Bremner.

17. PRO, CAB 44/9, The Times, 29 Jan. and 13 March 1917.

18. PRO, CAB 44/9, 45/31C; Fendall, EAF, 99-101.

19. WP, Movements and General Staff Plan; PRO, CAB 23/2, p. 129, War Cabinet minutes, 23 April 1917; van Deventer was asked, not ordered, to take the command, showing that it was a political appointment, as Brigadier-General Fendall (EAF, 101)

and Major Guy (CAB 45/33G) both say. It is clear from CAB 23/2 that the Chief of the Imperial General Staff, Sir William Robertson, took Smuts' advice in replacing Hoskins with van Deventer. CAB 45/33, comments on Smuts' claims to have trained new KAR units; Army Diary, 205.

20.   WP, General Staff plan; Downes, Nigerians, 226, gives the casualties as 2,700 out of 4,900; von Lettow, Reminiscences, 211-212; Moyse-Bartlett, KAR, 381-382; PRO, CAB 44/10, for effects on the Lindi force.

21.   Hordern, Operations in EA, 393, 265, n. 4.

22.   WR. paras. 10, 13 and 16; also 61-62.

23.   Ibid., paras 23, 65-67; Hordern, Operations in EA, 217, n. 1.

24.   WR. para. 67.

25.   Ibid., paras. 69-70.

26.   PRO, CO 534/21/18914, Smuts to SSC, 19 April 1916; WR, para. 28 for discharges.

27.   Buchanan, War in EA, Chapter 5.

28.   Brett Young, Tanga, 191, 235.

29.   Hordern, Operations in EA, 277, n. 2, and 324-325: van Deventer to Smuts, 3 June 1916.

30.   Brett Young, Tanga, 139; Meinertzhagen, Army Diary, 97 and 194-195.

31.   Notes kindly given by Gervase Mutua.

32.   Notes kindly given by Moses Oyugi.

33.   Interview 13 Dec. 1969.

34.   WR. para. 27; author's italics.

35.   Hill, Permanent Way, vol. II, 167-169; see PRO, CAB 45/16, Major-General R. E. Ewart and subordinates, on unnecessary supplies blocking trolley line, clearing Dar harbor.

36.   PRO, CAB 45/16, Ewart to Dobbs, 2 Oct. 1916.

37.   See Chapter 10 below, "The Bishop of Zanzibar's Carrier Corps."

38.   PRO, CO 879/119, "Belgian occupied territory in German East Africa," 27 Oct. 1918; Hordern, Operations in EA, Chapter 12, 201, 208; see also Table 3 below.

39. Moyse-Bartlett, KAR, 332-336.

40. See n. 26 above.

41. PRO, CO 534/21/28724, Smuts to SSC, 18 June 1916.

42. Notes kindly given by Fred Katule, Machakos.

43. WR. para. 28.

44. PRO, CAB 45/34, Hoskins to WO, 30 May 1917.

45. Downes, Nigerians, 109-114; see also PRO, CAB 44/6, 92-94: four of the five stages were supposed to be by motor; Dobbs to the General Officer Commanding-in-Chief, 9 Jan. 1917, only 5,000 a day reaching Rufiji, when 50,000 were needed; later, it was worked by casual labor - 12,002 were recruited at "Summit": WR, Appendix 1, Table 11.

46. PRO, CAB 44/6, Dobbs to Smuts, 9 Jan. 1917.

47. WR, Appendices 1 and 2; PRO, CAB 44/9, plans for the 1917 campaign; CO 536/88/50149, Hoskins to WO, 17 March.

48. PRO, CAB 44/6, mem. by AQMG, 6 Dec. 1916.

49. WP, General Staff plan, Troopers London to Smuts (wire), 20 Dec. 1916.

50. Ibid., "Extract from Report by Senior Military Liaison Officer," n. d., anon., but almost certainly by E. S. Grogan, who was liaison officer with the Belgians.

51. Hill, Permanent Way, vol. II, 173.

52. WP, DAAQMG to Hannyngton, 11 Feb. 1917, also ADST Duthumi to IGC Dar es Salaam, 14 Feb. 1917.

53. WP, Secret General Staff Memorandum, 25 Feb. 1917.

54. Ibid., Hoskins to WO, 4 March 1917, also PRO, CAB 44/9. W. W. Campbell, East Africa by Motor Lorry (London: Murray, 1928), is an excellent and lively account of this work.

55. PRO, CAB 44/9, Hoskins to Chief of the Imperial General Staff, 4 May 1917.

56. WR. para. 35. See Appendix 2 below.

57. Ainsworth Papers, Rhodes House MSS Afr. 379-382: 381, Ewart to Ainsworth, 31 Jan. 1917.

58. Ibid., Hoskins to Belfield, 27 Feb. 1917.

59. KNA, Sec. Circ. No. 12, 22 Feb. 1917; see also 37/577, vol. 4.

60. KNA, Sec. Circ. No. 19, 19 March 1917; 37/577,vol. 4, Ainswor-th's circular to PCs giving instructions, 21 Mar. 1917.

61. NAU/SMP 4290 Part 2, ADT Entebbe to Ch. Sec. Uganda, 12 March 1917; Jackson to Belfield, 8 June 1915.

62. PRO, CO 536/85/30772, precis of meeting; wire Hoskins to WO, 17 March, in CO 536/88/50149; the precis quotes two wires from Jackson to Smuts objecting to recruiting. A third file is CO 536/86/52618; future references are to serial numbers only. Cotton was used as a stabilising agent with nitro-glycerine when filling shells and bombs; in both world wars it was a vital basic raw material (Detail kindly given by Mr. A.J. Malpas).

63. 50149, MCL to DAAQMG, 29 March 1917.

64. Ibid., Colonel Dobbs' notes, 11 April 1917.

65. 30772, Wallis to Hoskins, 14 April 1917, min. by Read.

66. 50149, Wallis to Admin, staff, undated; H. B. Thomas, letter to author 19 Jan. 1970, guessed that two out of three were unfit.

67. Ibid., MCL to DAAQMG 30 June and 2 July 1917, latter on poor medical standard of East Africa Protectorate men; but Inspector-General of Communications to DAAQMG 19 July 1917 denied that Uganda had high rate of unfitness.

68. WP, secret file, Ainsworth to Watkins, 31 May 1917.

69. Ibid., Watkins to DAAQMG, 30 June 1917.

70. PRO, CO 533/182/39828, Bowring to SSC, 20 June 1917.

71. 50149, letters between van Deventer and Wallis, 30 June to 18 July 1917, and van Deventer to WO, 28 July; but in H. B. Thomas Papers (RCSL), Spire (PC Eastern Province) urged DCs to meet quota, 18 April 1917; 50149, on WO complaint, 11, 23 and 26 Oct. 1917.

72. 52618, Wallis to SSC, 25 Oct. 1917, reply 31 Oct.

73. H.B.T. to author 19 Jan. 1970; Mr. Thomas kindly drew my attention to the obituary in East Africa, 14 March 1946; Wallis drew attention to his services and work on the Hand-book of Uganda - CO 536/93/2764 and 90/60006.

74. 30772, Jackson to Smuts, 3 and 5 Dec. 1916.

75. KNA, EAP Sec. Circ. No. 55, 8 Aug. 1917.

76. WP, Byatt to DAAQMG, 9 Nov. 1917; WR. para. 37.

77. WR, para. 73, and Appendix 1, Table 11.

78. Ibid., para. 41.

79. WR, paras. 42-45; WP, correspondence between Watkins and Stokes, April-June 1918.

80. WR, para. 72.

81. Interview with Musembi Kiindu, Kilungu, 3 Oct. 1970; interview at Kabati, 25 Nov. 1970.

82. and 83.   Notes kindly given by Felix Osodo; Ertiman Gendia and David Sperling kindly helped with the translation.

84. Notes kindly given by Vitalis Ojode (Maende), at Homa Bay, South Nyanza; notes on Ngugi kindly given by Kinyanjui Gitao.

85. Interview at Kahuhia Church, Muranga, 29 May 1970.

86. Notes kindly given by Gervase Mutua.

87. Interview at Muthetheni, Machakos, 14 June 1969.

88. Repeated by another Meru soldier, M'Laibuni wa Baikwamba, notes kindly given by Zakayo Munene; see also George Shepperson, "The Military History of British Central Africa," review of Moyse-Bartlett, KAR, in Rhodes-Livingstone Journal, 26 (1960), 23-33; I am grateful to Mr. Charles Richards for the full version, heard in Nairobi.

89. Huxley, Red Strangers, 280.

90. S. S. Murray, A Handbook of Nyasaland (Zomba: Government Printer, 1922), 271; I am grateful to the Librarian, University of Malawi, for a photocopy of the relevant part; see also M. E. Page, in JAH, 19, 1 (1978), 87-100.

91. Meinertzhagen, Army Diary, 202-3.

Chapter 6
The Carriers' Pay

"My salary was 5 <u>pesa</u> (rupees). This money would either be given to me, sent home to my family, or saved for me."

(Josphat Muranga Njoroge, KMV)[1]

The Carrier Corps reflected pre-war labor problems. Government and private employers in the East Africa Protectorate disliked high military wages to attract carriers; the settlers wanted compulsory military labor, at rates which they dictated. But all except the War Office agreed after the war that wages due to missing carriers should be paid to the tribes.

THE PAY SYSTEM

In 1914, the headman of each batch of carriers sent to Mombasa or Nairobi was given a list of names by his District Commissioner, who sent the duplicate to the Carrier Depot Officer (CDO). But as many men deserted or joined friends in other units, the lists seldom tallied, and military and civil records differed, "which led ultimately to much friction and confusion."(2) So the improvised system broke down at once, and matters were made worse by the habit of changing names, often for reasons of custom, perfectly logical but misunderstood. There is always a contest of wits between employer and labor, and the Carrier Corps was no exception. "Men regarded in terms of 'lift' are an expensive form of transport." Though cheap to replace, they needed food, clothing, pay, medical attention and compensation if disabled. "They have moreover a human intellect mainly used for shirking their work, or avoiding sanitary and other regulations which contravene their habits and customs."(3)

There were two initial problems: how to register the carriers, and how to pay them. At first, the officer commanding a Corps kept the nominal role, notifying all payments and alterations to CC headquarters, which kept duplicates of the acquittance rolls, and drew cash from the civil treasury. This worked in theory, but not in practice, owing to the dispersal of the men.(4) Under the Carrier Section, the Depots kept pay records and paid balances to men on discharge. In March 1915 the new East Africa Pay Corps took over payment of labor units from the civil authorities. But the "unit" and "central" systems of control still conflicted; Force "C" units competed with each other, and wrote on each other's deserters. But this was less easy in Force "B" with its central control; however, accounts and records were kept with greatly varying efficiency. Despite the Depot system, still "it was possible for units to have on their pay numbers of natives who were not on any Carrier Depot books and of whom the D.A.D.T. Carrier Section had no knowledge."(5)

For instance, a certain Kamandu was signed on as a carrier headman with the KAR patrol during the Giriama uprising. His pay was Rs.20 a month, a porter getting Rs.15, both with posho (food) extra, as was usual with all wages. Kamandu served from September 1914 to mid-November, when he was dismissed at Voi for desertion, having only had Rs.10. He said he had deserted because the KAR had refused to honor his contract, their headmen being paid only Rs.15. Kamandu had a very good report from Dr. Wynstone Waters, both for his work and record at Malindi, the KAR were wrong to say that he was a porter and not a headman. Hobley demanded that he be paid at Rs.20 for the days that he had worked.(6)

Another headman, Nubi bin Safu, had been transferred to the machine gun section from Surveys in October 1914, and a month later to Carriers, at Rs.20. He claimed to have been underpaid by Rs.69.61; the District Commissioner of Mombasa said that he heard of such cases daily, and if Nubi was telling the truth, "it is not to be wondered at that we are finding the utmost difficulty in getting men to enlist in the Carriers." It also showed the problem of keeping track of movements "from one Military Department to another."(7) If other District Commissioners had this experience, many carriers must have been underpaid, and others overpaid.

That was what the military auditors found after the MLB was formed. A Zanzibari called Baruti, for instance, had started at Rs.25, but though by December 1915 his pay was down to Rs.15, his final payment was at the old rate(8) Advances were paid as required, rather than by the month, the man receiving the balance due to him at discharge. Rejects and repatriates were given vouchers showing the amounts due to them for payment by their District Commissioners, who were sent duplicate copies; receipts were thumb-printed and sent to Carrier headquarters.(9)

A tax defaulter, Bakari bin Salimu, who was arrested in Mombasa in August 1915, declared that he could not pay, but that the Carrier Corps owed him Rs.80. The Carrier Depot Officer had no record of him, but he was found on the roll of CC 1, with the number 33. He said that his discharge certificate had been taken away by Mr. Kerslake Thomas, who had been a Carrier Officer and was discharged as unsuitable: Bakari was jailed for the want of Rs.3 to pay a fine; if his statement was true, said his District Commissioner, things must be put right, but if false, "I should be glad to be in a position to deny it."(10)

The dangers of being unregistered with Carriers were shown by Malashi, who worked as a sweeper with the 2nd Rhodesia Regiment; he had no number but had been "in other military employ" before. "He is now at Voi and can not doubt assist in tracing himself."(11) In practice it might not be so easy for a man to account for his movements, even when physically present; when absent, it must have been far harder. How could anyone be sure if a man, who existed only as a name and number on a roll, with perhaps Rs.40 due to him, was alive, dead, deserted or on another roll under another name?

Throughout 1915 the confusion over registration continued. The problem of pay rates has been touched on already. Wages had varied before the war from Rs.4 or 5 on a Kiambu farm (often without posho), to the Rs.10 or more (with or without posho) offered on coastal plantations, the Uganda Railway or Kilindini Docks.(12) When the East Africa Carrier Corps (EACC) was being formed, wages tended to compete with those offered locally; initially both officers and men were, it must be remembered, civilians. In Seyidie, carriers were paid Rs.10 unless they were Swahili, who expected at least Rs.12, or Rs.15 for military work.(13)   When the campaign was expected to last for only a few months, high wages for voluntary service naturally precluded the idea of conscription. Military labor was recruited on the whole by the usual peacetime methods, as described to the Native Labour Commission. On the coast, men were so averse to work that offers of Rs.20 by the military produced only three men at Malindi.(14)   Gun porters and other front-line carriers were being eagerly sought at Rs.15.(15)

So, before conscription under martial law came in, men had to be cajoled into the Carrier Corps. In the middle of 1915, upcountry porters were paid Rs.10 as they had to work outside their districts. Coast men, however, received Rs.15, and Hobley warned the Chief Secretary that if this was reduced to the lower level, "voluntary recruiting would end."(16)   Watkins had earlier remarked to Hobley that "the question of coast carriers is under a very fierce light just now," because of the reduction in the labor supply.(17) But the revived settler interest in the war ended the laissez-faire period, and Carrier wages were reduced to only Rs.5 for the first three months of service, and Rs.6 thereafter, unless already engaged or in special units like the gun carriers, stretcher bearers, intelligence or others.(18) The Zanzibar Carrier Corps, which had landed at Tanga, was disbanded soon after because the island pay rate began at Rs.20, too high for the liking of the General Staff.(19)

Two important procedures which were soon introduced were the paying off of discharged carriers, and the ominous death registers. Until Smuts began his drive south in February 1916, carriers served up to six or nine months.(20)   District Commissioners must frequently have been visited by batches of carriers for their final payments on their way home. The register accompanying one such party was the cause of an altercation between Watkins and the District Commissioner of Kisumu.(21) Stories like that of Bakari, who claimed not to have been paid but who could have been a deserter, must have caused complaints, of which Watkins was, however, skeptical. "I do not think you will be able to substantiate a single story of men discharged without pay. Deserters of course sing a sad song when they go back, but for that there is no remedy but an application to the deserter."(22)

He issued new instructions to Carrier Deport Officers (CDOs) whereby the most reliable man in a batch took the pay voucher to the District Commissioner's office. It was then up to the men to claim their pay. "Sometimes they prefer to go home first," remarked Watkins. "I am prepared to posho them to the place of paying off, but not until such time as they elect to turn up to get paid off."(23) Unless he had been underpaid, a carrier might have a reasonable sum to his credit when discharged, as he might have drawn none for a long time, if on active service.

Although generally the most final of all events, death was less decisive for a man's relatives if his name was not on a death register; they could not then be paid the funds due to him, because his death was not proved. Death registers were kept at each Depot, and monthly lists appeared in Carrier Section orders; a District Commissioner then paid relations, and sent in claims to the CDO.(24) There were complaints at the beginning of 1916 that the lists were not reaching District Commissioners, who would not then pay claims as instructed.   H. R. Tate, acting Provincial Commissioner for Kenia, presumed that this was due to the pressure of work resulting from "the ever-changing and interminable demands caused by the military situation." Watkins agreed that this was so, and that he was too short of staff to keep pace with his growing establishment, which now consisted of 20,000 men.(25)

The registering of deaths was far more difficult in the early days, when interchange of labor between units could not be prevented. After the opening of the Nairobi Carrier Depot it became necessary to have an NCO permanently at work on a "Unit Ledger." In this way there began what was called the Statistical Section of the MLB, responsible for supervising the labor strengths of military units, for compiling information about each death, "with cause and locality." It had "to summarise total enlistments, discharges and desertions." It was in full operation by the middle of 1916; deaths could be notified to the Paymaster, who filled in the amounts due, and District Commissioners could pay next-of-kin from printed lists.(26)

Credit lists were kept, so that at the end of the war it might be known how much was due to missing men, although it might be impossible to say how many were dead or not. In an imaginary but true-to-life story, it might be tempting for a Luo named Otieno to find, while working with the Carrier Section at Bura in 1915, that his close friend Obondo was with the East Africa Labour Corps (EALC) nearby on the Maktau road; Obondo's account left Otieno in no doubt that he would be better off there. One night, Otieno slipped out of the Carrier lines and paraded in the morning with the EALC, who were ready to sign on such a strong and willing recruit under the name of Onyango. Perhaps Onyango might be taken by a European as a personal servant; if he died, this sad but not unlikely event might never be known officially. Otieno with his number had vanished, and there would be many Otienos and Onyangos on any list of Nyanza carriers.(27)

If the men and their relations were to be sure of their rights, there had to be a system proof against the human foibles of "Otieno" and thousands like him; proof also against accidents, and against that interference by military officers which so greatly increased the problem of control. Also, Watkins had twice heard of District Commissioners supplying labor direct to the military, without reference to the Carrier Section. "This process falsifies statistics of porters in military employ, and is apt to lead to confusion of identity and loss of pay among the natives"; men might also be "issued to officers with no authority to pay them." If a District Commissioner ever had to issue men direct to a unit, the Carrier Section must have a list of names; but if the supply of men was not urgent, previous authority must be obtained. The names of sick or dead porters must also be sent in.(28) This scheme had of course to be passed by the Chief Secretary, who no doubt did so; but only the setting up of the MLB in February 1916 stopped unauthorised labor recruiting.

Clearly an identity system was needed, which had already been discussed before the war for civilian labor:

> The original method was a numbered disc to which, for the Gun Carriers, was added a pay book. The facility with which these were lost or exchanged by their illiterate bearers was the cause of much confusion and loss in the accounts, and shortly after the formation of the M.L.B. staff was sanctioned for a finger print section which fully justified its existence......
> Desertions were prevented and frauds constantly detected, while many * unfortunates whose death or lunacy occurred under circumstances which left their identity obscure were identified and credited with their dues. If a man lost his identity disc he was at once renumbered at the first Depot at which he applied for pay, and given a small advance. His finger prints were sent to the Central Office which identified his previous number and caused his previous credits to be transferred to his new number.

The Finger Print Section was so successful that by February 1919 it had traced 10,000 lost disc numbers and re-registered their owners. A man might now draw pay anywhere, and the local paymaster would notify the man's Depot by voucher. At the Depot a pay card was kept with its owner's account.(29) The Depot was thus a vital part of MLB organisation; only the Nairobi Depot, for example, could issue a new disc or kipande for a Kikuyu porter, because it kept his account. The word kipande, meaning a piece of anything before it was used for an identity token, gained an emotional significance in post-war politics because of its use under the Registration Ordinance.

Just before the MLB was set up, Watkins proposed the centralisation of all carrier pay ledgers under an Assistant Paymaster, at Race Course Road Camp - the Nairobi Carrier Depot. Men were to be discharged and paid off at their depots of origin, which would also be told the amounts due by the new pay office. Only CDOs in the East Africa Protectorate could now write on labor recruited in the Protectorate. No man could be paid unless he had a disc, a depot number, and a place on the establishment. The Assistant Paymaster (Carriers) and the CDOs now had, in theory, complete control over registration, pay and discharge.(30) The MLB took on the payment, in July 1916, of all non-combatant personnel.(31)

To prepare for these changes, an East Africa Pay Corps officer began to investigate the registers in January 1916. He pointed out that many advances made to natives had not been entered in the registers; he thought that the only way out of this was to accept a man's statement as to the amount received. A second paymaster was put onto the arrears of work, but Watkins, with his numerous duties, did not get the work done as fast as the military auditors would have liked. In July 1916 pay cards were introduced, but as records were still in arrears, the MLB continued to accept carriers' statements of pay received, when they were discharged. "Overpayments ... will not amount to anything like the cost of food, pay , etc. if we keep the natives until vouchers are entered up." The card system then failed to catch up with the avalanche of work created by the mass levy, so that by mid-1917 there were 70,000 unbalanced cards at Nairobi Depot, needing fifty extra clerks to get them straight. Of the thirty-two MLB accounts staff at that time, ten were ineffective.(32) In addition, the officers at the depots which proliferated in German territory became "Field Disbursing Officers for the whole Force," from whom all units drew their cash, and not only the non-combatants taken on in July 1916.   The mind boggles at the work involved, and it is not surprising that the MLB could not catch up, when they were rather like a man running up a descending escalator. The comings and goings of carriers increased depot work, ad did "the fact that the active service life of a Carrier is very short, and ... the discharges and enlistments are very numerous."(33)

At the end of 1917 the numbers being paid off were so great that there was a grave shortage of currency to pay them. Charles Bowring, acting Governor of the East Africa Protectorate, suggested a special issue of one-rupee notes. It was estimated that 100 lakhs of rupees would be needed - a lakh being Rs.100,000 - but the local banks were only going to provide twenty-five lakhs. The Colonial Office turned down the idea, partly because of the difficulties experienced as a result of a similar scheme in Ceylon. A special issue of Indian notes was made, because the Indian Government was reluctant to allow coin to be exported; and it was anyway thought likely that large numbers of these notes would find their way back to India in the normal course of trade. But carriers preferred coin, and there was a riot on one occasion when notes were offered.(34)   This all showed that the East Africa Protectorate was still dependent on India for currency, reform of which would come after the war.

It was also assumed that repatriates would spend most of their money at Indian dukas (shops). "Those repatriated were, as expected, robbed on all sides by unscrupulous traders; money seemed no object to the former, but I understand that many returned to their homes sadder and wiser men, for they very soon realised that they had been fleeced."(35)   Certainly the war had caused a great increase in wage-earning. In Meru, for instance, Corporal Muthanya spent his pay freely, alleging that "we were promised more money later, but the government did not keep their promise."

But not all men wasted their pay. Asembo Odera was able to pay for three wives and with his Rs.500; being disabled, he needed their labor. His neighbor, Odandayo Agweli, bought many cows and blankets. Mbwika Kivandi, of Kilungu, put his askari's pay towards his dowry of goats and beer.   In South Nyanza, the stretcher bearer

TABLE 2

PAY

1. Rates of pay for African followers, maximum per month

Grade		Pay including rations
Unskilled labor	1st 3 months	Rs. 5
" "	subsequently	6
Armed Scouts		20
Transport Drivers	1st grade	20
" "	2nd	15
" "	3rd	10
Veterinary Dressers, Syces, Herds	1st grade	12
" " " "	2nd "	10
" " " "	3rd "	8
Mountain Battery, Machine Gun and Bomb Carriers		15
Stretcher Bearers (at training depot)		10
" " (trained, with units)		15
1st-Line Transport		10
Signal Section	1st grade	15
" "	2nd "	10
Cooks		25
House Boys		20
Hospital Dressers		15
Ward Orderlies and Sweepers		12
Office Boys		15
Interpreters		30
Mail Runners		10
Pier gangs	1st 3 months	10
" "	subsequently, if approved	12

2. Daily rates of Artisans, with rations:

	Indians	Swahili
Carpenters	Rs.2-3.50	Cents 75-Rs.2
Blacksmiths	Rs.2.50-3	Cents 75-Rs.2
Masons	Rs.2-3	Cents 75-Rs.1
Fitters	Rs.2-3	Cents 75-Rs.1.50

Sources: MLB Handbook, para. 51; KNA, 37/577 4, Ainsworth to Hobley, 28 May 1917; Meinertzhagen's scouts were paid out of secret service funds, Army Diary, 191-192.

Nguka Nyaoke used Rs.60 which he brought home to buy a big bull; a machine gun carrier, Okech Atonga, brought his father Rs.500 to pay tax.(36) The KMV men at Kahuhia said: "We bought cows, sheep and goats. Those of us who were young went back to school, and others got married." Some carriers had spent their advances of pay to supplement their diet in the field, on "food in the areas we were fighting in, and snuff especially," said Muasya Maitha, ammunition carrier, and Umoa Mbatha, headman, both of Muthetheni, Machakos District.

COMPENSATION AND UNPAID WAGES

Having lost his leg, Odera was "pensioned by the government, and even to this day I still get some money. I wondered very much what happened to the salaries of my friends who were unlucky enough to die, because their relations got nothing." But Muasya and Umoa recalled an example of the working of the death register system through the District Commissioner: "An announcement was made, asking the relatives of people who did not come home to go to a baraza. Kyethe's wife went, crying. Umoa had broken the sad news to her, but she had not believed him. He had died of dysentery. She was given his money." A carrier's next-of-kin could collect his unpaid wages and personal effects if his death was registered, like Kyethe's. But as the fate of so many was unknown, their balances could not be claimed.

KAR Regulations did not at first expressly include carriers in compensation for "Followers," though this was corrected in April 1915, carriers gaining the right to compensation.(37) The Governor of the East Africa Protectorate then approved compensation for the relatives of those who died on active service.(38) In due course it was laid down that "the wife or non-adult children of a soldier or follower who had died in action, or from wounds received in action, or from disease contracted while on active service" should be compensated, as well as a man who had suffered any permanent disablement; Odera's loss of a leg was "permanent partial disablement." In September 1916 the rules were applied to German East Africa. Claims could be paid before or after discharge, but only "provided that the wife or child....is not subject to tribal law or custom, or if so subject provided that the benefit of any payment.... will accrue to such wife and child, and not to any other member of the deceased's family." A District Commissioner paying a claim had to provide a medical certificate, and to testify that the applicant was "the wife of non-adult child," not subject to tribal law, or if subject the sole beneficiary, "and that there are no other children who may claim."(39)

Forms were issued to District Commissioners certifying claims for disablement, and for the payment of balances and compensation to the next-of-kin of dead carriers. In an example from Gazi District, only a few could be verified, and not even these conclusively. Moreover, the wording of the Command Order did not include the phrase whereby the District Commissioner could certify "to the best of my belief that the claimant is the right and only heir." Pagden, the Assistant District Commissioner, refused to pay the claims, the sums being quite large, unless the military first indemnified him against wrong payments.(40) Next, General Headquarters made a condition ignoring the principle on which District Commissioners had hitherto paid compensation: that Government owed blood money to the bereaved, for having sent a soldier or follower to his death. The District Commissioner's certificate was now worded that the deceased was not subject to tribal law, because he was "a professing Christian or Mohammedan."(41) The military were thus trying to stop money passing, under tribal law, to the male next-of-kin, as well as to the widow or children who originally received it. European and African custom differed sharply over the question as to who were the proper heirs. The War Office and Treasury persisted in this prejudice, when it was proposed to pay unclaimed wages into tribal funds.

Ainsworth referred Pagden's protest to Military Audit, also the new distinction between "pagans" and "non-pagans." Must a district officer really certify that a claimant was the only heir, when in most tribes this meant the eldest surviving male relative? Ainsworth arranged that the Administrator-General of the East Africa Protectorate should deal with the estates of Christians and Muslims.(42) But the military, and their masters in London, were for some reason determined to stop payment by tribal custom.

When those grim but vital documents, the death lists, finally began to come out, payments to relatives could begin. List No. 8, of January 1916, showed a group of eight men killed at Mwele, in Gazi District, whose District Commissioner (G. H. Osborne) had personally engaged one of them: 3380 Kinga Kome's balance of Rs.49.50 was paid to his brother as next-of-kin.(43) But in another example, Rs.22.40 was paid to Simeyu Kadu, brother of a driver with the East Africa Mechanical Transport Corps named Nasanairi Mayanja, who had died of dysentery at Dar es Salaam on 4 July 1917. Sir Apolo Kagwa, Katikiro (Prime Minister) of Buganda, sent Simeyu in a vain attempt to claim compensation as well.(44) A brother could only have unpaid wages; compensation was reserved for widow and child.

In 1918, after consultation with General Headquarters of East Africa, the Legislative Council of the East Africa Protectorate, to expedite these payments, passed the Military Labour Corps Distribution of Pay and Personal Property Ordinance. Money and effects were to be given to sufficiently convincing claimants, according to credit and death lists sent out to districts. Under Section 13, balances unclaimed in three years were to revert to the benefit of the tribes concerned.(45) This section was to be at the centre of the bitter dispute which now ensued. "Owing to an oversight in the Colonial Office, the consent of the War Office was not sought, as it should have been, since the expenditure would [mostly] fall upon Imperial funds."(46)

In October 1918 the Senior Paymaster Military Labour Corps (MLC) put out his credit lists as of 31 August, which were passed to the provinces and districts. The District Commissioner of Voi, W.A.F. Platts, pointed out that only 137 out of 337 men on his list were Taita; the others were "a medley" from elsewhere, including German East Africa, and could not be paid unless their District Commissioners were traced. Major Leonard (an ADML) commented that many Taita had been registered at depots in German East Africa; as very often only the name of the man and his father were given, it was impossible to know the tribe or district. Recruiting in German East Africa had been haphazard and carried out by the military; it was feared that hardly one in ten of the names could be traced. The only solution was to put a man on a list according to the name of the Depot on his kipande; whatever his tribe or district, a man with a Dar es Salaam kipande, for instance, appeared on a List compiled at that Depot. The names of Voi claimants who were not on the Voi list were therefore sent to Dar es Salaam, where search could be made on German East Africa credit lists. Most of the Taita who died in German East Africa were probably with Military Railways, which was separate from the MLC, and had no comparable statistical section.(47) Taita had been the scene of much fighting and varied military labor activities, so that the statistical system was in much difficulty here; but it must have been worse in German East Africa, which no doubt helps to explain why there were such huge numbers of missing carriers in that country.(48) Officers setting up the new administration there were trying to discover how many men had been registered in districts other than where they had been enlisted. To prevent confusion and fraud, MLC lists were being kept at the Treasury, Dar es Salaam, while matters were sorted out.(49)

In 1919 two Force Orders made pensions for disablement applicable to the MLC and to other non-combatants, such as the Uganda African Native Medical Corps, the Veterinary Corps, Pioneers, Intelligence, Interpreters and Road Corps; these soon applied to Tanganyika and Zanzibar, as well as Uganda and the East Africa Protectorate.(50) But the military ruling of 1917 made it virtually impossible for widows who were not Christian or Muslim to claim pensions. The Kabaka of Buganda himself protested at this, as others beside Christians and Muslims had been called up; nor did the application of the orders of Uganda in 1920 help much. Major Scott, formerly MLC and now Civil Secretary for Native Affairs, and the Chief Secretary both tried to have the 1917 order rescinded for Uganda, but General Headquarters refused. Scott then recommended that a standard Rs.90 be paid to widows and children of carriers, only half what KAR widows received. Pensions would be dropped, as they were not paid to KAR dependants. Despite the limitations of the 1917 order, district officers had been signing claim certificates with little regard for the religion of the claimants. The Colonial Secretary finally approved a sum of Rs.25,000 for pay due to missing carriers whose heirs could not be traced, to be paid into the funds of the Lukiko (Parliament of Buganda), for the benefit of the tribes concerned; proven claims were to be paid up to 10 June 1922.(51)

There was an invidious distinction between soldiers and followers in the matter of war gratuities; soldiers were eligible, followers not, though some may have expected them. Corporal Muthanya complained at not having had his; perhaps he had never received or seen a notice to apply to the District Commissioner. Askari were warned not to travel to Nairobi for gratuities which might be less than the cost of the journey.(52)

Payments were therefore being made, under the zealous scrutiny of the military authorities; Section 13 of the 1918 Ordinance was causing friction between them and the civil governments. The former said that because of the massive overpayments, these sums must be deducted from the balance due to the missing carriers, but the Kenya government disagreed, as the overpayments could not be traced. The dispute spread to London, where the Treasury protested to the Army Council, which put pressure on Lord Milner, Colonial Secretary; he now ordered the Kenya government to repeal Section 13.(53) A storm of protest was led by Ainsworth and Watkins, who saw it as a breach of faith between himself and the men whom he had led. Milner was urged to reconsider the ruling, first, because until May 1916 there was no finger print section to identify the mass of mostly illiterate men who had passed through the books. Secondly, there had been a choice between a special and expensive military staff to pay claims after the war, or the procedure adopted, of paying claims through district officers, and "crediting unpaid balances to the tribes in accordance with the customs of tribal life." Thirdly, "the agreement of G.H.Q. was given in all good faith and with the apparent concurrence of the War Office." Fourthly, the principle used was that of the Regimental Debt Act of 1895, whereby anything remaining of a dead soldier's estate went to the dependants of soldiers dying on service. Finally, had the opposition of the War Office been anticipated, Section 13 would have been omitted, and a commission set up to do its work "at great expense to the Imperial Government." A similar protest came from Uganda. A staff officer in Nairobi, closing down wartime accounts, said that Section 13 should have been referred to the Finance and Accounts Department of the War Office, since Imperial funds were involved. Incredible though it may seem, this omission was made a reason for refusing any settlement of the unclaimed wages.(54)

Winston Churchill, who now became Colonial Secretary, had to defer to the Treasury and the War Office, though he sanctioned payments under Section 13 until its repeal.(55) Meanwhile in Kenya the Native Trust Fund Ordinance had received royal assent in 1921, supporting Section 13 in paying unclaimed wages to the tribes.(56) In November 1922 amending bills presented to the Legislative Council drew spirited protests from officials, the Protestant Missionary Alliance and the Convention of Associations (the settler body). In the House of Commons, Mr. Ormsby Gore declared that the attempt to repeal Section 13 was "a breach of faith," and Churchill announced that claims might still be presented and met. This fresh attempt to find claimants was approved by the Treasury and Army Council.(57) A Department of Native Affairs circular said that since the Army Council had repudiated the original agreement to pay balances to tribes "as having never been referred to them," district officers must find the heirs by all possible means.(58) The Senior Commissioner for Nyanza, H. R. Tate, angrily declared that if the amending bill passed, "all unclaimed pay and property belonging to deceased natives who were members of the Military Labour Corps will escheat to the Home Treasury. The Native Trust Fund will not benefit by a penny."(59) The debates in Legislative Council had produced protests from both European and Indian elected members, but the governor, Sir Robert Coryndon, had to give his assent to the amending ordinance.(60)

Therefore, by 1923 the first attempt to secure payment of

balances to tribal funds had failed. In all the countries concerned, payments were made to claimants wherever they could be found, and so long as they conformed to military requirements. An example which arose in 1923 was of an African official in Uganda, who had died from disease, contracted in the course of some sort of war work. The Uganda government recommended compensation, which was paid on the orders of the Colonial Secretary, the rate being that paid to the relatives of a KAR askari, and the affair was brought to the attention of officers in Kenya.(61)   If the man had been an official of the Kabaka's government, which he probably was though it is not clear, it would be necessary to prevent political repercussions, and to pay relations who were not "wife or non-adult child."

The Kenya government now protested that money would remain unclaimed because "this Government had no right to legislate for the disposal of what were described as Imperial funds." The war had put the Colony in debt, and the refusal to allow the payment of balances to tribes was a negation of the Devonshire Declaration, in the White Paper of 1923, on the paramountcy of African interests.(62)   Later, in 1924, the first Labour Colonial Secretary presented the claim anew to the War Office, summing up the arguments already made; if payments were still refused, the prestige of the British Government might suffer, especially in Tanganyika, where it had to prove itself superior to the Germans.(63) But the War Office rejected the proposal to pay £150,000 to natives "who do not claim to have earned it." The Regimental Debt Act was no analogy. There had been many desertions, and many overpayments to missing men, or to men who had changed their names. If the claim were admitted, the sum would have to be reduced, but in any case the Army Council would not reopen the matter.(64)

Throughout 1925, the attitude of the Colonial Office and governments remained unchanged.(65) In 1926 the Colonial Secretary, Leo Amery, pointed out that though military and civil authorities had agreed about unpaid wages going into tribal funds, the War Office had dissented; he strongly emphasised the fact that the military had failed "to provide a special organisation for the administration of the Military Labour Corps." The campaign would have been impossible without the carriers, and the retention of the money due to them or to their dependants was unjustifiable. Though the Imperial Government "had refused to agree to a systematic search" for claimants, which would have been a vastly more expensive operation than simply paying the balances to the tribes, its liability remained. In reply the War Office repeated its former arguments, and deprecated reopening the question.(66)

In the Colonial Office estimates for 1927-1928, the claim was reduced to £100,000. The Treasury denied "that the British taxpayer had an obligation of honour to pay to tribal communities money which is due to missing individuals." Amery roundly declared that "the payment was a debt of honour incumbent upon His Majesty's Government to meet, and he did not accept the decision made."(67) The final date for the payment of individual claims was fixed at 31 March 1931.(68) While final attempts were being made to trace claimants before the deadline, the question of the unpaid balances was resumed. Lord Passfield, Colonial Secretary in the second Labour

Government, reluctantly concluded that it would not be practicable
to pay these balances into tribal funds.(69)

There followed a very forcefully worded protest, signed by the
Acting Governor of Kenya (H.M.M. Moore), and based on prior
consultations between officials in Nairobi and Whitehall, giving the
whole history of the dispute. Passfield's decision would undermine
the whole doctrine of trusteeship, and call in question the good faith
of the Government towards "people not yet able to stand by
themselves under the strenuous conditions of the modern world,"
quoting the words used in the Covenant of the League of Nations,
which had also appeared in a recent White Paper. "The effect of the
wholesale destruction of native social life which naturally followed
upon the absence of the able-bodied males of the community is one
from which the tribes have not wholly recovered." The men were
widely employed as military labor throughout East Africa, "and
sometimes against orders in the firing line." The methods of
recruiting were outlined, and the problem of ensuring correct names
in Africa explained. A "false" name might be a nickname
commemorating some feat, and in tribes like the Nandi and Lumbwa
with fine war records, custom forbade a man to give his true name.
Choice of names might be limited; Njoroge was very common among
the Kikuyu, and Onyango among the Luo. Consequently it was
almost impossible to make correct registers. The government of
Kenya had never accepted the decision of the Army Council, "and
its attitude has received unqualified support from Your Lordship's
predecessors.....the Kenya Government submits that no principle of
Imperial honour, obligation, prestige or even of gratitude can have
operated in the decision made. In its opinion mere casuistry has
been employed to defend a doubtful pecuniary advantage." The
German government had sent a commission in 1926 to investigate
claims both in Tanganyika and in Kenya. The claim for £100,000 was
formally renewed.(70)

The Germans had paid out £300,000 in Tanganyika, said its
Deputy Governor; it was "a grave breach of faith with the natives of
these countries....inciting most unfavourable comparison with the
action of the German Government." Claims now had to be pushed
through before the deadline, and matters were made worse by an
erroneous belief that 31 March 1931 was for payment of claims, not
for their presentation.(71)

Colonial Office officials were "at one" with the East African
governments, "but no Chancellor of the Exchequer, let alone the
Army Council, wants to pay away £150,000 or even £100,000; as
those to go short are merely African natives, the WO and the
Treasury are not interested." But these ministries would have to be
consulted before the matter could go to the Cabinet. Moreover,
during the slump, Passfield probably thought it an inopportune time
to approach Philip Snowden, the Chancellor, who was irascible, an
economiser, and in bad health; officials agreed that it was useless to
press the government in the present financial situation. But Passfield,
better known as Sidney Webb, was acutely uncomfortable: "it is
rather terrible that HMG should leave the Kenya natives under this
grievance, in addition to their other complaints against their white
'oppressors'!" (72)

The matter ended in 1934 with the report of the Kenya Land Commission which recommended that the British government, should pay the £50,000, which it was said to owe towards the unclaimed wages of Kenya carriers, as part of its contribution towards the cost of various recommendations concerning land. The War Office was accused of retaining "the money which had actually been earned by porters, and which should have been paid to them or their heirs." Legally these men had been "protected foreigners"; they had been forced to help their protectors in a war which was no concern of theirs. Though they might at first have been defending their own country, this was certainly not true of the invasion of German East Africa in furtherance of Imperial policy." In Kenya all sections of the community were in full agreement. If the Regimental Debt Act applied to the families of dead volunteers, it should apply even more strongly to the relations of unwilling conscripts who had died "fighting the battles of another people"; also, "the tribes of Kenya have suffered a grievous loss of men, and it would be but bare justice that they should receive the money these men have earned in obedience to their chiefs." The failure to have a proper registration system had saved the British government money. Finally, not meeting the claim was "a much more serious violation of the principles of trusteeship to the natives" than land alienation, the result of "ignorance of their needs and of their land tenure systems."(73)

The Imperial Government gave its conclusions in a separate White Paper. In summing up the pros and cons of the porters' claim, it was regretted, "that the Commission should have expressed their views on the merits of the question without affording opportunity for the presentation at first hand of the arguments on both sides of the case" - surely an absurd statement when all the arguments had been presented ad nauseam since 1919. "But it has been represented.... that whether rightly or wrongly there is a strong feeling among the natives of Kenya that they have not received fair treatment in this matter." The Government "had decided to ask Parliament for an ex-gratia grant of £50,000 to enable the Kenya Government to carry out the Commission's recommendations."(74)

The Colonial Secretary, Sir Philip Cunliffe-Lister, told the Governor of Tanganyika, Sir Harold MacMichael, that he had only been able to get anything for Kenya because the sense of grievance was far greater there. The War Office were as obdurate as ever; they said they could prove that 90 percent of the Tanganyika claimants were deserters. Unlike Tanganyika, Kenya had had no grant-in-aid since the war; to have fought a losing battle for the former might have involved Kenya in defeat. "I refrain, with difficulty, from expressing an opinion," commented a Tanganyika official.(75)

Was the £50,000 for unclaimed wages, or to fulfil the Commission's recommendations? Lord Lugard thought it highly ambiguous; in a letter to The Times he firmly endorsed Amery's description of the claim as a "debt of honour," likewise the Commission's views on the violation of the principles of trusteeship.(76) Lugard's doubts on the settlement must remain. The conquest of German East Africa had been Imperial policy since 1897. Despite the advice of Kitchener, and of other officers who

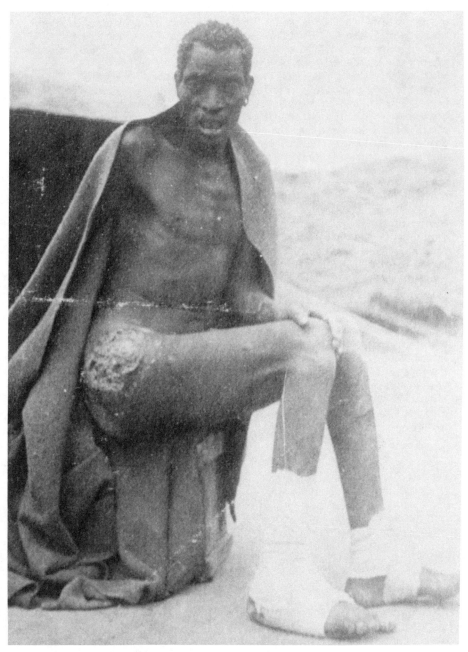

"Grievously earned money." A sick Carrier, with a tropical ulcer
by courtesy of Dr. Clive Irvine

knew East Africa, this policy was carried out, although no thought or preparation had been taken for the enormous transport problems which would ensue. The blame must rest on the War Office, who then in concert with the Treasury refused to pay a sum minute when seen in the context of the war itself.

Perhaps the War Office were simply concealing their responsibility, stubbornly refusing to admit their mistakes. The most brutal war in human experience must have deadened sympathy and coarsened feelings; perhaps injustice to African carriers seemed a small matter set against the slaughter on the Western Front. Rigid post-war economics also helped to defeat the porters' claim, which there was, however, little excuse for denying, when Africans were used to further an Imperial policy declared by Sir Edward Grey, Foreign Secretary, when war began: to attack "all German colonial possessions," despite the Berlin Act of 1885.(77)

The East African governments tried to secure justice, but the Bishop of Northern Rhodesia, Alston May, is said to have been very angry with his government for neglecting ex-servicemen.(78) An example from this country shows that individual cases might occur up to World War II. Joseph Mwenya, from Kawambwa near the Luapula River, had been a carrier with the British South Africa Police, but had not been paid a penny. Losing his company at Iringa, he became servant to a South African officer, and was wounded at Mahiwa. After the War, he spent many years at Tanga, where his wounded leg was finally amputated at the government hospital; this was reported to the Secretariat, Lusaka, in response to a request for information from the District Commissioner of Mufulira in 1938. Mwenya was of course not under the MLC; it is not told whether he got compensation, but probably he did. The evidence was very clear.(79)

It is now time to end the story of the Carriers' grievously earned money.

NOTES

1. The KMV remitted money home; see 241 below.

2. WR. para. 7.

3. Ibid., paras, 63 and 94.

4. Ibid., para. 95.

5. Ibid., para. 98, also paras. 59-60 and 96-97; see also CGL, Nairobi, Report on War Expenditure, by Lieutenant-Colonel H.C.E. Barnes, Director of Military Audit: Head 6, Civilian Subordinates, CC Accounts to 31 Dec. 1915, para. 42.

6. KNA, 37/577 1, Nov.-Dec. 1914: Hobley, Watkins, Officer Commanding KAR Voi, two DCs; Waters was MO with the EACC, and at Mjanji in 1917 - Chapter 5 n.66

7. Ibid., Crisford (DC) to Watkins, 24 June 1915, and Watkins to Hobley, 27 June.

8. CGL, Report on War Expenditure, enclosure 02.

9. KNA, 37/577 1, Watkins to DCs, 31 Oct. 1914.

10. KNA, 37/577 2, Dundas (DC) to Watkins, 10 Aug. 1915; for Kerslake Thomas, see OG, 1914, 1124; see also 38/582, "Labour Requirements and Recruiting," and 37/577 5, 767, where his foreman was convicted of assault while recruiting.

11. KNA, 37/577 2, Watkins to Platts (DC Voi), 23 Aug. 1915.

12. Clayton and Savage, Government and Labour, 58; see also Chapter 2 above, n. 26, Josphat Njoroge.

13. KNA, 37/577 1, Hobley to ADC Rabai, 15 Dec. 1914, and Director of Surveys to Hobley, 16 Jan. 1915, complaining that competing with carrier wages would put up his wage bill by £3,000 per annum.

14. 37/577 1, DC Malindi to Hobley, 4 March 1915.

15. Ibid., Major H. de C. O'Grady to Hobley, 10 March 1915.

16. 37/577 2, Hobley to Ch. Sec. 12 July 1915.

17. Ibid., Watkins to Hobley, 1 July 1915.

18. Ibid., 2, Watkins to CDOs and PCs 21 Sept. 1915.

19. WR, para. 17.

20. Ibid., para. 28.

21.   See Chapter 4 above, n. 53.

22.   KNA, 37/577 2, Watkins to Hobley, 1 July 1915.

23.   Ibid., Watkins to CDO Mombasa, 23 Aug. 1915, and to Hobley, same date.

24.   Ibid., Carrier Section Circ. No. 35, 16 Sept. 1915; see also MLB Handbook (2d. ed., 1917), 22-24.

25.   KNA, 37/577 3, Tate to Watkins, 5 Jan. 1916, and reply, 11 Jan. 1916; see also McClure (DC Nyeri) to Tate, 14 March, and Tate to Hobley, 30 March 1916.

26.   WR, paras. 105-106.

27.   Ibid., para. 107.

28.   KNA, 37/577 1, Watkins to Ch. Sec., 20 May 1915.

29.   WR, paras. 103-104; MLB Handbook, 20-22.

30.   See Chapter 11 below, "War and Protest Politics."

31.   KNA, 37/577 3, Carrier Section Circ. Mem. No. 1, Feb. 1916; 37/577 37/577 4, Hobley to Seyidie DCs on remittances to dependants; WR para. 99 on paying non-combatants.

32.   CGL, Report on War Expenditure, paras. 41-52, and enclosures N1-Q3, especially N3: Power (Paymaster, MLB) to Watkins, 13 Sept. 1916, and 03 on extra clerks.

33.   WR. para. 102; CGL, enclosure 03.

34.   PRO, CO 533/185/54206, "Coinage for payment of Carriers"; Dr. Anthony Clayton kindly mentioned the riot.

35.   KNA, PC/NZA/1/14, Nyanza AR, 1918-1919.

36.   Notes kindly given by Richard Siaga, 26 Aug. 1970.

37.   NAU/SMP 4404 1, "War with Germany: Grants of Compensation to Native Levies and Porters," 3rd. Asst. Sec. to Wallis, 23 March 1915, and Wallis to PC Buganda, 7 May 1915 (RPA, War F/1/2).

38.   KNA, 44/952, "Deaths on Active Service," Ag. Ch. Sec. to Watkins, 30 June 1915, and to PC Kenia, 30 July 1915.

39.   Command Order No. 764 - Handbook, 22-24, para. 49.

40.   KNA, 37/577 5, Pagden to Ainsworth, 16 Oct. 1917.

41. NAU/SMP 4404 1 (RPA War F/1/2), Scott to Ch. Sec. Entebbe, 5 Nov. 1919; Ch. Sec.'s circ. to PCs and DCs on General Routine Order 581/17; author's italics.

42. KNA, 37/577 4, Ainsworth to PCs, CDO Nairobi, Oct. 1917.

43. KNA, 45/1048, "Military Labour Corps - death lists," Osborne to Hobley, n.d., and other correspondence.

44. NAU/SMP 5162, "War with Germany: Casualties among Native Personnel Lent for Military Operations" (RPA War F/1/2).

45. EAP, Ords. Regs. No. 35, 1918.

46. Leo Amery (SSC) to WO, 8 Nov. 1926, quoted in Kenya Govt. Despatch No. 83, Ag. Gov. to SSC, 7 Feb. 1931; this is the definitive document on the Porters' Claim. For original, see PRO, CO 822/34/26018; for copy of duplicate sent to Govt. of Tanganyika, see TNA, W1/U 19351, in RPA War F/1/3. Unless otherwise stated, all despatches cited are quoted in this document.

47. KNA, 45/1048, correspondence between Platts, Ainsworth, Leonard and Ch. Paymaster EAPC, Nov. 1919 to May 1920.

48. See Appendix 3 below and Table 3 (Statistics).

49. TNA, W1/U 19351, "Unclaimed Wages (in respect of War Services) due to Natives" (RPA War F/1/3).

50. KNA, 37/566, "Pensions and Gratuities to Native Ranks, K.A.R., Labour Corps and other Units," 1919-1922.

51. NAU/SMP 4404 1, H. H. Daudi Chwa and three ministers to DC Buganda, 20 Oct. 1919, and Scott to Ch. Sec., 5 Nov. 1919; see also Circ. of 19 Jan. 1920, and Minute No. 229 of 18 June 1920 (RPA War F/1/2).

52. KNA, 37/566, CNC to SCs (PCs), 13 Jan. 1922, circ. 5.

53. Lord Milner (SSC) to Gov. Kenya: No. 136 of 20 Feb. 1919, and No. 1847 of 20 Dec. 1920.

54. PRO, CO 533/261/38087, Lieutenant-Colonel W. K. Notley, Ag. Gov., to SSC, 7 July 1921, also quoted in Despatch No. 83, 1931.

55. Winston S. Churchill (SSC) to Sir Edward Northey (Gov. Kenya), No. 95 of 1 Feb. 1922.

56. Ordinance No. 46 of 1921, s. 6(5).

57. Churchill to Gov. Kenya, 31 Aug. 1922.

58. KNA, 45/1048, DNA Circ. No. 104, 18 Dec. 1922, copy in NAU/SMP 5317, "War with Germany: Ordinances in Connection with Military Labour Bureau" (RPA War F/1/2).

59. KNA, SC Nyanza to DCs, 19 June 1922, on Govt. Notice No. 200, in 37/566.

60. Leg. Co. Minutes, 1922, 46–47.

61. KNA, 44/952, "Deaths on Active Service," DNA Circ. No. 33, 19 May 1923, to admin. officers, with copy of CO Despatch No. 521, 18 April 1923.

62. Kenya Govt. Despatch No. 243, 24 Feb. 1924; the White Paper was Cmd. 1922.

63. CO to WO, No. 14289/24, 15 July 1924.

64. WO reply, No. 0165/1738 (N.1.) 8 Dec. 1924.

65. Ormsby Gore (SSC) No. 359 of 17 April 1925; Northcote (Kenya Govt.) No. 828, 3 July 1925; Leg. Co. Debates (Kenya), 1925, 2, 641–643.

66. Amery to Gov. Kenya, 8 Nov. 1926, No. 1053: enclosing Note to WO and reply.

67. Amery to Gov. Kenya, 13 April 1927, enclosing Note by Treasury, 2 Dec. 1926, and his reply, 1 April 1927.

68. Scretariat, Nairobi, to Ch. Sec. Dar es Salaam, 3 Oct. 1930, in TNA, W1/U 19351 (RPA War F/1/3).

69. Ibid., Passfield to Cameron (Gov. Tanganyika), No. 876 of 8 Nov. 1930.

70. Kenya Govt. Despatch No. 83, Acting Governor of Kenya (H.M.M. Moore) to Lord Passfield (SSC), 7 Feb. 1931.

71. TNA, W1/U 19351 (RPA War F/1/3), Dep. Gov. Tanganyika to SSC, 30 March 1931; Uganda protest 16 May 1931 (Cmd. 4556, para. 2050); Kenya Sec. Circs. No. 3 of 7 Jan. 1927, and No. 8 of 21 Feb. 1927 on German commission, ask for returns from district officers. None were made in Nyanza (KNA, PC/NZA/3/57/1).

72. Minutes on Despatch No. 83, CO 822/34/26018, WO claimed to have been more generous than the Germans, who had in fact paid out £300,000.

73. Cmd. 4556, Report of the Kenya Land Commission, 1934, paras. 2041–2068.

74. Cmd. 4580, Summary of Conclusions reached by His Majesty's Government on the KLC Report, paras. 27–28; I am grateful for comments and assistance from Mr. S. H. Fazan, who was Secretary to the Land Commission.

75. TNA, W1/U 19351 (RPA War F/1/3), SSC to Gov. of Tanganyika (private), 14 May 1934, and minute.

76. Ibid., Lugard to editor of The Times, 13 Feb. 1935.

77. PRO, CO 537/28, Foreign Office to CO, 13 Aug, 1914. I am grateful to Mr. Lewis J. Greenstein for drawing my attention to this despatch.

78. Information kindly given by Mrs. D. J. Ruck, for which the author is most grateful; she was for many years a missionary with UMCA in Northern Rhodesia.

79. TNA, Secretariat File 26366, "Application for Compensation by Joseph Mwenya" (RPA War F/1/3).

Chapter 7
Recruitment and Repatriation

"When they were caught by force we were left
weeping, mourning."

(Leah Nyamuiru Karuga)

The war extended the pre-war problems of raising, paying and looking
after labor. As the war went on, and normal labor demands had still
to be met, it became much harder to raise enough carriers. The
political effects, events in the districts, and repatriation are
considered.

GOVERNMENT, SETTLERS AND RECRUITING

The war brought more pressure on government by the settlers,
who wanted representation, and Crown Colony status. Their demands
for compulsory recruiting of labor were voiced through the
Committees of Supply and the War Council; their effusions in the
press were studied by literate, mission-educated Africans.(1)

Government and private employers of labor were affected by
military demands. Were these to be met by the theoretically
voluntary method, as government wanted, or by compulsion, as the
settlers demanded? This was brought in by the Native Followers
Recruitment Ordinance in August 1915; some officials reluctantly
agreed with the settlers that compulsion should continue after the
war. The new pressures drove men from the reserves to European
farms, which suited the settlers, as it gave them more labor.

Carrier recruiting did not interfere much with the settlers' labor
supply during the first years of the war. In June 1915, the
government and the military agreed to give legal powers to native
authorities for compulsory recruitment.(2) The resulting Native
Followers Recruitment Ordinance was greeted with rapture by the
settlers, though the labor shortage was not much graver than usual.
All labor was to be on the books of the Carrier Section; native
authorities were responsible to district officers for recruiting any
native under thirty-five years of age. Refusal to comply might cost
a headman six months imprisonment, or a fine of Rs.300, or both; a
recruit was liable to two months and a fine of Rs.75.(3) The number
on the books was down to 10,823 in August 1915, 5,000 short.
Monthly drafts were at present 1,500 (raised with difficulty), and

must be increased to 3,000. A Colonial Office official thought that "the urgent necessity for keeping the carrier corps to its full strength is sufficient....to authorise the Governor assenting to the Bill in H.M.'s name before it has been referred home."(4) The settler press was very enthusiastic about this ordinance and its probable results, while pointing out that it could have been secured without any wartime pressures. Whatever might be said about the military in other contexts, here they were "seeking power to dominate the native carrier difficulty."(5)

Next came the Theatre Royal meeting and the War Council. The duties of the Council were to advise the governor on matters connected with the war, including legislation on compulsory service for all, and on how best to carry out the Registration of Persons Ordinance for Europeans and Asians, so as to put the community on a war footing.(6)   Enthusiastic press comments reflect the significance of the War Council, even if they exaggerate slightly: "we may almost regard the War Council as the Government," said the Standard, and The Leader felt that "we must congratulate the Administration on [its] high and liberal attitude."(7) Certainly the Secretariat implemented the Council's suggestion that natives who left work without their employers' signatures on their passes should be conscripted.(8)

Compulsory service for Europeans and Asians came at the end of 1915; the government could form any military corps from men aged between eighteen and forty-five, registered with district committees, whose lists showed whether men could be spared for service or were in reserved occupations.(9)   The year ended with a considerable increase in settler power and influence.

Pressure on the labor supply increased during 1915, especially on the coast. At Mombasa, shortage of dock labor led to a proposal for a Stevedore Corps. Plans were also made for the Public Works Department (PWD) and water works to have carrier rejects.(10) The improving effects of conscription on the labor supply moved - The Leader to say in February 1916: "There is more than enough labour freely offering for plantation work, which is a great novelty for the coast."(11)   But the big push in the Kilimanjaro area was due to start within a month. As animal and mechanical transport might break down in an offensive during the rains, 10,000 more carriers were needed, with forty officers and eighty NCOs.(12) It was now suggested that a medal should be given to chiefs and headmen after the war for their services, compulsory recruiting being a great strain on their loyalties: for energy in producing labor and livestock, for assistance against trouble in the reserves, or for any other service.(13) District officers were asked to refer in their annual reports to headmen who had done specially well, including donations to war funds; they were then asked to submit lists of chiefs with special claims to the proposed medal.(14)

Though the settlers were at first pleased about compulsory recruiting, there are signs that they, especially the coast planters, and government were feeling the labor shortage more and more. The PWD at Mombasa were constantly asking for labor, to be paid at Carrier Corps rates, although in September 1915 these sank below PWD rates. Labor might be scarce, especially in Nyika District owing to carrier recruiting, but employers could still lower wages to the Carriers' level.(15) Earlier in the year, the Colonial Office had heard complaints about the labor problems in Seyidie, particularly around Malindi and on the Magarini plantation.(16) All Mombasa labor now had to register with the District Commissioner, who was to run a labor exchange, and issue metal badges to all who registered.(17) Finally, Hobley received a deputation of planters, and promised them that District Commissioners would help with labor; he agreed that the settlement of Giriama squatters on plantations was "advisable, and also advantageous to the natives, especially as regards their health."(18) An incident showing how military recruiting helped the private supply was when a planter had asked Hobley to renew carrier recruiting in his neighbourhood, as then "he could get any amount of labour because they came to work for him while the recruiting efforts were being made....He further complained that they left him a couple of days after the recruiters had left the area." Hobley commented on the planter's admission that he was conniving "to shelter labour which Government needs."(19) Though examples are lacking for the highlands, things cannot have been good, since it was stated in Executive Council that military recruiting had drained the tribes of all suitable material.(20) This was an exaggeration, as the numbers raised in 1917 were to show.

War conditions, especially carrier recruiting, encouraged squatting on farms; an attempt to control it by a Resident Natives Bill in 1916 was withdrawn after settler pressure.(21) During 1915 and 1916, the Assistant District Commissioner for Dagoretti gave several reasons for emigration to Rift Valley farms, the most important being to escape from the authority of chiefs, and from impressment into the Carrier Corps.(22) Government was always concerned to maintain the chiefs, as its agents in the reserves, but settler opinion was the exact reverse: "We all wish to [make the native] a worker under European control. We see no provision [in the Resident Natives Bill] for exempting those natives who require emancipation from their chiefs, and who have a right of freedom of residence."(23) But, while recognising that there were complaints, government wanted not to stop the drift from the reserves, but to control it and prevent "kaffir farming," an abuse condemned by the NLC, whereby Africans lived almost unsupervised on farms, and paid either in kind or a nominal rent. Lord Delamere emphasised the need for squatter labor, of which many settlers were short; Bowring agreed, and said that it should not be enacted after the war.(24) Before the mass levy in 1917, an attempt was made to recruit labor from white farms, where there were supposed to be many not in regular employ; "the supply of native labour from the reserves for the Carrier Corps is becoming practically exhausted."(25)

It was agreed that the European community must provide officers for the mass levy porters, because men from the East Africa Protectorate knew something of the porters they would lead, and spoke Swahili, unlike South Africans who were, said Watkins, "at first quite useless. The result is an increased mortality among the natives and a diminished output of work." They would either work with first-line carriers, or with wharf and construction gangs, or do clerical work at stores and depots.(26) "It is most important," as

Belfield told the Colonial Secretary, "that our porters should be effectively supervised by competent officers." The need for 200 European staff would mean conscription, despite the risk of dislocating East Africa Protectorate industries.(27) London and Nairobi did not fully agree on this; the Colonial Office felt that the proposals went beyond the degree of compulsion allowed by the Munitions of War Act of 1915 in Britain. It was finally agreed that, as a compromise, employers should not be allowed to take on new employees.(28)

Should natives be conscripted as combatants? Bowring, now Acting Governor, wanted to amend the Compulsory Service Ordinance to cover them, but could not positively assure the Colonial Office there would be no violence or unrest; he did, however, not think "that there is the remotest chance of trouble." The Colonial Office had to be content with this equivocal answer, and KAR conscription could begin.(29)

As Military Commissioner for Labour, Ainsworth had to persuade the settlers to agree to recruiting on their farms, if the reserves could not supply enough. Porters from the East Africa Protectorate were thought more reliable than those in German East Africa who were near enough to their homes to desert more easily. In return he would make available "those found unsuitable for Military Transport, but who are otherwise medically fit."(30) So there were three categories: fit for the MLB, fit for farm work, and unfit for any work. "Because we are not living in normal times," men in the second category should be available for government or private labor.(31)

The Church of Scotland doctor, H.R.A. Philp, called this "an iniquitous proposal," saying that he himself only rejected the totally unfit. To supply such labor to farms would in his view be unfair to employers as well as to the men; the farmers would not get their money's worth, and those who were really fit would be tempted to slack at the expense of those who were not.(32) Ainsworth disliked injustice and inhumanity as much as Philp, but sometimes totally unfit men did go to farms. A Seyidie plantation manager called Jensen said that he had been sent "several hopelessly ill with consumption. One wonders why such people are rounded up, when big hefty loafers are allowed to walk about freely." It could be a question of whether or not one was a relation of a headman.(33)

The coast planter feared fire as the dry season advanced, and needed plenty of labor to prevent it. Jensen suggested martial law recruitment, with overseers picked by government headmen but paid by planters, who approved the scheme, and advised a South African-style pass law with it. Hobley of course rejected it, as the administration had no martial law powers.(34) The Magadi Soda Company had also been hit by the labor shortage, and claimed to be "a scheduled trade of national importance," as soda was used in explosives; it was exported to the Calcutta chemical works. However, when the mass levy ended in August 1917, the problem grew less acute at Magadi, though Bowring admitted that "the work is not popular."(35)

Mombasa Port and the Uganda Railway were the two largest employers of strategic labor in the country. An attempt to form a

Stevedore Corps of 1,000 men, with two officers and four NCOs, to work Kilindini and the Old Harbour seems to have come to nothing. The mass levy scared all labor out of the port. A serious situation arose, because dockers could not be distinguished from other men, and a tribunal was set up to decide whether natives employed as dock labor should be exempt from the Carrier Corps; it consisted of C. S. Hemsted (District Commissioner), and the two main lighterage managers, but broke down promptly when Hemsted accused one of the managers of using labor which had not been certificated by the Labour Office.(36)

In July 1917 the Colonial Office agreed that Asians and Europeans must have employers' approval before leaving their posts; the District Committees and War Council had "overriding authority." Compulsion also applied to natives, Arabs and Baluchis, but Hobley's suggestion that the two latter groups be liable for the Carrier Corps was turned down by Bowring.(37)   By August 1917, Ainsworth's military duties had ended; he was responsible for the repatriation of carriers, and became Adviser on Native Affairs. He was also appointed to the Executive Council.(38)   In announcing the end of the mass levy, Ainsworth said that compulsory recruitment must have been "most distasteful" to the district officers and native authorities, "being entirely opposed to the Government policy with regard to labour."(39)

Though little notice was taken in Britain of the carrier recruiting and mortality, criticism did appear in the Manchester Guardian. There was a South African Native Labour Contingent in France, which was undoubtedly well run by experts in labor management, with a low rate of death and sickness. Why, it was asked, was mortality so appalling among Africans working in their own country? Ainsworth, when asked to comment, pointed out that in France, the men were in permanent accommodation, had regular hours of work, and were well behind the front. None of this applied to East Africa, where conditions were much more exacting and unhealthy, and porters were often on the move. There were very few experienced caravan porters left; even in peacetime, ordinary porters were liable to suffer a high rate of sickness and death.(40) He could, of course, speak from experience of the 1899 tragedy, and might also have said that climatic conditions in Africa vary greatly.

The competition between the KAR and military transport also embarrassed the colonial governments. In 1916 it was proposed to augment the expansion of the KAR by using picked carrier recruits from "fighting tribes." Three new battalions, totalling 3,000 men, could be drawn from the 30,000 carriers who were on the books in April 1916. Nyasaland could produce two more battalions, and Uganda an "almost unlimited supply" - surely an over-optimistic statement. The administrator of Northern Rhodesia was unwilling to allow Bemba to be recruited for the 2nd KAR, because so many carriers were needed on the long haul from the railway to the German border.(41) Nothing came of negotiations by the Foreign Office to recruit in various non-British territories.(42)

In his researches into the recruitment of askari and tengatenga in Nyasaland, Dr. Melvin E. Page has revealed interesting details to show why the KAR raised so many men there. The apparent imminence of German invasion made many feel that they must defend their land. There was also a widespread feeling of deference to chiefs. Others wanted the money, just as if they were going to the mines in South Africa. Others were stirred by their own warrior traditions. Many were inspired by the bands which marched around the country; they wanted to wear the uniforms, play the instruments and share the military glamour. The realities of war brought disillusionment; it was thangata, pain and effort without real benefit.(43)

In recruiting KAR askari from carrier depots, fine, upstanding men were taken, like Mwaura Ng'ang'a of Kabati. They were kept at KAR depots for a month, and returned if found unsuitable or unwilling; the idea was to overcome the prejudices against military service of men from "the wilder tribes," who preferred "the more prosaic if better understood occupation of carrying loads." But there were men from the Eastern Province of Uganda who had been promised by their District Commissioners that they would not go as askari, and who felt that this period of probation was a breach of faith. Direct recruiting was therefore resumed in that area, and no more were taken from the carrier depots. By mid-1917, the KAR staff officer for recruiting reported: "B.E.A. can be considered as almost played out as far as recruiting for the KAR is concerned."(44)   Ainsworth was simultaneously reaching the same conclusion for the Carrier Corps.

No doubt men volunteered for the KAR as the lesser of two evils, as well as for more positive reasons. In Mombasa, for example, men who had previously shown little interest in the KAR were now joining in fair numbers.(45) Asembo Odera said: "Soldiers from Uganda came to Bunyala, and the Chief asked all people who wished to join them to do so. I joined voluntarily, because I would still be forced into it. Many people were compelled to join the army later." The question is whether this really meant the Carrier Corps, if it is true that unwilling recruits were not taken by the KAR. Another point arising is how far the transfer of carriers to the KAR has falsified total manpower statistics by causing "plural enlistment."(46)

In Nairobi, settler demands for a pass law were sharpened in 1917 by an increase in burglaries, for which returned carriers may have been partly responsible.(47) A legacy of the Carrier Corps was the very device which had ensured that a largely illiterate labor force got its pay: the kipande, which was to cause so much discontent.(48) But officials saw that a system of exemption passes could protect the interests of bona fide workers, as well as of their employers, as H. R. McClure (District Commissioner of Nyeri) pointed out in a letter to the Standard.(49)

The grave labor shortage, rather than settler demands, began to make the East Africa Protectorate government think seriously about compulsory labor after the war. Some officials were in favor; H. R. Montgomery, District Commissioner of Kitui for most of the war, wrote: "Why not call a spade a spade and admit that labour....can only be obtained compulsorily?"(50) Bowring suggested to the Colonial Office that government labor might be raised by compulsion, but the idea was not well received; the settlers would resent it, and anyway Parliament would not allow it.(51)

RECRUITMENT IN THE DISTRICTS

There were four stages of wartime recruitment: the pre-war, "semi-voluntary" system, then selective compulsion with the NFRO, then the mass levy, and finally a return to the pre-war system, owing to the greatly reduced military demands after August 1917.

For the first year, labor was raised rather unevenly in the four recruitment provinces, with Ukamba making little apparent contribution. The District Commissioner of Machakos feared that large scale recruiting might cause "trouble with the natives which might necessitate military assistance."(52)   This fear was never absent, but never justified except for slight passive resistance in Kisii and Giriama. In both Nyanza and Kenia, recruiting and purchase of livestock went smoothly; in the first year of the war the Nyanza chiefs were particularly helpful and raised Rs.27,000 for the government.(53)   But there was growing reluctance to serve in the Carrier Corps, due to delayed discharge, failure to report or account for deaths or pay wages to next-of-kin, and above all to the bad conditions. One result was to stimulate the flow of voluntary labor.(54)   In South Nyanza, after the German raid and subsequent rioting, young men had to be rounded up by night to fulfil labor requisitions. Much as the District Commissioner disliked this, he saw no alternative until the general prejudice against leaving the district had died down.(55)

Throughout the war, however, men volunteered as <u>askari</u> or even as carriers. Labor demands and livestock purchases were often fulfilled with a readiness which drew the admiration of district officers. The Provincial Commissioner of Ukamba praised "the loyalty of the population despite recruiting and commandeering," both unpopular demands. The headmen had been cooperative except in Kitui, a backward district where "the nature of the country offers them unusual opportunities for evading orders which they find distasteful." Two years later, in more difficult times, came an even warmer testimonial: "We have asked without ceasing for two of the main assets and most cherished possessions of a native tribe - their young men and their stock - and we have received both in abundance."(56)   In Kiambu there had initially been no disturbance to normal labor, but by March 1916 "women and children are to be seen using <u>jembes</u> (hoes), an entire transgression of native custom which is that men break up the land." Far more men, however, were working on farms to escape the Carrier Corps.(57)

At first some may have felt the normal call of adventure. In Machakos "it was called the war of the quivers (Kau wa Mathyaka)....Here in Ukambani <u>anake</u> (young men) were collected and told to carry bows and arrows....This was how Kamba soldiers were called up before the British soldiers had been prepared," said Joseph Munyao, who seemed to know of Britain's traditional unreadiness for war. Mutiso Kanzivei told exactly the same tale; he served as a carrier, Munyao as a clerk at Machakos headquarters.(58)

In Nyeri the demands were met cheerfully, despite the halving of wages and low prices for stock. But McClure complained that, though officers were not consulted about wage levels, they had to do "much laboured and unconvincing explanation, while the central authority would have been spared the necessity of indulging in terminological inexactitudes when accounting to the public for this change of policy" - the use of Parliamentary polysyllables which mean "lies" implied considerable irritation.(59)   Officers in Meru and Kitui noted the bad effects on recruiting; in Kitui 1,667 cattle were supplied, more than was asked, and the order actually had to be stopped because of rinderpest.(60)

Districts with strong native authorities fulfilled military labor demands most easily, which applied to most of Nyanza. In Nandi and Lumbwa, most young men went into the KAR or Nandi Scouts; those in the Carrier Corps were always drivers or syces, never carriers.(61) The Maasai produced no men, but gave large quantities of livestock. Under Lord Delamere and other Europeans they also served as scouts and irregular fighters. The war must have given the moran (young Maasai warriors) much excitement, with opportunities for raiding across the German border, even with rifles. The Maasai gave 2,000 donkeys, but no drivers. The District Commissioner (R. W. Hemsted) thought the NFRO a dead letter without military enforcement; an attempt was made to recruit members of the Purko section as askari, but fourteen moran were killed in an attack on the KAR company concerned. The affair also stemmed from the postponement of the E-Unoto ceremony, held on the Kinangop plateau above Naivasha.(62) Apart from the Giriama uprising, this was the only time when troops were used to enforce recruitment, as opposed to police or tribal retainers.

Before the mass levy, recruiting was usually, as the District Commissioner of Machakos said, "a personal visit to each location in turn and an interview with the elders who, after the matter was put before them, usually supplied their quota of men."(63) The 1912 ordinance had strenghtened native authorities, which was to make carrier recruiting possible. "They were recruited by force," said the gun carrier Okech Atonga. "At least every house had to produce one young man....Their mothers were crying as they went." Leah Karuga gave the women's point of view: "The son of a man who was hated was taken. The son of a man who was respected was hidden by Kinyanjui wa Gatherimu....Ropes were put through their ears and tied together," a method often used by tribal retainers. Another also used by Kinyanjui's headmen had been mentioned to the NLC, and was recalled by Josphat Njoroge, of impounding the goats and possessions of defaulters.(64) Consequently, even before the mass levy "almost all have an intense fear and hatred of service with the Carrier Corps," wrote the District Commissioner of Kisumu, but "both chiefs and people have been loyal to the government," and had met the heavy demands for stock and labor "without any disturbance."(65)

Many deserted, either between their homes and the depot, or in the field, or if a man was near home and overdue for discharge; Watkins sympathised with some Taita who had deserted for this reason, but felt that they must be punished. They were caned - a light penalty for what they must realise was a serious offence, Hobley commented, but they would soon be recalled for work on the Voi Military Railway.(66) In Dagoretti, 857 recruits were sent in,

Map 2

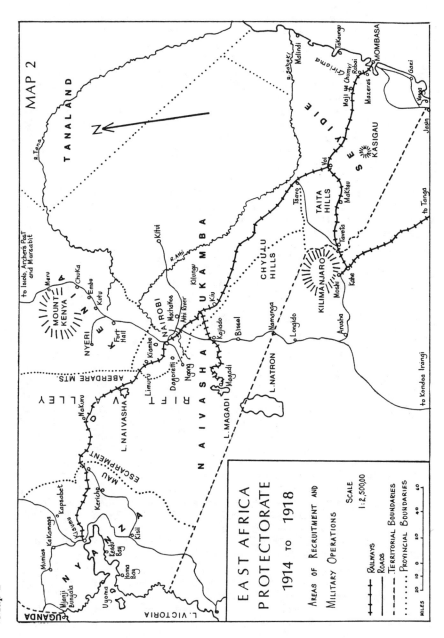

MAP 2

EAST AFRICA
PROTECTORATE
1914 to 1918

AREAS OF RECRUITMENT AND
MILITARY OPERATIONS

SCALE
1:2,500,00

+++++ RAILWAYS
——— ROADS
– – – TERRITORIAL BOUNDARIES
········· PROVINCIAL BOUNDARIES

MILES 20 10 0   10   20   30   40   50   60

168 deserted, and only three were caught; the rest hid on European farms or with friends.(67)   Later, the appalling condition of repatriates, and their grim tales, caused desertions "in the earlier stages of hospital development."(68)

The Swahili porterage tradition had at first turned attention to Seyidie as the obvious source of first-line porters. But despite an offer of Rs.20 only three volunteers appeared at Malindi; a nocturnal press gang produced only 200 "skallywags," according to the District Commissioner, M.W.H. Beech. Villagers now took to the bush if they saw an official. Beech's Assistant District Commissioner at Takaungu, R. F. Palethorpe, said that the porterage tradition had gone; a Swahili would work for an Arab, but not under an askari, and disliked porterage or long safaris.(69)

In fact Arabs were little different from Swahili; half the Malindi people were Arabs, who were above manual work, and physically incapable of it anyway, in Beech's view. In 1917 the District Commissioner of Gazi hoped that recruiting would instill some discipline into "youths who had only led loafing and parasitic existences previously."(70)   In February 1915 Wapshare was trying to raise 200 gun porters, which was finally achieved with the help of Sheikh Ali bin Salim, Liwali of Mombasa, who paid his headmen fifty cents per recruit; a staff officer said they were "of good class," but Hobley warned that as Muslims they must have preferential treatment over the pagans from upcountry.(71)

Thirteen of them deserted; three were Kikuyu, two Luo, besides several coast men and some Nyamwezi from German East Africa, including two former German askari, though they were all supposed to be Swahili. "It would be interesting," remarked Major O'Grady, "to know how these men came to be enrolled." There were many German East Africa natives about, replied Watkins, and German deserters would hardly risk recapture. Hobley doubted if men would deliberately carry guns off if their officers knew them well; "any native porters would probably drop them if they came under a hot fire." (72) General Headquarters now asked for 160 more gun porters from Seyidie, barring Kikuyu and men from German East Africa. Sheikh Ali was presumably given more money for fees, and when the demand was raised to 900, Hobley applied to the Provincial Commissioner of Tanaland. The answer was interesting: 160 locals were available, but the Pokomo were mostly canoemen, and all professional porters were Kikuyu.(73)   Here is a clear evidence of pre-war migration; Kikuyu and Luo who seemed like Swahili, people from German East Africa, and the story of Mwanyula Bikatana make one wonder how much traffic there was in other directions.

Beech said that, as German East Africa men were debarred, he could get voluntary Kikuyu "who have settled and become more or less like coastmen." But to allow men to refuse service with impunity would "most seriously impair the authority of the Liwali and headmen, to say nothing of mine." Men were also escaping into Mombasa. Only 40 percent of the Malindi recruits were fit for load carrying; "there is practically nothing left in the districts but Arabs, grey-beards and the medically unfit." An end to recruiting would help "to quieten down the people a little." The Native Followers Recruitment Ordinance, by applying equal treatment for all, may have relieved this district from the call for special carriers; also it was probably realised that Palethorpe's verdict was correct.(74)

Another result was flight; The Leader described with relish how bush was fired, and the unfortunates hiding in it captured. Also "a threat of dismissal and the Serikali Kamata (government arrest) is settling all sorts of labor troubles."(75) In Kitui that year, "whole locations would take to the bush when they heard that an officer was coming," and would not be easy to reach in the empty lands towards the Tana.(76) In German East Africa the people, who had already suffered severe requisitions from the Germans, "had a well developed system of avoiding conscription by abandoning their homes and fields, and living in the bush by the side of some isolated waterhole where game was plentiful."(77)

Two individual examples show the lengths to which men were prepared to go. "After the first [conscription], Waitha fled and lived like a wild animal for the duration of the war in the inaccessible fastnesses of the banks of the Tana River, below Tumutumu Hill. Thence he came out like the hyenas....to seek his food and scurry back."(78) At Kabati, Wabunya wa Kahindo said that men would try to hide locally, rather than in the Tana or Athi valleys, as the risk of being caught en route was too great. A friend who hid in a cave was caught, but Wabunya was evidently luckier or more cunning, and evaded capture.

Conscription increased the hold of white employers over Africans. Officers were warned to prevent employers signing on men who were trying to escape the levy.(79) For example, a servant was suspected of theft; the employer, who could prove nothing but wanted to get rid of him, was told that the man could be conscripted.(80) A syce at Kericho stole Rs.100 from his employer, Miss Buxton, who refused the District Commissioner's suggestion that he be whipped and conscripted, because of what she had heard and seen at Kampala of carrier conditions.(81) The District Commissioner of Kisumu considered sending an unsatisfactory young headman into the Carrier Corps for seditious attitudes towards his chief; it might also be the best thing for the undesirable retainers of Chief Onduso.(82) A nasty example of blackmail is given by Karen Blixen, whose cook Esa fled because a former employer, wife of an official, threatened to have him recruited as a carrier if he would not return to her service.(83)

The mass levy demanded all available males between eighteen and thirty years of age; Ainsworth estimated from the tax registers how many each province could produce, allowing for a medical rejection rate of 33 percent. District officers now had to supervise a "comb-out," and all other recruitment had to stop. Hobley planned a "capital draft" of 2,000 for March and April 1917, with 1,300 spread over the next three months; even the reluctant and harassed Giriama must contribute. Owing to the extreme difficulties of recruiting in Seyidie, Ainsworth counted men levied in March towards the capital draft. Labor had to be exempted for dock or special plantation work, and rejects were sent to the Coast Planters Association. At the end of May, Hobley reported that "Mombasa District may now be said to be swept fairly clean of available labour."(84)

In Machakos, district officers took charge, as the native authorities were afraid of claims for blood money from the relations of the dead; "the terrible mortality in the first six months of 1917, and the lamentable condition of repatriates returning home in May and June 1917, undoubtedly gave rise to their attitude." The previous year, members of nzamas had tried to avoid sending their sons. Only four locations escaped the levy.(85) "Selection of the people was strict," recalled Mulei Nguyo, an askari who later became a storekeeper. "A European came to a place called Kwa Kithembe on a horse, and the people were called out name by name (from a tax register). They selected strong men, but not fat ones, who then walked to Nairobi." The horseman, said Muindi Ngaui, a carrier headman, was a Mburu (Boer) who supervised the tribal authorities.(86)

Raphael Simigini Osodo, of Bunyala, was a clerk under Kadimu, a Wanga chief whose imposition on the Nyala people was a strong political grievance. His account of recruiting is of unique interest:

> My work was to record the names of all the people that were....sent to war. I did all the correspondence with the Government because I could read and write. Letters used to come to me stating the number of men we were supposed to send....I read the letters for the Chief, who....sent his askari to arrest the young men. At the beginning of the war the number we were required to produce for war ranged from 50 men to about 150 men; but at one time....about 500 men. [As the work increased, he had two men to help him, and would go with the askari] to different homes and capture the young men. Many of these young men used to run away and hide in the trees from us. They would only come down by night for meals when we had gone away....Some were very courageous and just joined without being forced into it. In those days there was a rumour that those who went to the war were eaten by the white men [so no more volunteered]. It was very hard for anyone to escape....because I had his name down and knew exactly where he came from.

The property of defaulters was confiscated, and the chief was not above accepting "a cow or two" to let a man off. This agrees with official accounts on the use of tax registers; it also bears out what the askari Agweli and Odera, who were in the same locality, said about volunteering. It also shows how closely Nyanza was administered, with much stronger native authorities than in Seyidie. Raphael Osodo worked as a clerk from 1911 to 1948; until the end of the war he was paid a cow or three goats a month. In World War II he recruited for Panyako, the Pioneer Corps.(87)

It is surprising that local authorities were ready to go so far, in defiance of local opinion, but not that recourse was had to stratagem. "A big law case was to be held at Karatina, and everyone was to attend." No doubt other chiefs besides Mwirigo wa Irimu (Muthengi in Red Strangers) were involved; men were caught and put inside a huge wire case, also described by Dr. Philp, in which they were divided into three batches. "One batch was called Fita, and these were sent to Nairobi with a guard of soldiers. The second, a small batch, was called Shamba, and they went to work for Europeans on farms close to Tetu. The third was called Rotha; these were the old and infirm and they were allowed to return to their homesteads."(88)

Twenty years after, at the time of Munich in 1938, rumours of war so alarmed people in Kisii that they feared another conscription. Very few spectators came to the District Sports. In the first war, young men had been tricked into coming into the station to cut grass, and had been taken for the Carrier Corps.(89)

Elijah Kaara worked as a clerk in the Nairobi Carrier Depot from 1914 to 1917, when he was sent to German East Africa as a carrier storeman. "I was able to save many Nyeri men by omitting their names. I would tell a man to carry a basket into the crowd and disappear." Apparently he had heard that Chief Wambugu wa Mathangani turned a blind eye if a recruit ran away; but, living only six miles from the Provincial Commissioner and District Commissioner at Nyeri, Wambugu had to be careful. The Scots missionaries disliked him, as Philp shows:

> He received the King's War Medal for his services, which consisted in turning out men to serve in the Carrier Corps. It was my lot to be the Examining Medical Officer for these recruits. Other Chiefs....produced hundreds and thousands of carriers. When Wambugu's turn came, his own men bolted like rabbits in the dark before his eyes, and Maclure [sic], the District Officer, had to confess that the great favourite had let the Government down.(90)

But was Wambugu really such a fool? Kaara did not think so, and said that he was trying to rescue those people who had not been circumcised; with the district officers "Wambugu was quite a tactful man....he was an intelligent man and he managed to keep his hands on everybody." In 1929 his District Commissioner, S. H. Fazan, noted: "a much abler man in every way than one would suspect on first acquaintance."(91)

The unsupervised activities of headmen and retainers tended to lead to illegality and violence. One example was of a series of fights around the Uplands Bacon Factory near Limuru, as a result of raids on people living on its lands. But in July and August 1917 when district officers held meetings with elders, and went through the hut tax lists, men were enrolled without trouble, where they were of age and had no reason for exemption.(92)   Another was during July 1917; an attempt was made to recruit Giriama who had moved illegally from Nyika to Malindi District, crossing the Sabaki River to the north bank whence they had been expelled in 1914. A young Assistant District Commissioner had sent some elders and retainers without notifying the District Commissioner of Malindi, Elliot; at Bura village there was a fracas with members of another tribe, the Kauma, one of whose elders was fatally stabbed by a Giriama retainer.(93)   A third affair was also in Nyika District, but south of the railway, where Duruma shot arrows at police and retainers from Rabai, and an elder threatened the Assistant District Commissioner with a bow. There had been no objection to poll tax, so Hobley sent Hemsted to investigate. His report was that, owing to the lapse of the Kambi (council) for many years, there was little authority in the tribe, and steps were taken to revive the Kambi. One elder had offended the other by forming a body of about forty relations as retainers.(94)   But it is clear enough that these events were exceptional, and that otherwise leaders and people cooperated with the government.

Undisciplined retainers were a nuisance. In Kisii in 1916 the District Commissioner, W.F.G. Campbell, complained that one headman, Nsungu, "is apt to surround himself with silly, gutless youths whom he describes as askari but who are quite useless." Campbell was able to conscript some of them after Nsungu's people had been assaulted by Mugori's.(95) An objectionable method used by retainers in Nyika and Voi was tying up the women, "which appears to be the only method of inducing a runaway to return," or so an inexperienced Assistant District Commissioner at Rabai thought, since the headmen were so weak. Hobley vetoed this and similar methods employed by retainers who were not supervised by an officer. It was all right if, after due consultation with an officer, the elders rounded up the cattle of recalcitrants. Hobley's advice to Elliot, after the Bura affray, was that "the obstinacy of these people cannot be overcome by making a hurried dash, and it will be necessary to sit down, and collect the elders, and talk about it."(96) Throughout the East Africa Protectorate, this seems to have been the secret of peaceful recruiting.

A growing demand for special workers fell mainly on Seyidie with its older technical traditions; they included "Motor Drivers, Sweepers, Cattle Herds, Grooms, Officers' Servants, Blacksmiths, Strikers, Tailors, Saddlers, Telegraph men, Winchmen, Watchmen, Stevedores and so on."(97) Canoemen were needed on river lines like the Rufiji and Rovuma, and were obtainable on the Tana, Sabaki and coastal creeks. Artisans would live a fairly easy life at base workshops, and canoemen would be used to their work, unlike most carriers. Higher wages were paid; Rs.10 for a canoeman, Rs.20 for an experienced donkey boy. Indian artisans were needed at up to Rs.100.(98)

After the end of the mass levy in August 1917, recruiting was again in theory voluntary. Any class of men whom Provincial Commissioners thought should go to the Carrier Corps should be sent if fit, said Ainsworth, "also any volunteers the D.C.s may be able to obtain either for Carriers, Maxim gun porters, K.A.R.s will be most welcome."(99)

Famine and the terrible, world-wide influenza epidemic much reduced the labor supply in 1918. During and after the mass levy, Hobley had incessant appeals for labor from the Medical Officer of Health and the PWD, which the long-suffering District Commissioners had to meet.(100) MLB rejects were called Class B labor, and were in demand for the new strategic road in Jubaland, linking Kismayu with Serenli, which had been suggested before the war as an alternative to the route from Meru through Archer's Post and Marsabit. One would have thought that such work, in dry thorn bush, was almost as arduous as that of a carrier.(101)

Recruiting produced a situation in Mombasa similar to that in Malindi in 1915. The District Commissioner E. C. Crewe-Read, agreed to try and get fifty-six casuals wanted by the Carrier Depot, but rigorous recruiting for gun carriers recently had denuded the town of all unemployed natives. He would ask the Mudirs and headmen to get a few, but held out little hope.(102) The recruiting saga ends with a numb sense of general exhaustion: district officers

A group of East Africa Protectorate Carriers
by courtesy of Dr. Clive Irvine

scowling at new and impossible labor demands, headmen vainly
scouring streets and villages, and Class B rejects toiling in the dust
of the Serenli road.

THE ROAD HOME

By 1916 cultivation was seriously affected in Giriama, on which
the coast relied for much of its maize. Homecoming carriers might
reap the crops, but there was no one to weed them. Two years later
W.F.G. Campbell, now District Commissioner of Nyika, said in his
forthright way that despite the uprising, the levy of "fine" porters,
the ineffectiveness of headmen, and "the incessant coast-cry of
'turn out the Giriama', I maintain that....the Giriama have done
excellently in turning out to work."(103) The Taita had suffered
both invasion and recruiting; they had built the Tsavo road and the
Voi Military Railway, followed by railway work throughout German
East Africa. By April 1917 they seemed to have reached the limit;
another thousand had gone to the sixty mile tramway into the bush
behind Kilwa, and to raise another 520 was impossible. In August the
new District Commissioner, A. E. Chamier, wrote: "I am afraid we
are just about at the end of our tether here."(104) In the New
Year, he asked that Taita carriers be released first, in view of the
state of the war-torn district; "I am constantly receiving petitions
from old people and women asking about the repatriation of their
kinsmen." Watkins said that the Taita should not have preference
over Nyanza, for example, as they had worked near home for the
first two years of the war. Many Taita were now skilled mechanics,
at high pay rates, especially on the Central Railway, and could not
be replaced. Later Hobley, moved by the distress of old people in
the Dabida area, tried again; because of the absence of young men,
hundreds of acres of land were too overgrown to bear bananas or
cereals.(105)

The situation was much worse in German East Africa. Horace
Byatt, Administrator at Wilhelmstal (Lushoto), brought the letters of
two of his officers to the notice of General van Deventer, "in order
that he may be aware of the conditions which exist." Military
recruiting parties had flogged men, women and even Jumbes (chiefs),
who with the Akidas (headmen) could not produce any labor on their
own. The death lists were bad enough, but Charles Dundas, in his
letter, doubted if they were final, "for to judge by the human
wrecks I have seen returning, I am convinced that numbers die after
discharge." A convicted criminal was better off than an honest man
sent as a carrier; justice and the work of political officers became
impossible. H. H. Bell pointed out that women with babies on their
backs could not keep up cultivation; another recruiting campaign
would be disastrous. Dundas ended passionately: "No political officer
would be fulfilling his duty if he hid these facts. I am firmly
convinced that we have earned the loathing of these people, we are
damaging our future prospects and establishing a most disastrous
foundation for our future administration."(106)

During 1918 military recruiting went on in Nyanza, including
4,000 porters with rations for Turkana. "The Chiefs, assisted by
tribal retainers, collected the quota without any assistance from the
district staffs, and the work they did reflects great credit on all

concerned." Cultivation was extended, due to the efforts of officers on safari, and the Lumbwa and Kisii, not previously great farmers, now actually exported food.(107) This testifies to the efficiency of Ainsworth's Nyanza administration, and it is also clear that Nyanza was much better off than Taita.

In Kiambu the air was full of menace: "a gloom spread over the native population, and in the writer's opinion....any spark might have caused a dangerous outbreak; the headmen were obviously perturbed and afraid" is a sample of the District Commissioner's sombre report. The administration was overworked and frustrated, and farm workers were sullen, giving "as much trouble as they dared."(108) This all explains that fear of uprisings which partly determined the end of the mass levy. It must have been alarming in districts drained of the able-bodied, undercultivated and with a latent feeling of unrest.

Early in 1918 a leave scheme for carriers was tried, parallel to one for the KAR, which some carriers might be induced to join as the Carrier Corps ran down. The idea had previously been rejected, but was now tried for hospital orderlies and gun porters, the latter being the best potential material for the KAR. But men were soon overstaying their leave, and disgruntled district officers complained of the extra work of rounding them up. By November 1918 Watkins was saying that, as the war was over, deserters should have an amnesty and be paid off, as from the date they went on leave. Many seemed to have a genuine grievance at being underpaid, through failure of officers to notify paymasters of promotions or higher rates. The scheme was not a success; only a quarter of the thousand who went on leave returned.(109)

The vast task of repatriating all these men remained. There were 64,622 on MLC books when the war ended; in six months 55,175 were successfully discharged, 30,527 through Dar es Salaam.(110) In fact, repatriation began in June 1917 with a plan by Ainsworth for the sick and convalescent. Often to retain men in hospital was literally heartbreaking; they "have a longing to return home, and non-compliance with their wish has frequently a fatal result." Convalescent camps, distinct from carrier hospitals, were to be set up; Ainsworth wanted them staffed by missionaries and other sympathetic people. as far as possible, for whose services he would be deeply grateful, both on behalf of government and "of the Africans who have done what they could to help the cause of liberty, and in doing so have suffered." The main camps were at Mombasa, Voi, Nairobi and Kisumu; they were staffed by the main Protestant churches, and by several Roman Catholic religious communities.(111)

Carriers were returning before the scheme started. At that time, desertions had increased on the outward road from Machakos to Nairobi "due to the deplorable state of discharged Carriers who began to be repatriated....in May and June." Complaints led to an improvement in July.(112)   There is a moving scene in Red Strangers where the first carriers return - gaunt, dazed, bearded, long-haired; "We who have returned have sworn an oath never to speak of what we have seen."(113)

Much was done to ease the road home. Transport meant rail journeys to the depots where they were paid off, with further trains

TABLE 3

OFFICIAL STATISTICS OF AFRICANS RECRUITED
BY THE BRITISH AS TROOPS AND FOLLOWERS
FOR SERVICE IN EAST AFRICA, 1914 TO 1918

(a) Recruitments, including Carriers for the Belgians

	TROOPS	FOLLOWERS			
		GUN PORTERS, MEDICAL STAFF	CARRIERS, ETC.	CASUAL LABOR (MLB)	TOTALS
1. East Africa Protectorate	10,500	16,611	162,578	10,961	190,150
2. Uganda	10,000	2,096	182,896	1,243	186,235
3. German East Africa	2,000	4,031	197,312	125,817	327,160
4. Portuguese East Africa	–	4	10,927	79,083	90,014
5. Zanzibar/ Mafia	1,000	111	3,404	27	3,542
6. Sierra Leone	–	–	5,005	9	5,014
7. Nigeria	6,216	812	3,987	–	4,799
8. Seychelles	–	–	776	–	776
9. Gambia	380	–	37	–	37
10. Gold Coast	3,976	177	204	–	381
11. Nyasaland	15,000	?	195,652	1,262	196,914
12. N.Rhodesia	3,437	?	56,000	–	56,000
13. S.Rhodesia	2,752	?	300	–	300
14. S.Africa	1,500	?	22	1	23
Urundi				8	8
TOTALS	56,761	23,842	819,100	218,411	1,061,353

Sources: See JAH, 19, 1 (1978), 116, "Official Statistics of Africans serving with the British Forces in East Africa, 1914-1918," which excludes those recruited for the Belgian Forces.

(b)   Deaths and Death Rates

	TROOPS OTHER THAN KAR	FOLLOWERS DEAD	DEATH RATE %	MISSING PRESUMED DEAD	TOTALS DEAD + MISSING
1. East Africa Protectorate	64	25,891	14.6	13,748	39,639
2. Uganda	113+	3,870	6.7	780	4,650
3. German East Africa	–	13,129	6.5	27,535	40,664
4. Portuguese East Africa	–	450	4.1	?	450
5. Zanzibar/ Mafia	?	213	6.1	349	562
6. Sierra Leone	–	808	16.1	44	852
7. Nigeria	589	814	20.4	20	834
8. Seychelles	–	222	28.6	–	222
9. Gambia	38	?	?	?	?
10. Gold Coast	400	75	25.0	?	75
11. Nyasaland	?	4,480	2.3	?	4,480
12. N.Rhodesia	200	2,300	4.1	?	2,300
13. S.Rhodesia	250	?	?	?	?
14. S.Africa	163	?	?	?	?
KAR	4,237				
TOTALS	6,000+	52.252	10.0+	42,476	c.94,728

Note: The mortality is based only on officially recorded deaths, and is in fact more like 22 percent for the East Africa Protectorate. Its men served longer and farther from home than those from Uganda, German East Africa, Nyasaland or Northern Rhodesia. During periods of desertion in German East Africa many local men may have reached home, "but many of those who preferred to adventure to B.E.A. across country must have perished" – Watkins Report, Appendix 1, Table 7.

onward if necessary; carriers from the Kenia districts could go to Thika, and for Machakos or Kitui to Athi or Kapiti. Carriers returned to their homes near Lake Victoria by steamer or lighter from Kisumu. Oxcarts were provided for the disabled or debilitated, rest camps being situated en route.(114) Medical officers were told that congestion at hospitals and camps must not be relieved by risking the lives of unfit men of the road. An extra means of help was the East Africa War Relief Fund started in 1915, partly at Ainsworth's instigation.(115)

Mwova Kataka (carrier) and William Nthenge (stretcher bearer) walked home from Athi River via Machakos. Raphael Osodo remembered the oxcarts for the sick and wounded from Kisumu to Munias. Okech Atonga, gun carrier, walked from Kisumu to Homa Bay. Asembo Odera was discharged from the 4th KAR at Bondo in Uganda, where he was impressed by the arrangements. Returning to Kisumu by boat, he was taken in an oxcart to Mumias, and was then carried home by men ordered by the Chief, like other disabled men. So, by degrees, the survivors made their weary way home.

NOTES

1. Savage and Munro, "Carrier Corps Recruitment," 319-322; T.H.R. Cashmore, "Studies in District Administration in the East Africa Protectorate" (Ph.D. thesis, Cambridge, 1966), Chapter 8, "The Impact of the First World War," by the author's courtesy.

2. EAP, Ex. Co. Minutes, 21 June 1915 (PRO, CO 544).

3. EAP, Ords. & Regs., No. 29 of 1915.

4. EAP, Ex. Co., 23-25 Aug. 1915; Leg. Co., 3rd Session, Aug. 1915; PRO, CO 533/156/50243, Belfield to SSC, 10 Sept. 1915, and minute.

5. Leader, 28 Aug. 1915.

6. OG 1915, War Council, 14 Sept; EAS 30 Oct. 1915.

7. EAS, 3 Dec. 1915, and Leader, 6 Nov. 1915.

8. EAS, 29 Nov. 1915; Sec. Circs. No. 91 of 8 Dec. 1915, and No. 94 of 10 Dec. 1915.

9. EAP, Ords. & Regs. No. 31 of 1915; see also KNA, 46/1067, "Compulsory Services of Europeans."

10. KNA, 38/585, "Labour for P.W.D. and Water Supply Mombasa," and 38/603, "Dock Labour for Mombasa Port."

11. Leader, 5 Feb. 1916, "Labour and Discipline."

12. KNA, 37/577 3, Watkins to Ch. Sec., 24 Feb. 1916, and Sec. Circ. No. 7, 8 Feb., 120 more Carrier Staff needed.

13. PRO, CO 533/167/20463, Bowring to SSC, 20 March 1916.

14. Sec. Circs. No. 30, 11 May, and No. 51, 21 June 1916.

15. KNA, 38/585, correspondence during 1916, also Clayton and Savage, Government and Labour, 83.

16. PRO, CO 533/157/2097, Mr. Cornfoot's complaints.

17. EAS, 22 Sept. 1916.

18. Ibid., 30 Nov. 1916.

19. KNA, 37/577 3, Hobley to DC Mombasa, 16 March 1916.

20. Ex. Co. Minutes, 14 Aug. 1916.

21. Clayton and Savage, Government and Labour, 95.

22. KNA, DC/KBU/1/9, AR 1915-1916, and 1/11, AR 1917-1918.

23. Leader, 9 Oct. 1916.

24. Leg. Co. Minutes, Oct. 1916 and Feb. 1917; Leader, 25 Nov. 1916, and Report of NLC, 1913.

25. Sec. Circ. No. 12, 22 Feb. 1917.

26. Sec. Circ., 3 Feb. 1917; PRO, CO 533/189/13242, WO to CO, 12 March 1917.

27. PRO, CO 533/179/14179, Belfield to SSC, 15 March 1917.

28. Ibid., 179/19516, SSC to Bowring, 16 April 1917; 181/23318 and 25760, Bowring to SSC, 5 and 18 May 1917.

29. Ibid., 180/19899, Bowring to SSC, 17 April 1917, and 181/25307, Bowring to SSC, 17 May 1917, and minutes.

30. EAS, 5 April 1917, Ainsworth's official letter.

31. KNA, 37/577 4, MCL to DADML Nairobi, 24 April 1917.

32. KNA, PC/CP4/1/1, Kenia AR 1916-1917, appendix by Dr. Philp, acting Provincial MO.

33. EAS, 30 July 1917.

34. Ibid., for Jensen's scheme; 24 Aug. 1917, evidence of Mr. Paton to Economic Commission; 27 Sept., Hobley turns down the scheme.

35. Ibid., 21 Aug. 1917; PRO, CO 533/191/31379, 19 June 1917, and /35533, 14 July (Magadi); 184/42707 (end of restrictions).

36. KNA, 37/577 4, nos. 369-375 on labor shortages.

37. PRO, CO 533/183/47071, 18 July 1917; KNA, 46/1068, "Recruitment of Arabs and Baluchis."

38. PRO, CO 533/183/40516-7.

39. Sec. Circ. No. 55, 8 Aug. 1917.

40. PRO, CO 533/185/59334, Man. Guard., 16 Aug. 1917; JAH, 19, 1 (1978), 61-86: B. P. Willan, "The South African Native Labour Contingent, 1916-1918."

41. PRO, CO 534/21/18914, Smuts on carriers and KAR; /28724 and /31670, Northey and North-East Rhodesia.

42. PRO, CO 534/20/45489 (Portuguese), /48699 (Congo), 22/2356 (French colonies), 21/47071 and 29/57165 (Abyssinia).

43.   See Chapter 1, n. 10.

44.   PRO, CO 534/22/2356, Major Critchley-Salmonson's report, 2 June to 18 Aug. 1917.

45.   KNA, 37/577 4, Hobley to Ch. Sec., 28 April 1917.

46.   See Chapter 4 above, n. 54, and Ch. 5 above, n. 60.

47.   EAS, 15 Aug. 1917, 19 Sept., 4 and 11 Dec. 1917.

48.   See Chapter 11 below, section on war and protest politics.

49.   EAS, 6 April 1917.

50.   KNA, DC/MKS/1/3/7, Kitui AR 1917-1918; McClure in DC/NYI/1/2, Nyeri AR 1914-1915. Montgomery was a brother of the Field-Marshal.

51.   PRO, CO 533/195/23117, 198/52514 and /54143.

52.   KNA, DC/MKS/10B/6/1, "The Italo-Abyssinian War and other Military Matters," DC to PC Ukamba, 23 Dec. 1914.

53.   KNA, PC/NZA/1/10, Nyanza AR 1914-1915.

54.   KNA, PC/CP4/1/1, Kenia ARs 1914-1916; reasons noted by ADC Chuka (sub-district of Embu); DC/NYI/1/2, Nyeri AR 1915-1916, McClure on voluntary labor, lack of information on deaths. See Appendix 1 below for results of recruiting.

55.   KNA, DC/KSI/1/2 C.E. Spencer handing over to W.F.G. Campbell, 1915.

56.   KNA, PC/CP4/2/2, Ukamba ARs 1915-1917.

57.   KNA, DC/KBU/1/7, G.A.S. Northcote (DC) in ARs 1914-1916.

58.   Extract from interview with Joseph Munyao, 1965, kindly given by Dr. J. Forbes Munro.

59.   KNA, DC/NYI/1/2, AR 1915-1916.

60.   KNA, DC/MRU/1/1 and DC/MKS/1/3/6, ARs 1915-1916.

61.   See Chapter 4 above, n. 42, and Appendix 1 below.

62.   G. R. Sandford, An Administrative and Political History of the Masai Reserve (London: Waterlow & Sons, 1919), 126-130; PRO, CO 533/198/59546, and DC/NRK/1/1, Narok ARs 1914-1919; Robert L. Tignor, "The Maasai Warriors; pattern maintenance and violence in colonial Kenya," JAH, 13, 2 (1972), 277: at the E-Unoto ceremony the moran drink milk, and can then leave their bachelor manyattas (huts), marry and settle down, giving up warrior status.

63. KNA, DC/MKS/1/1/2, AR 1915-1916.

64. The method of securing young men was seen by C. Dundas, African Crossroads (London: Macmillan, 1955), 19; it is mentioned by Marius Karatu, and in notes of interview kindly given by James Kuruga, Thomson's Falls.

65. KNA, DC/CN1/5/1, AR 1916-1917.

66. KNA 37/577 1, Watkins, Hobley and Platts, 11 March to 7 April 1915; 37/577 2, Judge Advocate-General to Watkins, 3 Aug. 1915, deserters to face military court.

67. KNA, DC/KBU/1/9, Kiambu AR 1915-1916.

68. KNA, PC/CP4/2/2, Ukamba AR 1917-1918; WR. paras. 29-30 and 80.

69. KNA, 37/577 1, Beech to Hobley, 4 March and 8 April 1915; 16/49, Provincial/District ARs 1914-1915 (Palethorpe).

70. KNA, 37/577 1, Beech to Hobley, 4 March 1915; DC/KWL/1/3, AR 1917-1918 (Gazi or Vanga District was later called Kwale).

71. See Chapter 4 above, n.n. 13 and 45; PRO, CAB 45/31; KNA, 37/577 1, O'Grady to Hobley, 10 March, Sheikh Ali to Hemsted, 29 March, and Hobley to Wapshare, 30 March 1915.

72. Ibid., Hobley, O'Grady and Watkins, 30 April - 31 May.

73. Ibid., correspondence June, and 37/577 2, O'Grady to Hobley 1 July 1915.

74. KNA, 37/577 2, Beech, Hobley and Watkins, July-Sept. 1915; also 37/577 3, Beech to Hobley, 7 Oct. 1915.

75. Leader, 15 Feb. 1916.

76. KNA, DC/MKS/1/3/6, AR 1915-1916.

77. WR, para. 30.

78. H.R.A. Philp, God and the African in Kenya (London: Marshall, Morgan and Scott, n.d.), 131.

79. KNA, 37/577 2, Hobley to DCs, 25 Sept. 1915.

80. Leader, 15 Feb. 1916.

81. WP, C. M. Dobbs (DC) to Ainsworth, 14 Aug. 1916.

82. KNA, DC/CN7/1, DC to PC, 25 Oct. and 25 Dec. 1915.

83. Blixen, Out of Africa, 242.

84. KNA, 37/577 4, 21 March 1917; Hobley to DOs, 23 and 29 March; Hobley to Ainsworth, 11 April and reply 23 April; Hobley to Ch. Sec., 28 April.

85. KNA, DC/MKS/1/10, ARs 1916-1918.

86. Notes kindly given by Philip Mwalali,Kiteta, 1969.

87. Notes kindly given by Felix Osodo, Raphael Osodo's grandson, who kindly arranged an interview, 4 July 1970.

88. Huxley, Red Strangers, 272-273; Philp, "The Wire Cage," in Kikuyu News, No. 66, (Feb.-Apr. 1918), 8-10. I am told by Mr. John Johnson, once District Officer at Kerugoya, Embu District, that this was the name of the circumcision group for 1917; in Meru it was apparently Kaaria - see Oral Source (Meru District) for M'Inoti and Muthanya.

89. KNA, DC/KSI/1/4, AR 1938.

90. Philp, God and the African, 108-112.

91. KNA, DC/NYI/6/1, Nyeri PRB 1, 8 Sept. 1929.

92. KNA, DC/KBU/3/5, Dagoretti PRB 2, 1913-1939, 87-88; for use of census, PC/CP4/2/2, Ukamba AR 1917-1918.

93. KNA, 37/577 5, Hobley to DOs, 7 Aug. 1917; /577C, Elliot to Hobley, 31 March 1917, copy in /577D.

94. KNA, 46/1074, "Duruma Opposition to Recruiting."

95. DC/KSI/3/2, "Histories and Customs of Kisii."

96. KNA, 37/577A, Hobley to Platts, 19 April 1917; /577C, Hobley to Campbell, 29 March, and to Elliot, 17 July; 577D, Campbell to Hobley, 16 March, Lambert to Campbell, 23 March 1917.

97. WR, para. 81.

98. KNA, 37/577 4, Ainsworth, Hobley and Hemsted, May 1917; 45/1023, "Sweepers and Canoeists for Military," and 51/1266, "Bootmakers, Carpenters and Tailors"; PRO, 533/195/22938, compulsory service for Asian car-drivers.

99. KNA, 37/577 5, Ainsworth to PCs, 2 Aug. 1917.

100. KNA, 38/585, "Porters or Labourers for P.W.D. and Water Supply, Mombasa."

101. KNA, 38/585, correspondence Hobley and Ainsworth, July 1917, and in 37/577 4; also 577 5; PRO, CO 879/105, Confidential Prints, African, No. 954.

102. KNA, 37/577 6, CDO to PC, 30 Oct. 1918, answer 31 Oct.

103. KNA, 37/577 4, Evans to Hobley, 26 June 1916, and 577 5, Campbell to Hobley, 22 Aug. 1917.

104. KNA, 37/577A, Hobley to Ainsworth, 13 April 1917; Platts to Ainsworth, 18 April, to Hobley, 24 April, on capital account requirement; Chamier to Hobley, 4 Aug.: 111 Class A, 61 Class B, 57 others.

105. KNA, 37/577 6, correspondence Jan. 1918, Hobley to Ainsworth, 17 July 1918.

106. WP, Byatt to DAAQMG, Nov. 1917, and enclosures.

107. KNA, PC/NZA/1/13, Prov. AR 1917–1918 (C.R.W. Lane).

108. KNA, DC/KBU/1/11, AR 1917–1918 (G.A.S. Northcote).

109. PRO, CO 534/25/17481, Bowring to SSC, 8 Feb. 1918, for KAR plan; KNA, 39/643, "Leave for Military Carriers or Porters."

110. WR. para. 129.

111. KNA, 37/577 4, Ainsworth to PCs, 15 June 1917, and other letters; 577 5, Ainsworth to DADML Nairobi, 16 July 1917, with plan.

112. KNA, DC/MKS/1/1/10, AR 1917–1918.

113. Huxley, Red Strangers, 278–282.

114. KNA, 37/577 5, Ainsworth's mem., 16 July 1917.

115. Ibid., Ainsworth to Gray (DADML Nairobi), 3 Sept. 1917.

Chapter 8
Rations and Medicine

Atalukugendere akusibidde etanda y'amanvu

He who will not accompany you on the journey has
provided ripe bananas (as these will soon become
inedible, he does not care how you will fare).

(Luganda proverb)

It has been supposed that carrier mortality was due to "deplorable
quartermastering, inadequate diet, and poor medical services."(1) So
far as this is true, it was due to the lack of an expert Department
of Native Affairs (DNA), and still more to the failure of the War
Office to have a proper transport corps, or other real provision, for
an Imperial aim, the conquest of German East Africa.(2) This was
not the fault of those whose devoted efforts greatly improved the
diet, medical care and working conditions of carriers.

THE PROBLEMS OF DIET AND MEDICINE

In 1914 there was still no "adequate expenditure on medical
provision for the native population" in the East Africa Protectorate.
Also, wrote Watkins, before the MLB there was no expert central
body of opinion such as a Department of Native Affairs. So the
Indian Army staff were much confused by "every variety of contrary
opinion" from officials and settlers, each of whom "was apt to be...
quoted as an authority by any military officer whose theories....he
endorsed." Moreover, military provision for a war expected to last
only six months was very sketchy; there was no precedent for
military labor on such a scale. Local opinion made false analogies
between civil and military labor conditions; it "constantly raised a
cry of 'pampering the native', that has only just begun to alter to
'frightful mortality'."(3)

African diet was much more varied than the average European
realised; Dr Norman Leys had told the NLC that lack of medical
care and of proper feeding greatly reduced the efficiency of labor.
The Kikuyu diet was wide and varied, and it was impossible for
labor to thrive on 1½ lbs. of maize and beans daily. Malaria was
rife, and 40 percent of Mombasa labor were affected by
ankhlystomiasis (hookworm). Chief Kutu said that men suffered from
bad water, unusual food, too much maize which was often bad, and
lack of vegetables. The Report agreed about the bad conditions,
without unduly emphasising the grave lack of medical attention.(4)

But over all there hung, unheeded, the ghastly warning of the Uganda caravan of 1899.

Europeans closely acquainted with Africans knew that they were not adaptable to climate, resistant to disease, or easy to feed. There is a difference between the hot coastal or Lake regions and the cool highlands where night frosts may occur at over 7,000 feet. Highland people are not resistant to malaria, from which Kikuyu migrants to the coast suffered, as well as dysentery.(5) People used to warm climates would catch pneumonia in the highlands. Bacillary dysentery was endemic among the Nyanza tribes, but south of the Central Railway in German East Africa the amoebic type was to prove prevalent. This was the greatest menace to the carriers, and was known to be brought on by unsuitable food.(6)

Throughout Africa the staple diet is still porridge (Swahili ugali), which today is usually made of maize meal; seventy years ago maize was still a comparative innovation inland. The Luo were turning to it from millet. In Uganda, the Ganda and their neighbours used many types of banana as their staple food, but especially matoke (plantain), which was cooked but could also be made into flour. A people so dependant on food usually eaten "green" off the tree tended to suffer severely from a sudden change to any kind of grain, which was apt to cause internal irritation, leading to diarrhoea and dysentery. The Ganda in those days also ate fish, meat, and many vegetables: sweet potatoes, maize cobs, peas, groundnuts, sugar cane and several kinds of bean.(7)

In the highlands, the Kikuyu and Kamba also ate a varied diet: millets, maize, yam, arum lily, and sweet potatoes. The Kikuyu were more fastidious about meat than others, usually eating only domestic animals, not fish or game; the Kamba, on the other hand, were less particular, and would eat meat freely, whatever its kind or condition. They also used more milk than the Kikuyu, but the warriors of either tribe, while herding cattle, enjoyed the Maasai custom of drinking milk mixed with blood from a live ox. Beer, whether made of honey, sugar cane, cereals or bananas, was and is an important part of the diet of country people in Africa.(8) So much, then, for European ideas in those days that African diet showed little variety.

Ugali or uji (gruel) might be made of flour ground from maize, millet or dried plantain; the commonest millets were wimbi and matama. Scott, the Uganda officer who was Watkins' main rations expert, preferred wimbi, which stored better than matama or maize. The Ganda were coming to like maize flour, as well as cobs; it was known either by its South African name of "mealie meal," or the Swahili mahinde. For cooked rations, beans were better than flours, especially mealie meal which soon ferments. Uganda carriers were well aware of the dangers of coarse flour; some Nyoro carriers in 4 CC had been buying their own sieves, which Scott recommended as standard issue. He thought mhinde and mpokya the most suitable beans, as they could be cooked in twenty minutes as long as they were not more than six months old; they tended to go weevilly in store, but could be treated with ash or spread in the sun. The bean called bijanjalo by the Ganda, and maharagwe in the East Africa Protectorate, took too long to cook, and however well prepared caused diarrhoea if over a year old. (The Meru servicemen M'Inoti and Muthanya both complained of this bean; M'Inoti blamed it for the deaths of many members of the Riungu age-grade.) Bananas were wasteful to transport as only half their weight was edible, and they only lasted four days after picking; the same applied to sweet potatoes, but they and matoke could both be made into flour. Rice, with which all but coast porters were unfamiliar, had first to be soaked before issue.(9)

Mealie meal soon became standard, but any meal would cause intestinal irritation, if dirty, gritty or undercooked; the coarser the meal, the longer it took to cook. In the field, with the enemy about, fires and lights had to be out about 6.30 p.m. with the onset of tropical darkness. Men were likely to eat a half-raw, indigestible mass of porridge, when they were exhausted by the day's march, and probably had too little water, firewood and time to cook properly. Cooking and the preparation of food were women's work, anyway; hungry men are impatient, and an exhausted man cannot digest a heavy meal.

Watkins' view was that "in cooking, feeding, cleanliness, sanitation and general habits we have to fight custom and superstition, breaking down cherished tribal distinctions to one level of reluctant obedience." Early in the campaign Dr. C. J. Wilson, medical officer and historian of the East Africa Mounted Rifles, noted the spread of "enteric fever" with the arrival of Nyanza carriers at Namanga. It was impossible to enforce sanitation, or prevent the pollution of streams; dust and flies further spread infection. After the war he condemned "the inhumanity and folly" of the view that porters needed only mealie meal. At camps like Bissell or Namanga, the spread of disease was encouraged by a sedentary mass of carriers fouling an area. No analogy was possible with the traditional safari of professional porters, not more than 300 strong, mobile and not an excessive burden on water supplies. They and the porters with small hunting safaris could be fed mostly on game while on the move.(10)

The lack of an expert peacetime DNA was soon shown by a bitter clash between, on the one hand, Watkins, the Senior Medical Officer (SMO) at Voi and Ainsworth, and on the other, the Central Committee of Supply, which represented the less enlightened settler viewpoint. Watkins and Captain Jolly, the Indian Army SMO, agreed that dysentery deaths at Voi among carriers were due to unsuitable food, pneumonia deaths being due to cold, exhaustion and malnutrition. They agreed on the need for a varied diet, and in condemning the widespread military interference with carriers, who were scattered about, used as a labor pool, and generally taken out of the control of their officers. Only verbal information could be got about part of 4th (Uganda) CC at Voi, where five were dead, and many in hospital.(11)

As quartermaster of the CC, Scott now carefully inspected samples of mealie, matama and wimbi flours; he said that one ton out of every six sent to Nairobi was a pure waste of transport. Only fresh grain should be used if possible; all must be well cleaned before milling, and sieved before issue, as some porters were already doing. The waste must be made good.(12) These findings enraged the Central Committee of Supplies (CCS), who maintained that the samples were what natives themselves would use. If military porters had a better ration than they would at home or in civil employment, it would create a new desturi (custom); in other words, it would lead to demands for better rations. The diarrhoea was attributed to insufficient cooking, the dysentery to some other cause.(13)

Watkins sent samples of flour to Ainsworth, with the acid comment that "we are up against the Nairobi mealie meal ring"; he particularly wanted Ainsworth's help in destroying the suggestion that the food was as good as the men would have at home. He pointed out to the Deputy Adjutant and Quartermaster-General (DAAQMG) that the efficiency of carriers depended on good health, for which a varied diet of their usual foods was vital. "We have to fight against a pernicious Nairobi tradition that unvaried mealie meal is the one food of all African natives." It was most important that supply officers refer to CC officers before buying local produce.(14)

The matter now went to the Director of Medical Services, Nairobi. Examples like the Uganda Mutiny and the Nandi Campaign meant that any recurrence must be prevented for military reasons, and as "our duty to the hordes of carriers." If food was the cause of recent dysentery, which medical officers thought it probably was, then "the Committee of Supplies will see the absurdity of appointing expert advisers merely to ignore their views." It was politically vital that carriers return home in good health. It was expressly denied that natives would see wimbi or other flour as carefully prepared as by their womenfolk for use at home. The difficulties of cooking in the field were reiterated; "to say that food needs long cooking is to condemn it for military purposes."(15) Captain Forbes, SMO of the EACC, explained that the husk of maize was not nutritious but entirely harmful, unlike the vitamin-bearing husk of wheat, which also promotes "rising" in the baking process; extra cooking would make no difference. He fully agreed with his colleagues and thought "that the attitude of the Committee is a cause for regret."(16) An examination of some Kisumu samples by the Government Analyst, which the Medical Officer of Health thought might cause dysentery, led to the conclusion that it was too coarse.(17)

"The Carrier Corps lost the battle," but a better diet was sanctioned, as was the use of sieves. Local milling and winnowing were not up to South African standards and

> local interests....strongly opposed any importation of flour or alteration of grade, [but with the change of staff following Smuts' appointment] orders were given to import all flour for human consumption from South Africa....in 1914 the opinions of Carrier Officers were worth no more than those of other residents. By 1916 their experience constituted a body of considered expert opinion.(18)

An example of this at work in 1917 was when Major Ernest Hill (of the South African Medical Service, and chief Medical Officer with the MLB), claimed that it was his duty to accept or reject locally cut sugar cane, which was not suitable, as it bruised if carried any distance, fermented and caused stomach trouble.(19) Hill and Watkins also agreed soon afterwards that it was for a local Carrier Officer to decide whether local mealie cobs were suitable, rather than the Inspector-General of Communications, Brigadier-

General W.F.S. Edwards, and greatly to that gentleman's annoyance. But Watkins, unabashed, pointed out that the rations were based on South African experience. "If I once agreed that it can be altered... without the formality of a reference to myself or to the Medical Officers appointed as advisers to the Department, the whole fabric falls to the ground, and we are back on the bad old lines of trusting to individual discretion in essentially technical matters."(20) The Carrier Corps had come some way for the DML to be able to make such a resounding declaration of policy.

THE UGANDA CARRIERS

"Uganda natives," wrote H. R. Wallis, "unless carefully dieted and accustomed to rice and flour for a considerable period beforehand, cannot be successfully employed away from their own country....when so taken a terrible mortality has resulted from intestinal diseases. Once they become accustomed to strange foods they render excellent service, but the proportion which can be so used is very small."(21) When a contingent of 3,576 was sent to the EACC in August 1914, Uganda people and officials may well have watched anxiously.

Kasoga, a porter of Chief Kimbuya of Kisonga, died on H.M.S. Nyanza bringing 500 carriers from Karungu in South Nyanza. "A rag of barkcloth was apparently his only personal effect. The body was in a state of extreme emaciation, the whole alimentary tract empty, the intestines and visceral peritoneum acutely inflamed, and the mucous membrane covered with ulcers. In my opinion death was caused by acute dysentery and lack of treatment." No one was in charge of the wretched porters, overcrowded on the deck and exposed to wind and rain. Sir Frederick Jackson complained bitterly of their diet, of their separation from their officers who understood their language and customs, and of "conditions which have called forth protests both from the Administrative Officers in Charge, and from the Medical Officers, either attached or who have been in touch with the Corps." A death rate of 23 percent, mainly from dysentery, had caused alarm recalling the 1899 disaster, and showed that the green food eaters of Uganda were not suited to service as porters outside their own country.(22)

Scott attributed the dysentery to unsifted wimbi flour, milled at Kisumu; after three months, 40 percent of the men had to be invalided. The findings made in November 1914 should have been final, and well known to the military staff. Yet Major-General Stewart dismissed Scott's verdict for "lack of evidence," and ascribed the dysentery to "want of ordinary sanitary precautions"; no doubt he listened to the pseudo-experts of the CCS rather than to the real ones on his own staff. Admittedly the death rate for wimbi-fed carriers on the Kagera front declined at that time, but the evidence for the bad effects of dirty or unsifted flour was overwhelming.(23)

Another dreadful case of callousness in transporting carriers occurred in February 1916. Eighty-eight recruits, unaccompanied by any officer, travelled for two days by open lighter and train from Masinde on Lake Kyoga to Jinja, where they boarded the S S Usoga for Sango Bay in the south of Lake Victoria. Their food was a mass of precooked wimbi and beans, dumped uncovered on the lower deck; it naturally decomposed. Seventy carriers fell sick, of whom fifteen died of ptomaine poisoning. It is not known what action was taken against those responsible.(24)

When it was suggested to Miss Buxton at Kericho that her syce be conscripted for theft she said: "I cannot consent to let any of my boys go into the Carrier Corps after the awful way in which they are killed at Kampala. Seven a day were dying of starvation owing to having been six days without food at all." A Court of Enquiry found no evidence to justify "the sweeping statement." She had evidently seen HMS Sibyl arrive at Kampala from Namirembe Bay with 700 carriers, of whom 500 were Carbels and 180 patients from Namirembe Hospital. Though they had been short of food, none were starving; the officer commanding Carbels, Captain E. G. Fenning, denied that any porters had died from starvation throughout the unit's existence. The Belgians had looked after them well, and had given them a fair share of food. The medical officers said that though this batch were worse off than most, deaths were due to dysentery and pneumonia, not starvation. Mrs. Katherine Cook, Matron at Mengo and wife of Dr. Albert Cook, remarked that these men had "wolfed" their first meal of soup and matoke without washing their hands, "which they are usually particular to do." Dr. Cook thought that Miss Buxton had mistaken dysentery patients for half-starved men (which one would think a very natural error); he said that the prejudice against strange food was so great among the green food eaters that it was extremely difficult to get dysentery patients to take enough to eat.(25)

The affair showed both the difficulty of feeding Uganda carriers, and the efforts being made to overcome the problems and to succour repatriates, in which Dr. Cook and his colleagues played no small part. During the advance on Tabora in the second half of 1916, a growing stream of porters were returning across the Lake. On 19 July Dr. Cook was warned of 329 men returning from Namirembe on H.M.S. Nyanza, and was asked how many he could accommodate at Mengo; Mrs. Cook replied, "Dr. Cook asks me to say that all 329 can be put up tonight." These convoys arrived twice or thrice weekly at only a few hours notice, and would always be met with great coppers of hot soup, arrowroot gruel, thickened milk and matoke which saved many lives, along with the careful nursing which the men received.(26)

Apart from the devoted work of European doctors and nurses. Uganda Africans themselves made remarkable efforts. Early in the war a Uganda Stretcher Bearers Company was formed by boys of the Church Missionary Society (CMS) High School, Mengo, with students of the Government Medical Training School as instructors. The schoolboys proved superior to peasant recruits at stretcher drill, nursing and first aid, and the Company then became the Uganda Native Medical Corps, 150 strong; it was encouraged by the Kabaka of Buganda, Daudi Chwa, and the Katikiro, Sir Apolo Kagwa. Being mainly Ganda, the men could not be classed as Followers, below the askari of other tribes, so they were called Troops. They were disbanded after the fall of Bukoba in mid-1916, but their work had been so good that a new African Native Medical Corps was started in March 1917, commanded by Major Keane, Royal Army Medical

Corps, and Captain Tomblings, a Uganda district officer. All high school boys of over sixteen joined it, including many who had previously served; a cousin of the Kabaka, Prince Joseph Musanji, served as a lieutenant. They worked mostly at the Carrier and Sewa Haji hospitals in Dar es Salaam, but Ganda NCOs were in charge of subordinate staff at many hospitals in German East Africa and Portuguese East Africa. For such a small body of men the Uganda African Native Medical Corps made a considerable impression, and the experience must have had effects on the later history of Uganda.(27)

Even this carefully organised unit suffered quite a high death rate, but had the misfortune to endure an epidemic of spotted fever (cerebro-spinal meningitis), with sixteen deaths before they left for German East Africa. This lethal disease was very prevalent in Uganda, and its virulence is shown by the shocking death of one of Cook's colleagues, Dr. W. Hillbrook, who was bitten on the hand by a patient. Up to 1916, it was second only to dysentery as a cause of death among Uganda servicemen.(28)

Wallis reckoned the true mortality in 1914 to be 32 rather than 23 percent, nearly half the 722 survivors having died.(29) He said that over 80 percent had been rejected during the mass levy in the Eastern Province, and tht his staff had produced as many as they could. Captain H. B. Thomas was an MLB officer at Mjanji Depot, to receive porters from Bakedi, Toro, Lango and Gulu districts; there were also the officer, Captain G.F.W. Gibbs, and Dr. Wynstone Waters, the former medical officer from Seyidie. "His examination of the porters," recalled Mr. Thomas, "....was to walk down the line of parade and, with a fly-whisk, indicate those unfit. I'd guess that 2 out of 3 were discarded. An outbreak of cerebro-spinal meningitis caused more losses. I've no notion how many were actually shipped across to Kisumu. By August the flow from up-country was coming to an end and Mjanji Depot began to fold up." Mr. Thomas was a battalion and column Carrier Officer until after the battle of Mahiwa, November 1917.(30) Dr. Waters rejected only some of those sent from the districts, where many had been rejected already. The Uganda government's reluctance to let any men go as porters in 1917 is quite understandable after the earlier mortality.

IMPROVING THE RATIONS, 1915 TO 1917

The 1897 plan had envisaged 1½ lbs. of rice and a few ounces of shark's flesh as a carrier ration; the average East Africa Protectorate settler was less generous, with only 2 lbs. of mealie meal or wimbi. South African and Rhodesian practice was far ahead. Mine experience had shown the need for a balanced diet: mealie, beans, meat, vegetables, groundnuts, salt, beer, and a pint of hot soup, coffee or cocoa after night shift. A Rhodesian committee on the prevalence of scurvy and pneumonia recommended preferably 3 lbs. of meat a week.(31)

The KAR diet was also poor; two companies were disbanded at Serenli after forty-one askari and two women had died of beri-beri, caused by insufficient mineral salts in the rice, the unvaried diet, the hot climate and lack of exercise. Dr. C. J. Wilson, though new to the country, produced a new and varied ration scale, which was rejected with the comment that maize had always been the food of the African and therefore an elaborate ration was unnecessary.(32)

The Carriers' initial ration was mostly flour or beans, of which no African, according to Wilson, would eat so much at a sitting. Though a more varied diet was arranged at the end of 1914, Watkins' attempt to include vegetables failed.(33) Since full rations could not be guaranteed in the field for anyone, the ideal was the same for Troops and Followers, which was not attained until 1917. The formation of the MLB in 1916 involved a South African medical staff under Major Ernest Hill, who brought about a vastly improved ration.(34) Officers were to notify Hill if any item in the new ration continually eluded them, or if local Supplies were coy about written explanations. Though Troops and Gun Porters had both rice and mealie meal, with dates as well as meat, the Carriers were in some ways better off, having vegetables and fats.(35) But this depended on Supplies, and on the willingness of combatant units to share and share alike, as the Belgians to their credit had done with Carbels. Cooking was crucial, and as the MLB grew larger, and lines of communication longer, maintaining rations became more difficult, especially when Smuts' last drive ended in the Rufiji floodwaters.

The main problems centred on mealie meal, until rice was adopted for forces in the field. Until Smuts' advance began in February 1916, the forces were more or less stationary, and problems of supply and cooking slighter. In February 1915 commanding officers were made responsible for seeing that their units were fully rationed; loads of food were not to exceed 50 lbs. and any which did were to be reported to Headquarters. Damaged food was not to be accepted .(36) Much food must have been wasted; if mealie meal gets wet it soon ferments and goes mouldy. Later on, waterproof bags were used. Had the order of February 1915 been enforced, all would have been well. But the discipline of the Force was so poor, and the difficulties of protecting carriers from outside interference so great, that it must often have been flouted.

In the Gazi sector, porter mortality had caused concern. The SMO had blamed the diet; the men needed more variety, and meat daily instead of thrice weekly. Kikuyu porters had suffered particularly, and were moved in August 1915, experience on the Msambweni Road having shown clearly how much the health of the men depended on full control by their officers.(37)

The food preferences of different tribes were hard to ignore throughout the campaign, but caused more difficulty in the early days, before compulsion put everyone on a level. Kikuyu would not eat fish, which the Taita and Nyanza tribes liked. Many porters would not eat beans, which were an important part of the ration. The raising of a Digo labor force to do the roadwork in Gazi led to some disagreement between Watkins and Hobley as to whether rice should be offered as an inducement; Watkins thought it would cause jealousy.(38)

When in April 1916 the meat supply for carriers working in Kilindini Docks broke down, dates were proposed as a substitute. The civil medical officer at the Carrier Depot Hospital said that men on night shift must have extra rations, and if meat was not available, they must have dates. He also spoke of the heavy loss of life among carriers on the coast, due to climate and unsuitable food. The failure of upcountry men to cook their food properly showed the need for gang cooks, "as is done in prisons."(39) Dates needed no cooking, so could be used on train or ship journeys, when mortality could be so severe. Dates and an allowance of parboiled rice (powa) proved to be best; if men were given two days rations before a journey, and told to cook them first, the result was likely to be a gorge with fatal consequences. Later, tinned meat and biscuits became standard train rations for all servicemen.(40)

Smuts' offensive in 1916 soon outstripped his supply organisation. To the east, at Msiha Camp and Handeni, troops lived on biscuit, mealie meal and fly-stricken trek ox. A medical officer wrote that the numerical strength of the forces led to a vicious circle. "It was impossible to feed the large number of troops, so that....sickness was increased by partial starvation, and the sick troops coming down.... consumed the supplies intended for those at the front."(41) Here, and during the drive to the Rufiji, the follower suffered most; the Carrier Officer with the 2nd South African Division at Iringa reported:

> Porters with advance have been rationed for ten days. Ration works out at ½ lb meat and 1/5 meat per day. Expect deaths, desertion and sickness will occur on large scale as work will be heavy as porters cannot stick it on these rations. Meal coming forward from Dodoma is not in waterproof bags so expect much will be sour as rains heavy.

Watkins sent this wire on to the DAAQMG, Brigadier-General C. P. Fendall, with the comment: "I desire to record my strong protest against the treatment being given by the 2nd Division to their Carriers." A second wire from the Carrier Officer said that bags issued at 50 lbs. contained only 40 lbs. Supplies refused to make good the deficiency. "Please protest against this." Watkins did so. "This if true means that losses through leakage and theft are being made good at the expense of the men's health and we are compelled to sign receipts for what we don't get." What they did get might still be unfit for human consumption, as was shown by thirty-six bags of yellow mealie meal at Voi, the entire stock in the Depot store, of which thirty were condemned on account of mildewed lumps, husks and sharps.(42)

In March 1917 there was controversy over the fat ration, coconuts being substituted for ghee (Indian clarified butter). The medical officer thought coconuts too indigestible. Ghee, being lighter, was used off the line of rail, where only coconuts were available. One officer complained that railway labor got more ghee and dates than MLB men, who needed them more as they had to make lengthy rail journeys. Ghee tended to be reserved for Indians; an alternative was sesame oil (sim sim). Coconut oil (which all upcountry men detested) and sim sim were produced by mills, driven by steam or even camels, as seen in Mombasa by Lazaro Maende, a carrier from South Nyanza. There were also mills at Dar es Salaam, Dodoma, Bagamoyo and Tabora. Some men said that sim sim, mixed with other food, gave them diarrhoea, but Scott thought that what they really disliked was having their food cooked for them. He advised discontinuing coconut oil altogether, and eventually the policy of mixing sim sim oil was quite successful. As ghee was unobtainable by September 1917, the fat in the final ration was presumably sim sim.(43)

The double standard in rationing, between Africans and Europeans or Indians, appeared again in April 1917 when the veterinary practice of passing measly beef as "fit for consumption by natives" at the Nairobi Carrier Depot was condemned by Hill: "that a Veterinary Officer should decide as to what disorders a human being may rightly be exposed is preposterous." Dr. W. H. Kauntze, medical officer at the Nairobi Carrier Hospital, wrote later that of 745 dysentery patients examined, 90.5 percent had up to five species of worm, whereas in non-dysentery patients the percentage was sixty-nine; dysentery encouraged helminthiasis, or vice versa. Tapeworm was very common, and a specimen of Taenia saginata, 250 feet long and with only one head, occurred at Nairobi Depot. After Hill's complaint, porters' meat was to be killed, inspected and issued as for the rest of the garrison, again vindicating the principle that Followers must be treated like Troops.(44)

The awful mortality in the year up to the mass levy, and the prospect of even greater numbers of followers, caused the MLB and medical officers to make strong recommendations to General Headquarters. If staging posts were used on lines of communication, wrote Surgeon-General Hunter, cooks working for gangs of twenty-five men could have meals ready for them on return from work.(45) It was almost impossible to train cooks, however, as a gang would only allow one of their number to cook, and they could not leave the depot until he was trained. Nor would the meals be as good as porters would have at home where, said Watkins, the standard was "as different from anything we can attain as a Parisian chef's efforts are from those of a camp cook."(46) Scott concluded that it was impossible to cook mealie meal properly in the field, when it had to be boiled for an hour and a half; it has to be put into boiling water for half an hour, covered and left to steam for hours over a slow fire. With limited water, firewood or daylight, or with the enemy about, this was impossible. A gang preferred to cook for themselves, as their only amusement in the evening; the cook was simply expected to get the water and firewood. Pots or petrol tins were used, each holding enough for five or six men; a cook could only look after four pots, as they had to be stirred while they boiled, but ideally it should only be one. With the largest available pot it would take six hours, needing more wood than was probably at hand, and with thoroughly unpalatable food as a result. When Scott tried cooking the best white meal for an hour and a half, the food was condemned by the Carrier medical officer. The problems could be overcome at posts, but were insuperable in the field; "at a time when the porters are particularly tired and in need of wholesome food, it is not procurable." Rice, which could be soaked and swollen before issue, and cooked in half an hour, was the answer; it was already in successful use by troops and front-line porters.(47)

Considerable progress was made with central cooking by September 1917. At the Dar es Salaam Depot nine kitchens were cooking for between four and seven thousand men, two of which were for the convalescent camp. The new methods at first caused

600 men to refuse their food, but they ate it the next day when they found that there was nothing else available. Though they would revert to the old method if they could, of throwing handfuls of meal into boiling water until there was a half-cooked mass of dough, Scott was encouraged by the progress, and by the prospect of bigger and better cauldrons from South Africa.(48)

Owing to the persistence of coarse and insufficiently sifted meal, the inspection system was improved; Watkins asked for an expert mealie meal tester from South Africa. He was coming to the conclusion that East African meal was not good enough. In May 1917 3,800 tons of meal came from East and South Africa, of which 1,800 tons were from Nairobi. Most was good, but some still badly milled; the Nairobi millers responsible were fined, and Lieutenant-Colonel Dunlop (ADST) agreed to a tester to help MLB officers to examine stores of meal. His name was Mr. L. McAuley, and he was given the rank of Company Sergeant-Major.(49)

Meanwhile, in June 1917, the German raid northward under Neumann interrupted the meat supply. It was suggested that carriers be reduced to meat thrice weekly, with substitutes on other days; Watkins presumed that "all other units are being reduced, and that the whole burden of shortage is not being put onto Carriers."(50)

Watkins and Hill now condemned the whole stock of yellow East Africa Protectorate meal; the white was less unsatisfactory, but would still not provide digestible food by present cooking methods. All East African meal should be replaced by South African, or only used in emergency. Dunlop agreed that the yellow be withdrawn altogether, and the white only used in Dar es Salaam, where it could be properly cooked. The MLB specification was for meal which would pass through sieves with a mesh of 400 to the square inch. Milling in the East Africa Protectorate seemed so inadequate that "unless East Africa can contrive to attain the standard set by South Africa they should drop out of the competition altogether." East African meal was therefore withdrawn, and only South African used, preferably only at bases where it could be properly cooked in large cauldrons.(51) But the shipping shortage limited the South African supply, illustrating von Lettow's success in forcing the British to commit precious resources.(52) In September 1917 a batch of East Africa Protectorate meal, issued in error, was reported at Mikesse, where it was condemned by Sergeant-Major McAuley at totally unfit for human consumption.(53) At last a fully comprehensive ration scale now came in, which included all African soldiers and followers, and offered both rice and mealie meal.(54)

Bread had been ruled out as an answer to the problem.(55) Beer was first considered following cases of scurvy at Dodoma, where the men had been without fresh vegetables for two months, suffering too from chest infections in the cold winds. Major Pitt, Carrier Officer at Kilwa, also advised beer as an essential item of diet, and not a luxury; it was issued by large employers in South Africa. He also drew attention to tapioca, eaten with groundnut sauce in Portuguese East Africa, which needed no cooking. Breweries were established in October 1917, but mainly for convalescents; beer "did much to restore tone, and combat the depression and nostalgia to which the sick native so readily yields, dying without a struggle because he can summon up no interest in a life in which he feels he will never be well enough to get home."(56)

Hill also secured extra sugar for carriers in hilly, sandy or swampy country, or in cold climates; though at best a carrier's labor might be "moderate," it was all too often "severe." Hill's work, "ably carried on by his successor Lieutenant-Colonel Bligh Hall, O.B.E., in organising the medical work for African followers would, if he had his deserts, make his name long remembered among them."(57) This tribute was deserved by all who worked for better conditions in the Carrier Corps.

MEDICAL PROGRESS

In 1914 there was a doctor for each Carrier Corps, or an assistant surgeon if no medical officer was available. It was less easy to provide medical officers as numbers rose in 1915, and the breakdown of control meant that Carriers became separated from their doctors as well as their Carrier Officers. It had also been proposed, when the Carrier Section was planned in December 1914, to have a carrier hospital at each base or depot; one had already been started at Mombasa, and "a Hospital came to be recognised as a necessary adjunct to a Depot." This was an advance on the pre-war position, where "the standard of medical comfort....recognised as the right of the natives was....a very low one."(58)

Where followers were separated from their officers or doctors, they "depended on the humanity of the Medical Officer of the post"; it was difficult to ensure that followers received equal treatment "with white men or troops." Under pressure, a medical officer tended to give askari precedence over wapagazi, or white patients over black. A convalescent white might even have more attention than a black in a critical condition; in other words, it was all part of "the great unresolved problem of Africa, the relation of Black and White." The only solution was for the MLB to have its own medical staff, but the shortage of medical officers became graver with the mass levy in 1917, which contributed to the heavy mortality. In November 1917, Hill's added authority as Lieutenant-Colonel and Senior Medical Officer enabled him to prevent the transfer of staff from carrier hospitals, and the requisition of Carrier medical equipment for other units. The carrier was "entitled to equality of treatment with the fighting man," in medical care as well as in rations.(59)

Despite all the progress by March 1917, the added burden of the mass levy made the problem of keeping down the appalling death rate seem insuperable. In all carrier hospitals, wrote Dr. Kauntze, "dysentery formed the cause of admission in at least 50% of cases, and led to one third or more of the total deaths." No treatment, no precautions against infection seemed to help. "It is almost impossible to picture the feeling of despair with which the unfortunate medical officer entered on his day's work, or with what relief he hailed his transfer to some fighting unit."(60) These transfers ended with Hill's promotion. Not only were a third of the deaths due to dysentery, but half were due to all kinds of intestinal infection. Pneumonia killed from 12 to 20 percent, mainly of those from warmer climates working on the higher plateaux; conversely, highlanders suffered severely from malaria. Smallpox and meningitis could push up the death rate sharply. In the early days the proportion of deaths from unknown or unspecified causes seems to have been higher than in

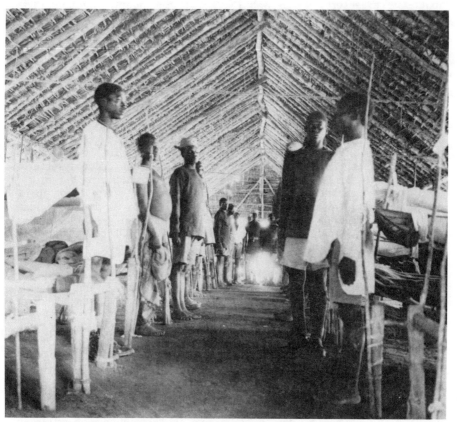

A Carrier Hospital, run by the Uganda African Native Medical Corps (This photograph is also in G. J. Keane and D. G. Tomblings, *The African Native Medical Corps*)
   by courtesy of Dr. Clive Irvine

Kauntze's detailed statistics for 1917, but doubtless often the reason was loss of the will to live.(61) In times of extreme hardship in the field some may have died of starvation or exhaustion, but very few carriers were killed in action; in this campaign disease killed more men than the enemy.

When Kauntze took charge of the Nairobi Carrier Hospital in September 1916, he consulted Dr. Pirie, Government Pathologist, about the dysentery, which was thought to be mainly amoebic. The two doctors decided that it was bacillary, which was further borne out by the failure of emetine treatment. Nor did other remedies like saline treatment reduce mortality as they should, and many cases became chronic. Pirie and Dr. Ross, Director of Laboratories, then made a vaccine, sterilized by a 0.4 percent solution of carbolic acid, which caused no reactions in the 76,000 porters who were given it.(62) It was tried first in a 1 cc dose, then in a 4 cc. Pressure of work made it impossible to ensure accurate returns, especially of causes of death. Up to March 1917, men from Ukamba, Kenia and Kisumu (who included the Uganda men) were given 1 cc; 5,000 could be inoculated in eight hours. Kauntze pointed out that his statistics showed deaths from dysentery only, not from post-dysenteric diarrhoea. All deaths were presumed to be from bacillary dysentery, until porters reached central German East Africa, where they might die of amoebic, which accounted for 70 percent of all cases in that area. The alarming rise in the dysentery rate in mid-1917, even among porters inoculated with the larger dose, could have been due to amoebic dysentery, as well as to the short period of immunity which, in the opinion of Dr. John Arthur, was given by the vaccine. Moreover, porters from Nairobi and Kisumu depots had less resistance than those from Seyidie or German East Africa; the swampy regions south of the Central Railway, where porters were so essential, were less healthy than the north. Whereas the uninoculated porters worked behind the front line, the inoculated recruits "were all exposed to the miseries of that advance by the Rufiji." When the supply breakdown caused semi-starvation, the inoculated men both ran a high risk of dysentery, including amoebic, and were more likely to die of debility than were those at base hospitals.(63)

The stronger dose gave a lower death rate than the smaller one. Though conditions in the field limited the success which the vaccine deserved, Kauntze was right to claim that it was highly successful; an outbreak of dysentery among the KAR at Mbagathi, near Nairobi, was almost entirely quelled by it.(64) Considering the unprecedented emergency in 1917, it was a considerable feat to have produced such an effective vaccine.

Convalescent dysentery patients were given fluid diets similar to those used by Cook at Mengo: milk, arrowroot gruel, sugar, rice jelly, bread and a little brandy. The full convalescent diet included matama, beans, mealies, meat, rice and vegetables. The East Africa War Relief Fund helped with cash for vegetables, snuff, tobacco and other comforts.(65) Men were sent home when they were fit to travel, not before, and not kept waiting, on light duty, for weeks until they were "worn out." A man was to go home if a month after discharge from hospital he was unlikely to be fit for general service. Men with eighteen months service or more had preference over those with shorter service, no doubt as they were more likely to be fatally

TABLE 4

THE DYSENTERY VACCINE, 1917

1.   Uninoculated Porters, recruited before vaccine introduced

	April	May	June	July	Aug.	Nov.
Total effectives	29,824	29,689	37,005	39,512		34,471
Total deaths	414	530	466	599	735	282
Deaths per 1,000, known causes	13.3	17.6	12.2	14.7		7.9
Deaths per 1,000, dysentery	3.7	4.0	2.4	4.9		2.1
Deaths per 1,000, all intestinal diseases	6.3	9.3	6.2	7.1		3.9

2.   Porters inoculated with 1 cc of vaccine

	April	May	June	July	Aug.	Nov.
Total effectives	8,882	7,232	6,151	5,000	4,551	3,625
Total deaths	832	805	496	281	103	39
Deaths per 1,000, known causes	90.0	108.2	78.0	55.6	21.8	10.8
Deaths per 1,000, dysentery	34.3	26.8	15.0	13.8	6.8	2.5
Deaths per 1,000, all intestinal diseases	58.2	69.4	43.9	29.8	13.6	4.7

3.   Porters inoculated with 4cc of vaccine

	April	May	June	July	Aug.	Nov.
Total effectives	30,854	41,779	36,517	34,637	30,461	23,393
Total deaths	123	976	2,366	2,354	1,702	424
Deaths per 1,000, known causes	3.8	22.0	60.8	63.0	54.3	17.7
Deaths per 1,000, dysentery	1.0	8.4	19.6	21.0	18.3	6.1
Deaths per 1,000, all intestinal diseases	1.6	12.1	36.2	37.1	32.4	10.5

Source: W. H. Kauntze, "A Polyvalent Vaccine in the Treatment of Bacillary Dysentery in East Africa" Journal of Hygiene 18, 4 (1920). Table 5; B.E.A. Porters from Nairobi, Kisumu and Uganda districts combined which fed the three Carrier Depots.

afflicted with home sickness. A porter arriving at Mombasa Depot from German East Africa was at once examined to see whether he should go to the Carrier Hospital or the Convalescent Camp.(66) Provision was also made for artificial limbs for the disabled, and an expert was sent from Britain to deal with the fitting.(67)

In Seyidie, 40 percent of the people were struck by Spanish influenza at the end of the war, and 4,500 died. The kimiri, as the Kikuyu called it, must have seemed like a final visitation of God to the suffering people; "he was angry because the young men had allowed themselves to be taken away to perish in the Europeans' war." It was said that "people would wake up cool and healthy, and within two days they would be dead." In the Carrier Corps the death rate shot up for a brief but horrifying moment.(68)

Concern about disease which returning servicemen might bring with them was fully justified. In 1916 and 1917 about 600 people in Meru District died of dysentery brought home by returning carriers. Ainsworth advised the Chief Secretary that areas to which repatriates were returning must be kept under strict medical observation for some time, so that any outbreak of disease could be dealt with promptly; the military might second doctors to help, or ask them to volunteer. In view of the poor physical capacity of the male population as a whole, government could "ill afford to add to the number" of the infirm. Medical examinations in the camps were consequently frequent and meticulous.(69) But all the care and devotion could only lessen the awful mortality, nor prevent the return home of men broken in health.

THE CARRIERS' POINT OF VIEW

Accounts of carriers at work are rare, because they were taken very much for granted, but the following, however dated and schoolboy storybookish in style it seems, is at least vivid: "At night they....seek the nearest derelict ox or horse and prepare their meals, with relish, from the still warm entrails. This, with their "pocha," the allowance of mealie meal or mahoga, keeps them fat, their stomachs distended, their bodies shiny, and spirits of the highest."(70) Eating foundered transport animals is often mentioned by Europeans, and no doubt Africans partook of such readily available meat. The Kikuyu may have scorned such fare, but others may have been less squeamish. Otochi Onduko, a gun carrier from Kisii, spoke of eating game; some people near Thomson's Falls had heard of this, but said that most Kikuyu would rather starve than eat unclean food.(71)

The KMV men at Kahuhia acquired a taste for fish, but this force was well fed, so never needed to scavenge; their schooling may have helped the mission followers to be less prejudiced against unfamiliar foodstuffs. The Kahuhia men, and Josphat Njoroge (a KMV man in Kiambu), said that the food was good and the same as for askari. The psychological effect of equal treatment, when it came, must have been profound.

The effects of bad flour and cooking were generally confirmed. In Ukambani, William Nthenge (stretcher bearer) and Nguku Mulwa (syce) remembered it; Nthenge said that the doctor would condemn bad meal, and Mulwa referred to dysentery caused by damp flour. Cooking problems were mentioned by several askari in Machakos

District: Mutiso Kanzivei and Mulei Nguyo, of Kiteta, and Nzioki Wambua, of Muthetheni, all spoke of cooking utensils abandoned when the enemy attacked, or of fires having to be put out or concealed.(72) Another Machakos man, Makau Nzibu of Iveti, said: "One of the troubles was that we were rationed very bad food such as dates and rotten grain. We were also rationed joggrey in place of vegetables for our maize flour which caused dysentery among the people."(73)

Like British tourists on the continent, servicemen complained about cooking oils. Kamau Kagimbi, an askari from Nyeri District who served through Smuts' offensive and the occupation of German East Africa, said: "A type of cooking oil upset our stomachs sometimes. We refused to eat this kind of fat and we had to starve for a short time."(74) It sounds like a food strike similar to the one reported by Scott. One wonders whether the oil Kamau objected to was sim sim or coconut; it could have been palm oil, liked by West Africans, but hated by East Africans. The latter take their fats, in which their diet tends to be poor, from meat, milk or groundnuts. Mutiso Kanzivei learned to use ghee for frying, useful because it was plentiful at home in Ukambani.

Both askari and wapagazi could be quite enthusiastic about their rations, but perhaps this would only apply to men who experienced the improved conditions later in the war. "Food, I must say, was marvellous," said Agweli, one of the Nyala askari. "We had rice with meat. We also had biscuits, especially during the battles." His neighbor Odera agreed, and said that they also had tea, though not as an official ration. Musembi Kilundu, ammunition carrier at Kilungu, Machakos District, said that they had mostly rice and meat, never flour, but sometimes dates; nevertheless he suffered from dysentery.(75) The Nyanza carriers Maende and Atonga said that there was no lack of food, though Atonga grew tired of it. Of course, during very severe marching and active operations everyone went short, which is very clear in accounts of the campaign like those of Brett Young or Buchanan. At depots this was much less likely; Elijah Kaara, whose experience was limited to depots, learned to like rice, for which he acquired a lasting taste. As a man of some education and pre-war experience he must have been used to novelties, and perhaps more ready to experiment. Kikuyu carriers at Ngecha, near Limuru, also liked rice, but detested dates.(76)

There were several accounts of hospital experience. Kinyanjui wa Mukura was very ill with diarrhoea at Dodoma; he also mentioned, as nobody else did, that they boiled and filtered their drinking water, as Watkins had been advised to do in 1914 by Lieutenant-Colonel Turner, Indian Medical Service.(77) Kinyanjui convalesced for four months in Nairobi before release; he remarked on the proneness of Kikuyu to malaria. Umoa Mbatha, carrier headman, suffered badly from dysentery, and spoke highly of the convalescent diet at Nairobi.

Marius Karatu was a medical dresser for the latter part of his varied service, and used to escort repatriates between Dar es Salaam and Nairobi. "I would go wherever there were people in a critical condition. I would write the names of the diseases from which the people were suffering, and I would take the record to the senior doctor." Karatu naturally thought the hospital attention good, but was borne out by the Meru askari M'Laibuni, and the Kamba askari Mulei Nguyo and Kimumo Kitui.

The unenviable record for the highest mortality was held by the small contingent of Seychelles stevedores attached to the MLB; they differed from other followers in that they could hardly be described as Africans, and may well have included more men literate in English than the rest of the carriers put together. They had no resistance to tropical diseases and were withdrawn after losing 222 men out of 776.(78) There are two letters to their Carrier Officer at Kilwa Kirinji which may be the only written protests by military followers. The first, signed by twelve overseers, complains that their supplies, promised in their terms of enlistment, had not been fully provided. If this was done, "we will work as hard as we can to give you satisfaction, and by our efforts to uphold the British flag for which we are ready to shed our last drop of blood if need be." In the other, signed by 215 men, with such names as Desiré Céleste, Jule Solin and Charles Rosette, it is stated that they had expected, when they signed on, to work at Dar es Salaam, not Kilwa. They had not been properly dressed; as to food, "we are accustomed to take our tea, coffee or milk every morning with bread or rice or biscuits then we are forced to take a small portion of hot water, half-sugared and sometimes obliged to start work without taking nothing in the morning till noon. Our meal scarcely can we bear it only boiled beef....We are English subjects, civilised and ought to be loved and cared tenderly."(79) They were used to a much higher standard of living than Africans, and more than likely were not given by the military what they had been promised when they signed on.

NOTES

1. Carl G. Rosberg Jr., and John Nottingham, The Myth of "Mau Mau": Nationalism in Kenya (Nairobi: EAPH, 1966), 30-31.

2. See above, Chapter 2,p.11 and Chapter 3, sections on strategic planning and the Kings' African Rifles.

3. WP, Watkins to Surgeon-General Pike, covering letter to the medical and rations correspondence (R); (the former is unfortunately missing), 6 Jan. 1918.

4. NLC, 270-274 (Leys), and 215.

5. Ibid., 85 (Hobley).

6. Staff Surgeon Dr. M. Taute, "Medical Treatment on the German Side," TNR, 8 (1939), 1-20; see also Clyde, Medical Services, 30: in 1908 there was no specific cure for amoebic dysentery.

7. B. A. Ogot, "British Administration in the Central Nyanza District of Kenya, 1900-60," JAH, 4, 2 (1963), 255; John Roscoe, The Baganda (London, 1911), 426-444.

8. W. and K. Routledge, With A Prehistoric People - The Akikuyu of British East Africa (London: Arnold, 1910) passim; C. W. Hobley, Ethnology of the Akamba and other East African Tribes (Cambridge: Cambridge University Press, 1910), 15-16; Gerhard Lindblom, The Akamba (Uppsala, 1920), 511-521; KNA, PC/CP1/5/1, Kenia PRB for diet in "Short Early History of Embu District"; WP, R25, ADC Chuka to Watkins, 26 March 1915, note on diet in this Embu sub-district.

9. WP, R9, Scott to Watkins, 19 Oct. 1914.

10. WP, Watkins to Pike, 6 Jan. 1918; C. J. Wilson, The Story of the East African Mounted Rifles (Nairobi, 1938), 44 - quoted Clyde, Medical Services, 58-59; WR. paras. 63 and 110.

11. WP, R3 and R5: 3 and 10 Oct. 1914; Captain Jolly eventually rose to be Lieutenant-General Sir Gordon Jolly, Director-General of the Indian Medical Service (Clyde, Medical Services, 73).

12. WP, R11 and 14: to Watkins, 17 and 19 Nov. 1914.

13. Ibid., R15, Sec. CCS to Dir. Supply, 27 Nov. 1914.

14. Ibid., private, 4 Dec. 1914; R16, 29 Nov. 1914.

15. Ibid., R18, 9 Dec. 1914, copies to Ch. Secs. Nairobi and Entebbe, Supply Officer Kilindini, and Ainsworth.

16. Ibid., n.d., attached to R18.

17. Ibid., R22, 16 Jan. 1915.

18. WR, paras. 110-111.

19. WP, Watkins to Assitant Director of Supply, 21 Feb. 1917, and latter's minute of 22 Feb.

20. Ibid., Watkins to DAAQMG, 19 April 1917, and letters earlier that month.

21. PRO, CO 536/90/60006, Handbook of Uganda (2d. ed., 1921), Chapter 21, "The Great War in Uganda 1914-1917," 356.

22. NAU/SMP 4290, Jackson to Belfield, 8 June 1915 (RPA War F/1/2).

23. Ibid., Scott to Officer Commanding Troops Kagera, 10 Sept. 1915; Stewart to Ch. Sec. Uganda, Oct. 1915; OC Kagera to Brigade Major, Nairobi, 30 Nov. 1915.

24. NAU/SMP 4290 (RPA War F/1/2), Officer Commanding Lake Detachment to Senior Naval Officer Kisumu, 4 March 1916.

25. WP, Dobbs (DC Kericho) to Ainsworth, 14 Aug. 1916, and Court of Enquiry at Kampala, 13 Oct. 1916.

26. Albert Cook, Uganda Memories (Kampala, 1945), 306-308.

27. G. J. Keane and D. G. Tomblings, The African Native Medical Corps in the East African Campaign (London: Richard Clay & Sons, 1920); Wallis, Handbook of Uganda, 17-21; C. F. Phillips, Uganda Volunteers and the War (Kampala: A.D. Cameron, 1917), Chapter 31; Clyde, Medical Services, 62, 77-78.

28. Keane and Tomblings, ANMC, 25; Cook, Memories, 308.

29. NAU/SMP 4290, Statement n.4 on causes of death, and comments by Wallis on Assistant Director of Transport Entebbe, to Ch. Sec., 12 March 1917 (RPA War F/1/2).

30. H.B.T. to author, 19 Jan. 1970.

31. PRO, WO 106/46; C. J. Wilson, 'Native Diet; A Lesson from Rhodesia,' KMJ, 2, 12 (1926), 337-342.

32. Discussion on Native Diets, intro. by Wilson, Kenya Branch of British Medical Association, KMJ, 2, 5 (1925); Moyse-Bartlett, KAR, 220 and note, referring to CO 534/15.

33. WR. Appendix 3, Table 1 (quoted Wilson, n. 32).

34. MLB Handbook, 37, 68-70; WR, paras. 112-113; see Appendix 4 below.

35.   See Appendix 4 below.

36.   WP, R23, Watkins to Assistant Director of Supply, 2 Feb. 1915.

37.   Ibid., R29, SMO Gazi to Watkins, 28 July 1915; see above, Chapter 4, 51-53.

38.   KNA, 37/577 2, letters 28 and 30 June 1915.

39.   WP, R34-9, SMO to CDO Mombasa, 27 April 1916.

40.   Ibid., R103-4, on new train rations; see also MLB Handbook, 12-14, and para. 19, "Duties of Carrier Officers."

41.   Hill, Permanent Way, Vol. II, 157.

42.   WP, R53-7, 23 Dec. 1916 to 21 Jan. 1917.

43.   Ibid., R58-69, March-April 1917.

44.   Ibid., R73-6, 17-21 April 1917; see W. H. Kauntze, "A Polyvalent Vaccine in the Treatment of Bacillary Dysentery in East Africa" (MD thesis, Pt. 1), The Journal of Hygiene, 18, 4 (1920), 417-425.

45.   WP, R60, DMS (EAF) to DAAQMG, 25 March 1917.

46.   Ibid., R115, Watkins to DMS, 20 July 1917.

47.   Ibid., R116-8, especially Scott to Watkins, 22 July 1917.

48.   Ibid., R152, Scott to DAAQMG, 5 Sept. 1917; new cauldrons could have tainted the food, which the author remembers happening in a new school kitchen in Zambia.

49.   Ibid., R77-81 (especially Watkins to DAAQMG. 19 April 1917), R88-91, 107-109.

50.   Ibid., R92-3, especially Watkins to DAAQMG, 7 June 1917.

51.   Ibid., R111, Watkins to DAAQMG, 16 July 1917.

52.   Ibid., R142, Scott to DAAQMG, 2 Sept. 1917.

53.   Ibid., R143-4, 153-161, McAuley to Watkins, 15 Sept.

54.   See Appendix 4 below.

55.   WP, R113-5, especially Watkins to DMS, 20 July 1917.

56.   Ibid., R132, DADMS Dodoma to Hill, 3 Aug. 1917; R157, Watkins to Ainsworth, 20 Sept. 1917, and R162-3; WR, para. 126; KNA, 37/577 4, Ainsworth to PCs, 15 and 22 June 1917.

57. Ibid., R131, Hill to Assitant Director of Supply, 3 Aug. 1917, and R135, Hill to MLB MOs, 21 Aug. 1917; WR, para. 132.

58. WR, paras. 115–119.

59. Ibid., paras. 120–125; WP, the missing medical correspondence is covered by a summary: M10, "Repudiation of C.C. [Central Committee of Supply] by both civil and Military medical" and M32-3, "Difficulty in keeping our stretcher bearers," 21 May 1915.

60. Part 2 of "A Polyvalent Vaccine" in Kenya and East Africa Medical Journal, 3 (1926-1927), 342.

61. See Table 4. also Appendix 5 below.

62. "A Polyvalent Vaccine," Pt. 1, 417–418.

63. Ibid., Pt. 2, 343–347; for Arthur's remark, see Nairobi Laboratory Report for 1917, 201.

64. Ibid., 298.

65. "A Polyvalent Vaccine," 427–431; KNA, 37/577 5, 716 (Menus), and Ainsworth to PCs, 11 Sept. 1917, also 43/918, EAWRF.

66. KNA, 37/577 5, Hill to Carrier Hospitals, Dec. 1917.

67. KNA, 37/577 6, Watkins to CDOs, 8 Jan. 1918; Ainsworth to Hobley, 20 July, and to PCs, 13 Dec. 1918.

68. Ibid., DC Voi to OC Voi Military Railway, 25 Nov. 1918, also 32/485; see Huxley, Red Strangers, 276-277.

69. KNA, PC/CP4/1/1, Philp's appendix to Kenia AR, 1916-1917; also 37/577 5, Ainsworth to Ch. Sec. 30 July 1917.

70. R. V. Dolbey, Sketches of the East African Campaign (London, 1918), 119; he was MO with a combatant unit.

71. Notes kindly given by John Makori (Onduko).

72. Notes kindly given by Raphael Thyaka (Wambua).

73. Notes kindly given by Dr. J. Forbes Munro.

74. Notes kindly given by Njagi Gakunju.

75. Interview 3 Oct. 1970.

76. Ngecha interview 10 May 1970.

77. WP, R17, 1 Dec. 1914.

78.   See Table 3.

79.   WP, 12 overseers to 2nd Lieutenant Whiting, 7 Jan. 1917, and 215 Seychellese to Whiting, 12 Jan. 1917.

Chapter 9
The Life and Work of the Carriers

Muthii onaga magothe

He who travels sees many things

(Kikuyu proverb)[1]

THE LOGISTICS OF PORTER TRANSPORT

"We are the porters who carry the food, of the porters who carry the food, of the porters who carry the food" was a marching song "current in Uganda soon after the return of the Baganda carriers from the advance to Tabora in 1916. It was....devised by Dr. G. H. Hale Carpenter who....had accompanied the force to Tabora."(2) It shows the crux of the MLB's problem: "A porter eats his own load in 25 days." His official load was 50 lbs. and he needed 2 lbs. of food a day. If he carried his own food and restocked at "Head" – the end of a line of communication – only half of his load would be available for other goods. If there was no food at "Head," his load would consist only of his own food, and he might as well not be sent, unless he could restock en route. Under good conditions porters could do twelve miles a day, taking fifteen days to reach "Head" on an average line 180 miles in length.(3) But on the 600-mile line from the Rhodesian railway to the German border, porters were expected to carry 60 lbs. for fifteen miles a day, on an unvaried diet of $2\frac{1}{4}$ lbs. of meal a day.(4)

In the East Africa Protectorate, government safaris carried meal from Nyeri to Meru in five days, whence it was taken on to Marsabit. If 100 loads of 60 lbs. each were to be delivered in this time, 100 porters would be needed for the loads themselves, and twenty more for as many loads to feed the food carriers and themselves. Thus an extra 1,200 lbs. was needed to get 6,000 lbs. to Meru: 1,000 lbs. for "the porters who carry the food," and 200 lbs. for the extra men, all at 2 lbs. per man-day. The formula gives an answer of 120 loads:

$$X = 100 + \frac{X \times 2 \text{ lbs.} \times 5}{60}$$

but on the MLB loading of 50 lbs. such a safari would have to be 125 strong in porters and loads.(5) The Nyeri-Meru safaris may well have been fed mainly en route, but after Meru the lot of carriers like M'Kongo wa M'Maitai must have been hard.(6) A porter had to carry his blanket, other belongings, tools (a jembe or panga), or perhaps a cooking pot, in addition to his official load.

This was known as the convoy system in the CC, and was ended by the enormous extension of the lines in 1916. It was replaced by the dumping system, whereby a line had permanent posts every twelve miles or so, where permanent labor was housed and fed. Besides the adage that "a porter eats his own load in 25 days" stands the other: "to say that food requires long cooking is to condemn it for military purposes." Coarse meal was wasteful of transport as well as medically objectionable; the new system ensured that meal was properly cooked, since "to a tired man raw mealie is poison."(7) Thus posts and dumping were vital to maintain the health of troops, as well as of the carriers on whom they depended.

Each post had fifty laborers for building bandas (huts), and for digging drains and latrines, for keeping up roads and bridges. On a line 180 miles long, 12,000 labor were needed: 11,216 carriers and 750 post labor. The system was that 730 men would hand over loads to an equal number at meeting place O, midway between their respective posts Nos. 14 and 15. the group returning down the line might take back sick and wounded. Loads would thus pass up the line, borne by diminishing numbers of carriers, until finally at meeting place A, 143 porters from "Head" would take over from the same number from post no. 1. The labor force used over 500 loads of food a day, over 25,000 lbs. leaving about 1,000 lbs. in hand. A third of them were reckoned to be off work every day, made up as follows: as percentages, four were headmen, four cooks, ten sick, fifteen on their weekly rest day.(8) This was never quite realised in practice, no doubt, what with shortage of labor, problems of terrain, or use of animal or mechanical transport. Figures of the 1917 campaign give a good idea of the amount of labor needed to keep troops in the field.(9)

The lines developed roughly as follows. Until Smuts' offensive, the northern forces worked on quite short lines based, except in western Uganda, on the railway. During the first phase of the 1916 advance, carriers were most important on the Tabora and Dar es Salaam lines. But during the second phase, south of the Central Railway, carriers became predominant on the two lines from Dodoma to Iringa, and from Mikesse to the Rufiji. The third advance, planned by Hoskins but led by van Deventer, involved four thrusts: from Iringa to Mahenge, from the Rufiji to Mahenge, from the Kilwa Railway to Liwale, and from Lindi to Masasi. While water, rail or motor helped at the beginning of some of these lines, the brunt was borne by the porters of the mass levy. Finally, in Portuguese East Africa, there were short lines based on Port Amelia, Lumbo and Quelimane.(10)

Many different types of transport might therefore be used on a line. A carrier could take 50 to 60 lbs. a donkey or an ox 120 lbs. a mule about 200 lbs. and a Ford light lorry or "box car" 700 lbs. not counting the driver and his kit.(11) But after the terrific losses in 1916 there was a grave shortage of transport animals; readers of Brett Young's Marching on Tanga will see that carriers featured as gun porters and stretcher bearers, the main transport being mules, oxen and lorries. The animals died fast of tsetse and horse-sickness, and south of the Central Railway the country was even more unhealthy. Motors were scarce, and there might either be no roads at all, or too much mud for motors to move.

The notorious Mikesse-Rufiji line dissolved into mud in January 1917, becoming almost impassable even for carriers. Heavy lorries on the forty-one miles from Mikesse to Summit, carrying up to 60,000 lbs. daily, may have made things worse. Light motors were supposed to carry for the next thirty-five miles to Duthumi, and mules and animal transport carts the next forty-five miles to Kimbambawe. But in practice the carriers, who were supposed to carry only on the last lap to the Rufiji, seem to have been on all sections. The first two stages were precarious for lorries even before the rains, and only 5,000 lbs. daily had been coming through during the two weeks after Christmas 1916.(12)   The officer in command on the Rufiji sent increasingly curt messages to Dar es Salaam about the meagre rations reaching his men. But he later found the Duthumi road "sufficiently formidable" even after the rains, and apologised in person at every office in General Headquarters, as "now that he had seen the road his only wonder was that anything at all had been got up."(13)

The Dodoma-Iringa line was almost as bad; on one stretch porters "had to carry nine miles mostly waist-deep in water, much of it on raised duck walks made of undressed poles laid side by side." By March 1917 an alternative route to Iringa from Kilosa was being used, despite "heavy casualties among porters and donkeys, and much sickness among the white personnel." The original route was not used again until May.(14)

As to the Dodoma line, we are given one of the very rare accounts of porter work by Dr. J. W. Arthur, whose KMV force started work on it in July, conditions being far from idyllic but at least tolerable. He shows how the dumping or relay system worked, and how even in fairly level country the exact placing of posts depended on supplies of water and firewood. In very hilly country, as it was near Iringa, posts might be as close as seven miles. The KMV had brought up loads of salt and food; they then camped at Muhanga Mission, forty miles from Iringa. From here, they picked up loads from the dump or meeting place half way from the previous post at Magazine Hill. The first thirty miles from Iringa to Observation Hill were covered by ambulances and lorries, the next four miles to Magazine Hill by donkeys. Carriers next took goods on to a dump half way to Muhanga; as these posts were seven miles apart, the KMV carried for a round trip of seven miles. The next post was Big Gun Fort (Boma Mzinga), six miles away, the length of a "round carry" to the usual half-way dump. Then the line fell steeply down an escarpment to the Kilombero Valley, and on to Mahenge, which the Belgians took on 9 October.(15)

The KMV started work on 2 August, C Company making camp. A and B Companies carrying from the rear dump, where they took over from the Magazine Hill carriers, past Muhanga to the dump where they handed over to the Boma Mzinga carriers. In practice, there never were the theoretical 33 percent of spare men, the growing pressure demanding the labor even of cooks and headmen. It was possible to rest 150 men on 5 and 6 August only. They began with a double lift of 640 loads: "320 loads back + 480 forwards = 800," noted Arthur in his diary, "480 forward + 400 back =880." The line closed in late November, when "countless numbers of bags of mealie meal, rice, sugar etc. and tins of oil which had been painfully carried forward over these ghastly hills were now taken as painfully back, and in addition innumerable odds and ends." During the advance, return loads were mostly sick and wounded; KMVs usually carried stretchers back to the Magazine Hill dump, returning with food and ammunition.(16) The relay work was clearly remembered by Samwel Ngoci of Kahuhia and his friends, also by Kaniaru of Ngecha and by Nathaniel Mahingu, who said: "We took loads of bullets and then carried them to those people whom we met, and then they took them and carried them about twelve miles away." Mahenge, he continued, was captured, and "the bullets which we were carrying were the same bullets which were used to defeat the Germans."(17)

The Southern Force, under General Edward Northey, depended on two very long lines of communication. The one through Nyasaland began with coasters from Beira to Chinde (in Portuguese East Africa), whence river steamers towing barges took stores on to the railway at Chindio. After railage to Limbe, lorries carried goods to the Lake, and after a passage by water to its head, carriers took over on lines which linked up at Iringa with the East African Force; it is important to emphasise that Northey's force was never under the East African Force, and its carriers not under the MLB.(18) The same applied to carriers on the other line, which ran from the Rhodesian railway north of Broken Hill to the German border, with a branch at Kasama to Abercorn and Fife. It is unique in having an excellent official description, and between Ndola and Kasama had a long alternative river route with carrier transport at each end. In the middle, goods were carried by canoes for some 400 miles up the Luapula and Chambeshi rivers. These canoes carried between 120 lbs. and half a ton; they were propelled by a corps of 12,000 paddlers from the Bangweulu Swamps and adjacent rivers who, in over a year, delivered 2,500 tons with little loss. This was the result of skilful political work by district officers among people with little previous experience of Europeans. On the main road, the first method was to send a convoy of thirty ox wagons to the border with 100 tons of stores, on the correct assumption that the oxen would just arrive before succumbing to tsetse. Motor transport then supplemented carriers on a hastily improvised surface on which Ford cars did well; but on the 900 miles round trip to Kasama and back, 150 miles short of the border, a car would use half of its 700 lbs. load on petrol. Thus the logistical problem was much the same for any kind of transport which could not live off the country. For carriers, the route crosses country which even today is sparsely inhabited. When food became scarce, difficulties increased rapidly. "When the route is through a country which cannot feed the carriers at all, the length of each section must be less than that of a 12 days' journey if anything at all is to be delivered."(19)

If the 450 miles from the railway to Kasama were divided into five day stages of seventy-five miles each, only one twenty-seventh of the original loads would actually arrive, with another 150 miles to the border. The logistics of delivering only one ton of stores a day were as follows:

At a distance of	With food on the road	With food also to be carried
150 miles	750 carriers	1,800 carriers
300 miles	1,500 carriers	7,150 carriers
450 miles	2,250 carriers	23,200 carriers
600 miles	3,000 carriers	71,000 carriers

The column needed ten tons a day. But it was never as bad as this, since food could usually be brought in, over up to 300 miles, and only once did the whole line have to be fed from base. During the dry season 40,000 carriers would be at work, and 20,000 or less during the rains. The loss of labor in the districts reduced their output of food.(20) On both these southern lines much of this porterage was seasonal, with men working for a few months at a time from their homes, and never going really far away, unlike those in the MLB.

It is hard to say how much of the stores carried was actually lost. When things were very bad, as on the Mikesse or Dodoma lines in 1916 and early 1917, with many porters dying and food getting soaked, the loss must have been great, and an instance is mentioned in official correspondence.(21) But this was more likely to happen in the convoy system; when dumping was used, as by the KMV, loads were only taken for a day's march by any one group of carriers, and were either brought into their post or handed on to the next post at the meeting place. Also, by the time the KMV were at work, packaging was better; "we carried things like beans, sugar and dates in waterproof packets," recalled Kaniaru, at Ngecha.

Each rifle needed one first- or second-line carrier, and two more on the line of communication. But there was also personal baggage; for Europeans, the allowance was 40 lbs. for an officer, 25 lbs. for an NCO. In practice, every man from officer to porter had little more than blanket. An ideal allowance was 10 lbs. for a man, 20 lbs. for an officer, but "no man can keep healthy on that scale for long."(22) Africans were superior to Indians or Europeans in needing much less baggage, but not less food in weight. Only the most hardened whites - veteran KAR officers or others inured to the bush - could really rough it. In the Nigerian Brigade, the allowance was two loads per European, and they were accordingly called the "bed and bath" brigade. Weekly "chop" boxes came from Fortnum and Mason, though not, presumably, during the hungry vigil on the Rufiji. Von Lettow thought it foolish of the British to send raw young whites to fight in such a climate, noted Colonel Beazley who, like others, queried the wisdom of trying to conquer German East Africa at all, rather than be content with securing the Uganda Railway: "K. seems to have been right."(23) The vast efforts of Carrier transport confirm that he was.

EXPERIENCE AND RELATIONSHIPS

"Few have written of the devastating effect of the war on the African himself," wrote Dr. Philp. Men left home for the first time, were drilled and medically examined, saw different countries and peoples. "Within four years these primitive tribesmen were forcibly educated, but with what an education!"(24) This education was summarised by Watkins; men whose previous experience of Europeans and their gadgets was nil, "have been trained to carry into action on their heads the field wireless or the latest quick-firing gun ... have been steadied till they learned to pull great motor lorries out of the mud."(25)

Experience like the latter could be enjoyable, as Driver Campbell noticed, seeing some men pushing a lorry: "Von Lettow, oh! Von Lettow, oh! Von Lettow, kwenda! (Go away!) Ah!" A mighty heave accompanied the last shout. It was a new experience, too, for Campbell's driver who emerged scared but unscathed from underneath his upturned Ford.(26) The war accelerated that exposure to new experiences, which was already in progress before the war on farms and plantations, in workshops and European homes. In Red Strangers, Matu had been terrified by a mowing machine, but his friend Karanja could not explain why the Europeans threw away the rich mowings off the lawn instead of feeding them to cows: "they have no sense, and do many foolish things without reason."(27)

Prejudice goes with ignorance and incomprehension; but, while Dr. Dolbey was ill-informed about porters, he at least showed interest in them, and his description is colorful:

> Clad in red blankets or loin cloths or in kilts made of reeds and straw, they struggle on ....grass rings temper the weight of the loads to their heads ...., Winding snake-like along the native paths, they go chanting a weird refrain .... Here are ....porters from the mountains, "shenzies" as the superior Swahili call them .... Good porters these, though lacking the grace of the Wanyamwezi.(28)

The coast man could show prejudice towards his upcountry colleague; similarly, Major Lyon of the West African CC thought the Ibo carriers inferior to the Hausa soldiers, or even the Mendi first-line carriers from Sierra Leone, where he had been a district officer.(29) Brett Young, another doctor, was probably the most gifted and sensitive writer with the Force; he showed a sympathetic interest in his Nyanza stretcher bearers:

> When they march at night they huddle close together for the sake of a little fortuitous courage; but they are by nature a happy people, cheerful under the most distressing physical conditions, and with the fear of darkness no longer brooding over them they soon begin to straggle over the track. The harsh fumes of native tobacco rose in the air, and I ...., saw that one of them was carrying .... the dry centre of a mealie cob. With this slow-burning tinder he had nursed a smouldering fire all night.(30)

Modern knowledge makes people of all races realise that there is no basic intellectual difference between the many races and nations on earth, but in those days there was less evidence available. The war provided plenty of experience, and the mutual enlightenment which resulted must have been beneficial.

There could be two opinions about an incident told by Campbell. Twelve white drivers, wilting in the heat of the Rovuma valley, were forced by a bullying European overseer to help Africans unload stores. Their protests were unavailing, but after a quarrel with one of the

Africans they slipped off.(31) Such incidents may well have helped Africans to feel superior to Europeans who could not work as well in the broiling heat; it may also have bred sympathy. War is an educator as well as a leveller. The white man, wrote Philip Mitchell, lost his fabulous aura when an askari was told that he must kill a mzungu (white man) on the other side. In the field, everyone slept on the ground, and the whites "dressed and undressed, washed and shaved in the presence - usually the very near presence - of the multitude".(32) No better example of the levelling effects of war can be quoted than Brett Young's story of how he spent a night, huddled in the bush with wounded Indians and Nyanza stretcher bearers, hiding from the Germans who had rushed their clearing station.(33)

War stories are a mixture of horror and humor; as time seems to cleanse the memory, humor may even predominate. Reri's story in Red Strangers is of unrelieved horror; the train journey and the sea voyage were terrifying, especially when a fear-maddened man leaped overboard.(34) But his ship does not sound as disgusting as the Lake steamers, nor as the Wang Hai 1, on which thirteen porters had died, and 100 more within four days of arrival at Mombasa, in April 1917. The supply of ships was always inadequate; the MLB may have been lucky to have two wheezy transports, one after the other, and its own hospital ship. The Wang Hai 1 or "One Lung," once the City of Edinburgh, may have been exceptionally bad; none of the men interviewed had any adverse comment to make about ships.(35)

Stories of contacts with West Africans tend to be garbled by rumours of cannibalism, probably spread by Europeans to discourage fraternisation. Kinuthia, of the KMV, said that near Dodoma they were given guns for fear of an enemy attack:

> These Europeans, they are as cowardly as birds! MaKorogothi [Gold Coasters] accompanied us; they were very bad people. The Europeans told them that if they associated with us, we would eat them [and vice versa]. We didn't believe. Between us and the Korogothi, there was a barbed wire fence. We became like wild animals, each group being afraid of the other. Kikuyu are very brave people. We told them that we were not cannibals.... We became friends. We bought some of their things because we didn't need money very much. They were being paid but they needed money more than we did because, unlike ourselves, they had their wives with them.

This clinches it; these were not Gold Coast men but Congolese, who according to Grogan were accompanied by their women. The Belgians were responsible for the line from Dodoma to Iringa, and the Gold Coast Regiment, who cannot have had wives with them, were hundreds of miles away on the Kilwa line. Josphat Njoroge, also KMV, said that Belgian troops (called Bolomatari, breakers of obstacles, a nickname of H. M. Stanley) were supposed to be cannibals, though several other witnesses associated the practice with the Gold Coasters.(36)

Musembi Kiindu, ammunition carrier, said that he and some friends had actually come upon some cannibals in the act, and their European officer had incurred their wrath by kicking the nyama ya watu (meat of people) into the bush; the Kamba carriers had to come to his aid.

Kiindu thought they were Nigerian soldiers, but again this can be ruled out, because the latter were Hausa, mostly Muslims, as were their front-line carriers. The West African Frontier Force as a whole was well officered and highly disciplined. The Belgian forces were large and poorly controlled; they may well have included Manyema from the Lualaba, who were said to be cannibals. Reports of the practice were so widespread that there was actually a Force Order threatening disciplinary action against any British officer or other rank who disparaged the Belgian allies in this way; there was even a report of a meal being cooked on a station platform.(37)

These meetings all showed that lands inhabited by black people were far vaster than East Africans can have supposed. The KMV fraternisation with the Congolese was probably exceptional, as on the whole carriers seem to have kept to their tribal groups. There may have been periodic brawls, as reported by M'Inoti wa Tirikamu; "we, the Meru carriers, killed two Kavirondo boys in our camp at Rongai. The cause of the brawl was the high-handed behaviour of the Kavirondo boys." The latter might have said the same of the Meru. Jonathan Okwirri, for two years a superior headman at the Mombasa Depot, said that Luo and Luyia, Kikuyu and Kamba, kept to themselves. But the Kamba askari Mbwika Kivandi said: "We Africans have a very easy way with strangers; we used to make friends with our colleagues." Kinyanjui wa Mukura said: "We were all united. If you became ill, whatever tribe you came from, I would look after you and cook for you. Everyone usually spoke his mother tongue, though there were people who spoke Kiswahili frequently." Very many must have learned Swahili, and with it a wider knowledge of the world. Okech Atonga learned it; so did Kivandi, who also learned to write it a little.

As for what they discussed, many felt that talking about homely things, like tribal ceremonies and customs, might only increase their homesickness, as for example did Mulei Nguyo and Nyuka Nyaoke. But many liked to sing, as Nguku Mulwa remarked. Some songs may have been traditional, but others were about the war, like this ditty about a one-eyed corporal who was cruel to the other askari; it was sung by Nguyo's neighbour, Mutiso Kansivei:

Musikali wi Nthongo
Nthongo isu yootwika to-kongo
Kana ukalika ndutu ukanyeewa!
Soldier blind in one eye,
blind eye that might become like a furrow (or gully),
or get an insect in it and become itchy! ++

But future bliss, recalled Mbwika Kivandi, inspired the following: "Iuvi Nzama! Iuvi Nzama! You Council, maliciously taking me from home, you thought I was going to die, Council; that I will not do, but will go back home to enjoy the company of beautiful women!"

Only those at depots in large towns like Mombasa can have had much opportunity for girls. In the field and on lines of communication there can have been little chance, anyway. Agweli and Odera, askari, both said they talked mostly of home. Agweli said they discussed

++ Translation by courtesy of Augustine Kavyu and David Sperling.

their own customs no doubt in the light of unfamiliar ones, but also "we talked a lot about women." Like Kivandi and thousands of other young men, they had marriage to look forward to if they survived.

The destructiveness of modern war must have been particularly shattering. Ndansi Kumalo, an Ndebele, who looked at the Imperial War Museum in London, thought it was unfair and unmanly to shoot afar off, without knowing who might be killed, with weapons from which one sought cover in vain; "we prefer to fight man to man."(33) This touches on the political effect of the war on the white man's position in Africa. The old servicemen were, however, unanimous that they did not discuss politics, having no modern views about it. Marius Karatu, active in politics after the war, said: "We hadn't much to talk of because there was no time"; he and his mates were too busy with the sick. He did, however, have some political discussion with Indians, but "we were not politicians then....what was worrying us was the war."

Jonathan Okwirri had much to say about spare-time activities. In Mombasa, carriers were allowed to live their normal village life, with their own tribal music and dancing after working hours, tribal groups keeping apart. With special leave a man could go into town from the Depot near Kilindini Docks, but within a radius of four miles and a time limit. There were "others who would hire themselves out just to go around with girls." But they mostly amused themselves within the compound, with songs, dances, football and discussions. They would talk of themselves, the Europeans and others whom they met: Arabs, Zanzibaris, other kinds of Africans, and even Chinese whom they called "twins" because they were so alike. Probably these were members of a stevedore company who later worked at Dar es Salaam. Also they discussed their own problems, and the sickness and suffering so evident in the broken men returning by sea, for treatment in the hospital and convalescent camp.(39)

No doubt travellers' tales are often tall stories, which cannot be verified, but which lose nothing in the telling. One of the wazee at Ngecha repeated an exceptionally bizarre anecdote; he said that at Mwanza, the German port on Lake Victoria, "there were some trees, the smell from which caused madness." On many facets of Carrier history comment is superfluous; here it is impossible!

STATUS AND ACHIEVEMENT

When men are forced into a way of life unwillingly, most will accept it unless it is unbearable; they may even take a pride in their work, and strive for promotion. Head porterage was contrary to the customs of most carriers; in Nyeri, about 1903, "people were amazed to see warriors behaving like women" and carrying loads with headstraps, the method still used by Kikuyu women today.(40) Numerous photographs in various books make it clear that carriers placed their loads on their heads, in the traditional manner. Those upcountry men who had taken to portering before the war may have been developing a professional pride; it offered young men a chance to prove their stamina. Meinertzhagen bet an official, who fancied himself as a walker, that a Swahili porter would beat him over eighteen miles with a sixty-pound load, the official "carrying nothing beyond his huge bulk." The porter won the race and Rs.10 by a mile!(41) It was also regarded as women's work in Northern Rhodesia, where a chief told a district officer that "when we go to war our women carry for us. Now we shall do your women's work."(42)

In 1915, Wapshare's gun porters were an élite grade: of picked physique, specially treated, uniformed, and brigaded with the KAR. As soon as they arrived at the Gun Carrier Depot, "saw their uniforms and heard that they were to be drilled like askari, they were delighted; we shall probably get another hundred."(43) The Nairobi depot for first-line carriers was moved from Race Course Road to Kwa Maleve, near Ngong, with similar depots at Dar es Salaam and elsewhere, where the élite of the Carrier Corps were trained, including stretcher bearers and signal porters. A Carrier Police force of 1,500 men was formed, initially to stop desertion on the line from Mikesse to the Rufiji; they were armed, and relieved troops of many guard duties. The KAR, Native Medical Corps and Transport Corps recruited freely from the MLC, many of whose "most promising men became soldiers of these formations." Carriers also became skilled stevedores, and builders of the huge numbers of bandas or temporary shelters which were needed, made of poles, grass or coconut thatch; the Royal Engineers were entirely relieved of building work.(44) Even today, one can look with admiration on the neat structures which young Africans can rapidly put up with saplings and long grass; this was a skill which many carriers had already.

Gun Carriers, Stretcher Bearers, Intelligence Agents, Armed Scouts and Carrier Police wore the military tarboosh, which must have given a strong sense of status. Others who were uniformed and drew Rs.12 and more were headmen, syces and drivers; Nguku Mulwa emphasised the fact that as a syce he was uniformed. As a superior headman, Jonathan Okwirri was paid Rs.12 and had extra clothing - a special woollen shirt called a magari, also a badge of rank. He tried unsuccessfully to join the KAR, as did James Beauttah, a civilian telegraphist. Machine gun carriers in both British and German forces tended to look upwards to the askari's exalted status; in the closely integrated German companies, men became gun porters when aspiring to become askari. British gun porters had to be warned off displaying KAR cap badges, which they preferred to their own official patches of yellow cloth. Gun porters were already drawing the same rations as askari, when the common dietary for all African servicemen was established in 1917.(45)

The heavy machine gun needed a team of ten and later fourteen followers, including drivers for oxen or donkeys as well as carriers for barrels, tripods, ammunition and spares. They had to be well disciplined, or panic and chaos would ensue; "there would be delay in finding parts of guns, belt boxes etc. and getting the guns into action." A load of ammunition weighed 60 lbs., as did the barrel. Such loads could not be divided, which explains why gun porters had to be picked for their physique. The same applied to Lewis guns, mortars and their bombs, wireless sets and parts of mountain guns; the supreme champion of the Carrier Corps could well be the Nigerian giant, with the wheel of a 2.95" mountain gun on his head, and iron tyre across his shoulder, total 70 lbs. The use of oxen and donkeys must have declined steadily; an ox or ass could carry as much as two men, but could not stand tsetse fly. The donkey's noisiness was a drawback which has already been remarked on; a

A Nigerian Battery Carrier, with a 70 lb. load, consisting of the wheel of a 2.95″ mountain gun, its steel tyre being slung across his shoulder
from W. D. Downes, *With the Nigerians in German East Africa*

TABLE 5

EQUIPMENT

	A.	B.	C.	D.	E.	F.	G.	H.
Boots or Sandals	1	1	–	1	1	1	–	1
Brassards (Medical Units)	1	–	–	–	–	1	–	–
Chevrons	–	–	–	–	–	1	–	1
Coats, Warm Followers	–	1	–	–	–	–	–	–
Discs, Identity and Cord	1	1	1	1	1	1	1	1
Frocks, Khaki	–	1	–	1	–	–	–	–
Jumper with Shoulder Pad	–	–	–	–	–	1	–	–
Jumper	1	–	1	–	1	1	1	1
Putties, pairs	–	1	–	1	1	1	1	1
Shirts	–	1	–	–	1	–	–	–
Shorts, Khaki	1	1	–	1	1	1	1	1
Tarboosh and cover	–	–	–	1	1	1	–	1
Blankets	1	1	1	1	1	1	1	1
Haversacks	1	1	1	1	1	1	1	1
Waterbottle	1	1	1	1	1	1	1	1
Blanket Straps	–	–	–	–	–	–	–	1

Notes.

A. African followers and transport boys.
B. Transport headmen and Cape Boys.
C. Carriers.
D. Native Intelligence Agents.
E. Armed Scouts.
F. Maxim Gun, Stretcher Bearers and Signalling Porters.
G. Africans of Telegraph Section, graded as workmen or linemen.
H. Carrier Police.

Source: MLB Handbook, 35.

Kamba medical orderly, Silvano Mutiso Mwoloi (who had been under fire several times), said that they were kept well to the rear for this reason. He served for about four years, which implies that donkeys were not used in the later stages for guns or ammunition, when trained gun carriers were available.(46)

Front-line carriers became used to being under fire, and won the whole-hearted admiration of Europeans for their courage. Recognising it was a problem; Watkins feared that monetary rewards for acts of bravery might cause discontent among other carriers and the KAR, but Hobley pointed out that a laden porter could not take cover as fast as an askari.(47) He had been in military operations in North Nyanza in the nineties. Porters were also unarmed. East African carriers were never eligible for the Military Medal or Distinguished Conduct Medal, as were West Africans, whose first-line porters were more integrated with the rifle companies, more like the Germans than the KAR.

After his company commander was mortally wounded, the Nigerian gun carrier Awudu Katsena held up the enemy with rapid rifle fire, though untrained, and got the Military Medal. At Mahiwa he fought with Downes' rifle, "one of the pluckiest men it has been my good fortune to meet." Osuman Bauchi brought shells for a mountain gun at Mahiwa, joined the detachment as the gunners fell, defended the gun with a rifle and won the Distinguished Conduct Medal (DCM). So did the stretcher bearer Langala Katsena, always there with his stretcher whenever it was needed, "showing utter disregard for his personal safety, even under the heaviest fire."(48)

Despite the regrettable lack of such anecdotes for East African carriers, there is every reason to think, from the glowing praise bestowed on them, that there were Bauchis and Katsenas among them. In 1938, Captain Thomas Anderson praised the wonderful work of porters and personal servants upon whom the troops at Kibata had depended for creature comforts; "the regularity with which these undisciplined men ran the gauntlet of rifle, machine gun and shell fire, bringing up food and ammunition to the various outposts is worthy of all praise."(49) Though under fire porters might drop their loads and disappear, "more often the laconic record runs 'at this point the....porters bringing up ammunition came under nasty shell fire, but duly delivered their loads'."(50) Dr. R. R. Scott, who has taken so much interest in this book, was present at Mahiwa, and has spoken more than once of the bravery of his Kamba stretcher bearers. It is certain that many must have shown the debonair courage of Lance-Corporal Sowera, DCM, 2/2nd (Nyasa) KAR, who fired all day with his Lewis gun from a tree, and then danced an ngoma to hearten his men.(51) Nor is there any reason why East African carriers should not have behaved like some Gold Coast colleagues, who helped their regiment, the 40th Pathans and some naval Lewis gunners to extricate two pack guns which were in danger from the enemy, and who were with difficulty restrained from attacking the enemy with their machetes (pangas).(52)

An immoral practice, which occurred more than once on the Kagera front, to the west of Lake Victoria, was to use carriers as decoys. In once instance, to distract enemy attention from Bukoba before the raid in 1915, 1,000 porters were used as a feint to simulate troops in full view of the enemy.(53)

Carriers might be killed in action, especially if they were front-line. Sickened by what he had seen, and horrified by being soaked with the blood of a man shot dead by his side, Reri actually "walked about seeking a bullet that would kill me, but I could not find one."(54)Musembi Kiindu carried ammunition for machine guns; on the Lindi front he was sick and, like Reri, desperate, so he stood up in front of the Germans to be killed, but "Boy, cheka cini!" shouted an officer. "Lie down!" When his platoon was overrun by the enemy William Adiang (a Nyanza askari) said that he smeared himself with a comrade's blood and feigned dead, which showed considerable courage and presence of mind. Many front-line porters must have been wounded; Adiang's neighbour, Lazaro Maende, lost a finger while carrying ammunition, and a Kiambu gun carrier, Ngugi, while carrying a load on his head, was shot through the arm by a bullet which also scraped his upper lip. (He was very well treated, he said, by the European nurses, and spoke also of the cleanliness of the hospital ship.)(55) No doubt many others bore honourable scars to their graves, as memorials to their devotion to duty.

DISCIPLINE AND CONTROL

At its peak, the MLB had over 220 officers, about 600 British other ranks, about 120 Indian clerks, and over 100,000 men; probably it was bigger than all other units together. But its highest officers were only Lieutenant-Colonels: Watkins with fourteen majors, 134 other officers and 380 NCOs and clerks, and Hill with 89 Medical Officers (there had been 113 earlier), and 432 NCOs and clerks; this was on 31 March 1918.(56) The unit had collected, fed, paid, equipped and given medical care to a vast number of men, with depots and hospitals in six countries, and its Pay Officers had handled huge public sums with very little loss.(57) It is high time some recognition was made of the organisation which made all this possible.

It would have been impossible without discipline, which is determined by the overall command of an army. The discipline of the East African Force was never good, either before or after the South Africans came into it.(58) The administrative chief was the Deputy Adjutant and Quartermaster-General, who at first was Brigadier-General Ewart, and later his deputy, Brigadier-General C. P. Fendall. The latter cannot have been an easy man to work with, and there is a note of growing friction in his dealings with Watkins, whose difficulties were greatly increased by his being only a Lieutenant-Colonel: equal, despite his enormous responsibilities, to the growing number of young officers of this rank who were promoted with the expansion of the KAR, and "who already are inclined to ignore any regulations of this Department with regard to labour," as Watkins said when arguing his case for a full Colonelcy. The MLB Paymaster, who handled far more cash than the KAR paymaster, and the two deputy DMLs all ought to be Lieutenant-Colonels.(59) This suggestion was rejected.

So Watkins had to run the largest unit in the Force with an inadequate rank. By the end of 1918 his relations with his superiors seem to have reached a very low ebb. Fendall had, for example, angrily demanded the withdrawal of a letter in which Watkins had drawn attention to the lapse of disciplinary proceedings against an officer. Watkins, threatened with "disciplinary steps....for bringing false accusations," withdrew his remarks, adding that if he had thought that the accusations read into his minute were justified, "I would have faced any proceedings rather than withdraw them." Again, Watkins protested bitterly against what he felt was a severe reprimand over a technical and inadvertent breach of regulations, involving the shipping of a car; this treatment of an officer, "for so long Head of an important Department", seems strangely petty after the end of the war. To judge by remarks in his unpublished diary, Fendall was not a tolerant man.(60) None of this can have helped the interests of the carriers; when Watkins described his officers and NCOs as "fearless champions" of their men, it implies that the interests of these men were frequently in jeopardy.(61)

During the Rufiji offensive, commanding officers were forbidden to march troops unnecessarily in the heat of the day, and otherwise to neglect health precautions and invite heat exhaustion, fever and dysentery. Subject to military exigencies, troops were not to be marched between 10 am. and 3 pm; there must be reasonable stages and proper halts. Water discipline was to be enforced. Though carriers were not mentioned, this plainly includes them, and is in the MLB Handbook. In June 1917 column commanders were warned against waste of labor, which must be properly distributed through the MLB, and that all available natives were to be collected.(62) All too often, water supplies were inadequate for troops, followers and trek animals; carriers could all too easily not have their share for drinking, let alone cooking.

Carrier officers were told to be "rigidly fair and just" in their dealings; labor was like a machine which would break down if not properly fed, if overdriven or neglected. Much suffering would have been prevented if combatant officers had been similarly instructed. Food must be properly cooked, sanitation enforced, and proper latrines dug, rather than rely on disinfectants. A tip still worth knowing is to use white ant hills as soakaways; "their capacity is almost inexhaustible." On the march, spare carriers were to go at the tail, with stretcher bearers to help any who could not march, which was mentioned by a Luo carrier, Yohana Ojwang', and also practised by Bishop Frank Weston.(63)

"Officers are reminded that, apart from all questions of humanity, the efficiency of labour depends upon the well-being of the men." This meant supporting their interests in every way: keeping loads down to 50 lbs. "marching and working in the cool of the day, where possible, to save naked feed from blistering sands." Food, cooking and water arrangements must be adequate at all times. Officers were twice ordered to report disregard of their advice to the DML: "forced marches without reason," or any differences with an officer commanding a post. Officers must not leave personal contact all to headmen, who might not distribute food fairly unless given bakhsheesh (bribes) by the men. "Accessibility, justice and good temper will make an African native stand by his Officer in a very tight place. An Officer with no direct control will be deserted at the first excuse." Popular fallacies about labor were to be perpetually contested"; men must not be worked in the noonday sun, must have well-balanced meals instead of just a daily gorge of mealie porridge, and must be given time to acclimatize to unfamiliar climes and altitudes. These essentials about porter management were understood by Dr. Dolbev, who was also aware of the special problems of Uganda carriers.(64)

For discipline, carriers were under the 1912 KAR Ordinance. A commanding officer could order up to twenty-four lashes, and forty-two days imprisonment with or without hard labor, and up to twenty-one days loss of pay. A detachment commander was limited to fourteen days imprisonment, or ten days loss of pay. Lashes were supposed to be given on the buttocks covered by a wet cloth, and with a broad kiboko or leather strap twelve hours after sentence and under medical safeguards. The brutality of KAR floggings in 1903 so disgusted Meinertzhagen that he refused to have any man of his flogged again, unless he was then discharged. A Meru askari, M'Laibuni wa Baikwamba, exhibited his scars, uninvited, to his interviewer! Marius Karatu was caned for desertion at Moshi.(65)

Captain Maxted, Staff Officer at Kisumu and not of the MLB, grossly exceeded his powers in sentencing two carrier headmen to eighty-four days imprisonment each, with hard labor, for theft and assault, his powers being limited to forty-two days. Scott tried to find out why Maxted had exceeded his powers, and why the Carrier Officer had not dealt with the case; the DML would like a copy of his instructions, if any. Maxted furiously informed his superior officer (Line of Communication, Dar es Salaam) that "as long as I am Post Commandant here I will not be dictated to by anyone but you." This thwarted Scott's attempt "to call Maxted's attention to his having exceeded authority without calling down on him official thunders. Maxted doesn't seem quite overcome with gratitude."(66) It is significant that a mere captain felt free to treat the DML with contempt, a lieutenant-colonel and a departmental head, more especially when the captain had blatantly ignored regulations. His superior officer seems to have reproved Maxted for this, to judge by the friendly tone of his letters to Watkins. Still, it all goes to show that it was nearly impossible to protect the interests of porters when junior officers of other units felt free to behave like this.

Several witnesses, like Lazaro Maende, spoke of the enforcement of "lights and fires out," and "no talking" after sundown on active service, leaving insufficient time for cooking when men were too tired anyway. Muumbi Mulei, a Kamba medical orderly, mentioned the punishment of being made to run about carrying a bag of salt. Odera remembered having to march to and fro with a gun for several hours. Jonathan Okwirri, who was concerned with distributing loads according to the size of the carrier, said that a 60-lb. load might sometimes be given as a punishment, but with his kit and other items a man's load must usually have totalled 60 lbs.(67)

On the whole, carriers thought that their officers were reasonable. Two men, Askari Kivandi and Gun Carrier Atonga, spoke of very cruel white officers or NCOs being killed by their own men. Atonga was with 4th (Uganda) KAR. Some officers were kind, others not. One, called Kibaya (Bad Little Man), was killed after maltreating his men for a year. Kivandi said that a white NCO used to beat the askari every morning at reveille, to wake them up. They plotted revenge, and at 6:30 one morning the whole company fell on him and beat him to death. They then stood silently in three concentric circles until noon, when the commanding officer came out and said: "Ni shauri ya

vita tu," literally that it was "an affair of war," in order to prevent
a mutiny. The rapid growth of the KAR brought many white men who
were entirely new to Africa. Some of those sent out for the new
battalions were described as a "poor, shell-shocked lot" by a staff
officer, who said that the askari called them shenzi bwanas; a
sergeant-major of 2nd KAR asked: "Of what tribe do these new
masters come?" There may have been others steeped in white South
African prejudices. The staffing of the Carrier Corps must have been
even harder. But although there were no doubt many misfits, and men
who should not have been sent, the signs are that the new units did
well.(68)

The Meru postal carrier M'Inoti probably voiced the general
opinion when he said that though some officers were cruel, most
were considerate; he mentioned a very brave captain, nicknamed
Mwanoiba, who was killed in action. Nduma Mutie, a Kamba headman
of carriers, served with the KAR and other units; he named two
officers who were honoured members of the Kenya farming
community: Kitila (Major Frank Joyce) and Kiteng'e (Captain
Wilson).(69)

Ever since the days of Emin Pasha in Uganda, Sudanese have
served as soldiers in East Africa; it was some of them who mutinied
in 1897. They have been vital in the KAR; they are usually called
Nubians, and their descendants have recognised settlements at Bondo,
near Kampala, and Kibera, near Nairobi. Agweli thought the Nubians
very tough disciplinarians; there was a white officer called Bwana
Mukia (Mr. Tail), because of his fly-whisk, and NCOs who included a
Luo, an Arab and two Nubians. When the Arab, Sergeant Sefi, knocked
down Agweli's friend Ouma during a food strike, Agweli struck him
down too, and was given several hours extra drill by Bwana Mukia.
Though these incidents concern the KAR, not the Carrier Corps, they
may be taken as showing that Africans were not disposed to take
harsh treatment lying down.

MAJOR LYON'S STORY

This grim account of a Carrier Officer's trials shows much of what
has already been discussed, and needs little comment in the telling.
Major W. R. Lyon was a Sierra Leone district officer, transferred
"without any consultation" from 6th London Regiment to the Carrier
Corps, presumably because of his obvious qualifications to serve with
the West African contingent.(70) He was with the Nigerian Brigade
near Lindi in the bitter fighting in late 1917, when nerves must have
been very strained. In September he complained to the Adjutant, 2nd
Nigeria Regiment, that carriers of his own 8th Nigerian CC, the 7th
NCC and the Sierra Leone CC had been overloaded, had had no water
after a six-hour march because the troops had had it all, and that
200 of them had been sent back for more loads at 3 pm, having been
up at 4 am. "It appears that Carriers are considered as little better
than animals. May I draw your attention to the fact that carriers are
human beings, and that officers in charge of carriers are responsible
to their governments for their men?" While he would do all he could
to help the rapid movement of troops, the present treatment of
carriers was wasteful and short-sighted.(71)

No answer seems to have been given, perhaps because Lyon's charges were unanswerable. The Nigerian Brigade must have known the regulations perfectly well, including the fact, plainly stated in the MLB Handbook, that a Carrier Officer must "see that loads are kept down to 50 lbs."(72) After the battle of Mahiwa, Lyon asked if company commanders could account for thirty-nine carriers missing but not in hospital returns; again he regretted troubling these officers, but he had to maintain his records and his contact with his men. The reply was curt and unhelpful, nor did circulating the list reveal "the whereabouts of many carriers." Lyon repeated his request for accounts of carriers from the companies to which they were issued, as otherwise he could not make his returns to the DML. If this was done daily, replacements could be sent daily without altering ration strengths. He was told that it was the duty of his British NCO to see to this, but he later told Watkins that whenever he had sent the NCO, the carriers were never properly paraded, and difficulties and excuses were made.(73)

It had been a time of hard marching and fighting, with heavy loss of life; Lyon's frustrations must have been mounting. Finally he was in charge of a party of Mendi first-line carriers, from Sierra Leone, and of all the Ibo second-line carriers, who were to repair roads. The three Mendi headmen all spoke good English, said Lyon, and therefore must have understood his orders to parade at 5:30 am next day, at which hour the Ibo were ready, but the Mendi were drifting off in small parties. The headman gave the unconvincing reason that a native soldier had told them to do so; Lyon promptly gave two of them twenty-four lashes apiece for wilful disobedience. One of them reported to his officer, 2nd.-Lieutenant Despicht of C Company, that he had not only been flogged, but also threatened by Colour-Sergeant Rushby if he complained. Lyon and Rushby denied this, as Rushby had been asleep at the time; Lyon said that Goba, the headman, deserved further punishment for lying. The second headman who had been flogged, Sasi, and a third, James, who had not, had run off with ten carriers to friends in another column.(74)

Lyon had impulsively exceeded his authority, though the men had certainly been deliberately disobedient. But Lyon was very understanding with the Ibo carriers:

> The Adjt. and other officers of the 2 N.R. do not appreciate that with such men as the 8 N.C.C. to obey an order is not at all an instinct....to punish them is often mere cruelty as they do not understand what they are being punished for. They have, for example, carried loads all day. Their headmen have taken so long a time to divide their food that "lights out" has arrived before they can cook. They are tired, & know that if they do not eat they will drop on the road the next day. Consequently they make fires despite all orders the moment the European's back is turned.(75)

As well as describing the problem of the evening meal, this shows that Lyon was ready to make considerable allowances for those who did not understand: an excuse which an English-speaking headman could not make. Lyon may also have encountered that most explosive of all provocations, dumb insolence.

Lyon should have settled the matter quietly, if possible, with Despicht, but now most unwisely laid himself open to his enemies in the 2nd NR by referring the matter to their Commanding Officer, Lieutenant-Colonel Parr. This angered Despicht so much that he complained to Watkins; he had already resented Lyon's ignoring his authority by punishing his men, who had always worked well for him, and by reporting to Parr over his head. Parr and Major Fell, commanding the Right Half Battalion of 2nd NR, reported to Major Spencer, Brigade Carrier Officer, that Lyon was incompetent and unsuited by temperament for the performance of his duties.(76)

This opinion was based first on "personal observation in camp and on the line of march," but Lyon objected that no instances were quoted. Secondly, successive adjutants had found it difficult to do business with Lyon, who again complained of their failure to substantiate. "The reason which has made me difficult to do business with from the point of view of the 2 N.R. is that I have based my duties mainly on para 19 of M.L.B. handbook....it is obvious that the Adjt. and the O.C. Carriers must necessarily view the carrier from two entirely different points of view." Thirdly, Lyon absolutely denied "the fact that your subordinates cannot work under you"; there was no evidence of it before the Despicht affair. Finally, "the carriers themselves will not work under you"; Lyon was reminded that his authority was limited to twelve lashes, and to flogging men of his own company only. Lyon's version of the affair differed little from Despicht's; "If this is the only instance of (d) it seems to me to be a somewhat slender proof especially as Lt Despicht says the remaining 1 HM & 9 carriers are not with him. My carriers work for me as well as they are capable of working for anyone & they certainly keep better health when entirely under my charge than when split up among Coys." He regretted exceeding his powers. He had been a political officer in Sierra Leone for five years, and his temperament had been no disadvantage. He suggested that instances be quoted of people being unable to work under him, or of duties not carried out. But "since further correspondence on this subject" was refused, he chose to proceed with it through the MLB rather than through the General Officer Commanding Nigerian Brigade.(77)

Lyon had erred badly over the flogging and in upsetting Despicht, but the impression remains of an officer with a sincere devotion to the welfare of his men, who was thorough in such duties as keeping up his correspondence; his letters are all meticulous copies in a very clear hand, done on Army forms for want of other paper. (A friend of the author, Mr. John Say, remembers Major Lyon as a pleasant and kindly man.)(78) He was probably right in suggesting that the officers of the 2nd NR resented his adherence to his duties as a Carrier Officer. But, ironically, he neglected the one instruction which might have prevented this unhappy train of events at their inception: "Carrier Officers should never allow themselves to be drawn into an altercation....[but] in the event of a difference of opinion state quietly that they propose to refer it to the D.M.L." There is no sign that Lyon did this, which he plainly could and should have done in September, when his initial complaint produced no satisfaction. Though this letter is not couched in very conciliatory terms, the battalion were breaking every part of the General Staff order on the proper treatment of their men.(79) Lyon chose instead to bear a load of responsibility which finally broke him.

Lyon said that the wastage in 8th NCC during those three terrible months was 64 percent; on 9 September there had been twenty-two headmen and 396 carriers; on 9 December there were eight headmen and 142 carriers left. These figures are borne out by the official death rate of 20.4 percent for the Nigerians, and 16.1 percent for the Sierra Leone carriers. When Watkins received Lyon's dossier, he must have been angry both at the callous treatment of the carriers, and at Lyon's failure to inform his earlier. The wastage must have seriously reduced the efficiency and mobility of the Nigerian Brigade, which also suffered huge losses: 528 out of the 1,750 engaged at Mahiwa alone.(80) The problems of ill-treatment of carriers, and of interference with their management, recurred constantly throughout the campaign. This episode is unique in its description by Major Lyon, showing vividly and clearly "some of the difficulties with which I have had to contend."(81)

NOTES

1. Barra, 1,000 Kikuyu Proverbs, 69.

2. H.B.T. to author, 28 May 1971, kindly lending The Nile Quest - Speke Centenary Celebrations 1962 (Kampala: East Africa Literature Bureau, 1962), including his article "The Logistics of Caravan Travel," 12; see also Philip Mitchell, African Afterthoughts (London: Hutchinson, 1954), 49; Dr. Hale Carpenter later joined the MLB.

3. WR, para. 51; MLB Handbook, Appendix 2, Formulae.

4. PRO, CAB 45/14, "Transport Difficulties."

5. KNA, DC/NYI/3/5, "D. C. Nyeri, Safari Handbook 1916."

6. Notes kindly given by Zakayo Munene.

7. See Chapter 8 above, especially the section on medical progress; MLB Handbook, 54, Departmental Order No. 209, 1917.

8. MLB Handbook, Appendix 2, "No. of Porters required on line to move x loads"; formulae are given for convoy and dumping systems.

9. See Appendix 2 below.

10. WR, paras. 24-43; Chapters 4 and 5 above.

11. PRO, CAB 45/14, 1.

12. CAB 44/6, Chapter 14, "Advance to Rufiji," 92, and AQMG to General Officer Commanding-in-Chief, 9 Jan. 1917.

13. Fendall, EAF, 91-92.

14. WR, para. 28; Downes, Nigerians, 96.

15. EUL, J. W. Arthur Papers (GEN. 763, Box 2): Diary, 14 July to 1 Aug. 1917, and J.W.A. to Kikuyu Mission, 5 Sept. 1917; Kikuyu News, No. 66, Feb-April 1918, "Doing our Bit."

16. Arthur Papers, Diary: 2-10 Aug. 1917, letters to Kikuyu, 5 Sept. 1917 and 1 Jan. 1918.

17. Interview with Mahingu and Mukura, June 1969.

18. Lucas, Empire at War, vol. IV, 267-273;   Murray, Nyasaland, Chapter 19, 271.

19. PRO, CAB 45/14, "Transport Difficulties."

20. Ibid.

21. WP, R53, Watkins to DAAQMG, 23 Dec. 1916.

22. Mitchell, Afterthoughts, 40; MLB Handbook, para. 62; PRO, CAB 45/30B, Beazley to Director, 19 Oct. 1937.

23. Downes,Nigerians,55;PRO,CAB 45/30B von Lettow, Reminiscences, 113 quoted. K. refers to Kitchener.

24. H.R.A. Philp, A New Day in Kenya (London, 1936), 32.

25. WR, para. 131.

26. Campbell, Motor Lorry, 185.

27. Huxley, Red Strangers, 206-208.

28. Dolbey, EA Campaign, 118.

29. WP, Lyon to Watkins, 11 Dec. 1917; see the section on Major Lyon's story in this chapter.

30. Marching on Tanga, 43-44.

31. Motor Lorry, 124.

32. Afterthoughts, 34, 40.

33. Marching on Tanga, 138-166 for this story in full.

34. Huxley, Red Strangers, 283-286.

35. Rhodes House, Ms. Afr. S 379, Ainsworth's Diary, 15 April 1917; WP, Secret File, Ainsworth to Watkins, 31 May 1917; Downes, Nigerians, 163-164.

36. WP, "Report by Senior Military Liaison Officer."

37. Meinertzhagen, Kenya Diary, 242-243, incident during 1905 Nandi Campaign, involving a Nyema corporal in the KAR; Thomas Papers (RCSL), Confidential Memorandum on behaviour towards Belgians, by DAAQMG, 25 June 1917; Moyse-Bartlett, KAR, 325, n. 1 in The Golden Trade of the Moors (London: Oxford University Press, 1968), 83, E.W. Bovill (who served with the Nigerian Brigade in East Africa) writes that Nyam-Nyam used to be a common term for cannibal in the Western Sudan: the form Nyum-Nyum was used in East Africa to refer to cannibals, Musembi Kiindu repeating it with great disgust. It is of course similar to the Swahili nyama (meat).

38. M. Perham, Ten Africans (London, 1936), 78-79.

39. KNA, 38/603, Chinese Dock Labour.

40. Huxley, Red Strangers, 175.

41. Kenya Diary, 102.

42. PRO, CAB 45/14, 8.

43. Hordern, Operations in EA, 141, n. 2.

44. WR, paras. 78-83; see experiences of machine gun carriers.

45. PRO, CAB 45/30B, Beazley to Director, 19 Oct. 1937;
     MLB Handbook, 86-87, for Circ. No. 21, 2 May 1916, "Maxim
     Gun Carrier Badge"; Appendix 6 below, and WR, Appendix 3.

46. WR, para. 78; see Standing Orders and Regulations for
     the Forces (Thomas Papers, RCSL), from which Table 1 is
     taken; Downes, Nigerians, photo of mountain gun carrier.

47. KNA, 37/577 2, letters 18 Aug. and 30 Aug. 1915.

48. Downes, Nigerians, 78, 206, Appendix B.

49. PRO, CAB 45/30, to Col. Sec. Nairobi, 11 March 1938.

50. Lord Cranworth, Profit and Sport in British East Africa (London:
     Macmillan, 1919), 46-47.

51. Moyse-Bartlett, KAR, 392.

52. PRO, CAB 45/33, Lieutenant-Colonel Gregg, on draft of Chapter
     17; Hugh Clifford, The Gold Coast Regiment in the East African
     Campaign (London: Murray, 1920), Appendix 2 - 1 mg carrier
     won the DCM, 5 mg carriers and 2 stretcher bearers the MM. In
     CO 533/209/37253, Northey said it would be too difficult to give
     awards to Central and East African carriers.

53. Hordern, Operations in EA, 151, n. 1.

54. Huxley, Red Strangers, 285.

55. Notes kindly given by Vitalis Ojode and (Ngugi) by Kinyanjui
     Gitao.

56. WR, Appendix 1, Table 12, and Appendix 2, Tables 1-4; WP,
     Secret File, Watkins to AAG, 15 March, 1918 (staff strengths);
     Downes, Nigerians, Appendix B, omits the MLB.

57. WR, paras. 131-132.

58. PRO, CAB 45/31-32; Chapters 4 and 5 passim.

59. WP, Secret File, Watkins to DAAQMG, 15 March 1918.

60. WP, Staff File, Fendall to Watkins and answer, 19 Dec. 1918;
     Watkins to Asst. AAQMG, 21 March 1919.

61. WR, para. 131.

62. MLB Handbook, General Routine Order 10 of 1 Jan. 1917, 73; 80-82, circs. of 12 Jan. on recruiting, and 2 Feb. 1917 on wastage of labor; WP, Major-General Ewart, AAQMG, to column commanders, 20 June 1917.

63. MLB Handbook, 42-45, 54 and 73, also para. 48; see below for Bishop Weston on Stragglers; notes on Ojwang' kindly given by Vitalis Ojode.

64. MLB Handbook, para. 19, the basic advice for Carrier Officers, used by Watkins after the war for government labor management, in OG, 1921, 184-186, which Dr. Clayton kindly pointed out to me.

65. MLB Handbook, Chapter 8; Thomas Papers, mem. on discipline by DAAQMG, 26 Nov. 1917; Kenya Diary, 11; notes on M'Laibuni kindly given by Zakayo Munene.

66. WP, correspondence Oct.-Nov. 1917.

67. Notes on Muumbi kindly given by John Mang'oka.

68. Moyse-Bartlett, KAR, 332-336; WP, Staff Correspondence; PRO, CAB 45/31C, Chapter 2, Crofton to Hordern, n.d.

69. Notes on Nduma kindly given by John Mang'oka.

70. WP, Lyon's letters: to Watkins, 11 Dec. 1917.

71. WP, Lyon to Adjutant 2 NR, 11 Sept. 1917 (Utigere).

72. MLB Handbook, 6: "Duties of Carrier Officers."

73. Lyon and Adj. 2 NR, 24 Oct., 3 and 4 Nov. 1917, at Nangowa; the tone of the Adj., a Lieut., to a Major seems disrespectful; see Lyon to Watkins, 11 Dec. 1917.

74. Despicht to Lyon and reply, 7 Dec., to Watkins, 9 Dec.; Lyon to Watkins, 11 Dec. 1917, on flogging.

75. Lyon to Watkins, 11 Dec., on trouble with 2 NR.

76. Despicht to Watkins, 9 Dec.; Spencer to Watkins, enclosing Parr to Spencer, same date.

77. Lyon to Watkins, 11 Dec., on letter from Major Fell, 9 and 10 Dec.; Lyon to Fell, 10 Dec.

78. Lyon to Watkins, 11 Dec., complaints against 2 NR.

79. MLB Handbook, para. 19; General Routine Order No. 10, 1 Jan. 1917.

80. Table 3 (Statistics); Downes, Nigerians, 244.

81. Lyon to Watkins, 11 Dec. 1917 (60/a/17).

Chapter 10
The Missions and the Carrier Corps

"Advance in happiness, because it is God who has
directed thus"
(hymn of the Kikuyu Mission Volunteers)[1]

Early mission contributions to the war effort had been mainly
medical, like Cook and the CMS in Uganda. Government and mission
attitudes towards African progress showed slight differences, but
missions of divergent doctrinal outlook could disagree much more
sharply. Protestant missions in the East Africa Protectorate had tried
very hard before the war to prevent this; conferences were held both
in Nyanza and Kikuyu, culminating in the Kikuyu Conference of 1913.
The feeling was that, though African Christians might not yet be
ready to take part in such gatherings, a large native church might
quickly grow and must be united. Moreover, the feeling of being "all
one in Christ Jesus" in a pentecostal sense was very strong amongst
the CMS, Church of Scotland, Africa Inland Mission (AIM), Friends
and other smaller bodies who took part.(2)

One of the main leaders of the 1913 Conference was Dr. John
Arthur of the Church of Scotland; until his furlough in 1915 he was
only a layman, but his medical achievements, his knowledge of Kikuyu
language and customs, his zeal and gifts of leadership all made him
outstanding among the missions. But a jarring note was introduced by
a clergyman who did not take part and who accused Bishop Peel
(CMS) of heresy for participating in a joint Communion Service: Frank
Weston, Bishop of Zanzibar and a notable Anglo-Catholic. These two
very different churchmen thus became prominent in different ways,
through the Kikuyu Conference; both were to be leaders of mission
carrier corps.

THE BISHOP OF ZANZIBAR'S CARRIER CORPS

Despite the inevitable difficulties of the war, in the East Africa
Protectorate and Uganda it was "business as usual." But in German
East Africa, both the CMS and the Universities' Mission to Central
Africa (UMCA), for which Frank Weston worked, endured real
persecution. Though von Lettow was not held responsible for this,
opinion was less lenient towards Schnee on the general ill-treatment
of internees. Some British Christians were badly treated, and their
African followers exposed to great brutality.(3)

The invasion of Belgium had enabled the British to enter the war as a crusade, a feeling which was fed with atrocity stories, mostly false. But some of those current in East Africa were not.(4) Africans were told stories of German cruelty, as Kaniaru, of the KMV, remarked. The KMV at Kahuhia said of the war:

> The Germans and the British were fighting for power, each seeking....to have a larger territory than the other....We thought that the British would win when they drove the Germans out of Voi and Kisii, and then....captured Tanga and Dar es Salaam. The difference between [them] was the Germans were men of violence, and the British were men of thought.

Frank Weston saw the moral issue as follows:

> German theology had got rid of Christ....German ethics had rejected his teaching in favour of might....German psychology justified lust, impurity and shameful vice....In all this Germany was only representing Europe. In each nation you will find some or other of these sins; she has them all, and glories in them.(5)

It was a war against the decadence of European civilisation and not just against Germany. The High Churchman who was to arraign four fellow bishops for heresy, the prophet for whom the war was the consequence of the sins of Europe, regarded Africans as his children; "to pretend that they are within measurable distance of self-government is the highest folly." He accordingly condemned proposals to make Tanganyika a mandate of India, which was less qualified to rule than Britain.(6)

As the British began to overrun German East Africa, they recruited more porters, both in occupied enemy territory, and in Zanzibar; the island was the centre of the UMCA diocese, whose greater area was on the mainland. Weston was therefore heavily involved. When he and his Roman Catholic colleague protested against recruitment methods, he was challenged to form his own contingent. Flinging himself with enthusiasm into the task, he had 560 men within a few weeks, in June 1916. He drilled them himself, teaching them how to form line, lift and carry loads and stretchers, helped by buglers of the Zanzibar Scouts, and later by a Goan band; they were soon responsive to "a word or a whistle." The Bishop had the rank of Major, unpaid and ungazetted at his own request so long as he could command the force. Two mission laymen, C. M. Baker and A. A. Richardson, and a Zanzibar government official, B. C. Johnstone, were subalterns, assisted by Lieutenant-Commander Clarke, R.N. Four mission teachers came as clerks and evangelists: the Rev. J. B. Mdoe, William Swedi, Henry Kelezi and Alban Ali. The men, who had come forward eagerly to join the Bishop, were mostly Zanzibaris, Muslims predominating, but including Christians, catechumens and some pagans.(7)

Weston showed his practical sense of the men's welfare in two ways: first, knowing the chaos in the regular Carrier Corps at the start, he was careful to enrol men only under their right names, which he was probably able to do because of the trust he inspired. Secondly, his Corps would include more literate men than any group of servicemen hitherto; he therefore arranged for a supply of postcards. The result is one of our few pieces of evidence written in an African hand:

> Truly our Lord Bishop is a great man! Did he not call us and gather us all together? Did he not drill us, and go for marches with us every day?....Truly he is a great man, for he came over the sea with us, and when we reached the mainland he marched with us, he slept with us, he ate with us, and when we laid down at night, did he not pray with us? And when we arose in the morning, did he not pray with us again?(8)

The excellent discipline which prevailed is shown by the fact that, during the five weeks in Zanzibar, "we had only three police cases, not one of them serious."(9)

In July 1916 they moved to Tanga, finding it badly smashed up by the British naval bombardment which had preceded its capture. At Tanga they doubled their numbers to over 1,000, and had three tasks: "to enclose the town with barbed wire, to safeguard the camp," to work in the docks, and to help in policing and cleaning the town. Then, leaving Richardson to meet another 500 recruits from Mombasa, Weston and Baker set out with 1,034 men for Muheza, Korogwe and Handeni. More mission recruits were picked up en route, and at Korogwe the Bishop was able to inspect his own mission, where one of the UMCA priests was combining pastoral and political work. Here he had to hand over 300 men to the Royal Engineers, and his column set off with stores for Nderema Depot, near Handeni:

> Never was road like that Handeni road. I remember it as one of the show roads of the colony: broad, hard, and clean. We found about two feet of dust on its surface:....dust that made of one colour all races of men, and gave us all one common cough "to the pits of all our stomachs" as Kipling has it....And to the dust was added a stench that passes words: a stench now subtle and suggestive, now throttling and entirely disgusting; a stench that attracted one's gaze only that it might be repelled by visions of a sated jackal's half-eaten meal. For horses, oxen and mules have died by thousands....Truly, war is hideous even at its base.

Even in dry weather a road might become utterly disgusting; the beasts included those which had died on the march described by Brett Young and Buchanan. The Bishop's vivid description continues:

> Another glory of the road was its lack of water. I knew Zigualand from painful experience....But on my arrival I was given an official list of wells and watering places [made during the rains]....twice did we resolve to halt where the Army said good water was....And twice did we repent ourselves of our trusting and confiding spirit. On the first occasion it was midday....and there was no water at all: only a vast camping place where water had once been....The second day we had marched nearly fifteen miles and wanted food. The so-called well was....a museum of dead frogs....It remained to do another

six miles onward. And the man who had not had to do extra miles beyond his promised halting place, under tropical sun, has yet much to learn of what a broken spirit really means.(10)

This picture of the Handeni road, with its dust of death and empty wells, shows only too clearly the need for stringent water regulations, and confirms Major Lyon's later experience as to who suffered most when water was scarce. This was a commander's worst anxiety, wrote Major-General Sheppard; streams were few in the dry season. "Hunger is a trifle, but no water is death." Nor did the British know where to find water, as the Germans did.(11)

A later stage, of which "even the Army said there was no water at all," was done by night. Infantry had no option, according to Captain Anderson, because during the day lorries stirred up the dust, which was a foot deep; his account tallies with that of Weston: the rotting carcasses and befouled water holes on this hideous road. Weston combined saintliness and prophetic insight with remarkable gifts of leadership; he clearly understood a porter's work after so many peacetime safaris:

> Of course porters do not move quickly. They have their own food etc. to carry as well as the official loads....[perhaps made up to] say eighty pounds, whereas the porter requires fifty pounds or at most fifty-five....So that most men must either carry overweight, or share a load that is not up to the two men standard and so waste the "lift" of your column. The last lot of supplies I handled, very many thousands of loads, was almost entirely made up of 80 lb. bags, and 96 lb. boxes of ammunitions.

Watkins' anger can well be imagined when Weston told him of this, as he almost certainly did. But the large loads which Weston describes had probably been made up for mules and animal transport carts; the beasts were now dead, and ways had to be found of adapting their loads to porters. The Bishop was in a position to add great weight to the work of improving the porters' lot; they had to be rested,

> otherwise men fall out and get lost or run away, or get overtired and ill. And to rest a column of 1,000 carriers in single file, or at best in double file, takes time; with the result that two and a half miles an hour is very fast, and one and a half is not unknown....the stronger men get in well ahead of the last men, whose job it is to urge on the tired, look out for dropped loads, and gather up the sick. If there be a more weary work than coming last of such a column on a march of fifteen miles, I have not yet seen, heard or read of it. Yet it is not unuseful. Our men did very well on this particular work. We made a record for the journey both in time and accuracy. That is, we got our loads there quicker than other porters, and we got them all there. I gather this was not common.(12)

This comment on the related questions of lost loads and carriers dropping out is valuable. In very severe conditions, as on the Duthumi

A Column of Carriers on the March in German East Africa
by courtesy of Dr. Clive Irvine

line, if a carrier fell out his load would almost certainly be lost; it would also probably have to be abandoned if an exhausted carrier was put on a stretcher, which the Luo carrier Yohana Ojwang' remembered was the practice by his time.

There were deaths from pneumonia, dysentery and meningitis. It would be interesting to know whether the pneumonia was anything to do with the ghastly dust; respiratory diseases are often worst at the end of the long dry season. They returned to Korogwe and were joined by Johnstone, "a real tower of strength and a most pleasant fellow worker." They were suddenly given two days to return to Tanga, forty miles away, to embark for Bagamoyo. Their column, about a mile and a half long, was led by Weston, with Johnstone in the rear. They left at 4 P.M., torrential rain fell, and they followed the railway, whose bridges consisted mainly of sleepers "not too close together." Johnstone was almost carrying night-blind men across, but although one man fell into a pool none were lost. Only the fly sheets of tents could be put up, and many men slept under a goods train whose driver had to be told not to start until he had awakened them! Many fell sick, and one long delay was caused by the column splitting in two, but after a better second night they marched into Tanga at 7 A.M., "singing lustily and quite happy," Weston wrote. "Marching all night is no joke, and it is no uncommon thing to fall asleep as one walks, while Africans can go to sleep the moment they put down their loads, and need much persuasion to get out again."(13)

At Bagamoyo the Bishop was put in command of the Coast Column Carriers. He was told to provide 2,500, but despite being given another 1,000 they were still a few hundred short. The answer was to commandeer all the two- and four-wheeled carts in the town. Five men could pull a two-wheeler, carrying perhaps 500 lbs. Though some officers doubted whether the road would be suitable, "it was carts or nothing, since backs would not go round." Despite dust and a late start, they started well, but a night march had to be made to catch up the column. Soon after 1 A.M. they were stopped by the camp of the Supplies Officer and his staff blocking their path; a sergeant told the Bishop that "the oxen were wind-broken, the porters back-broken, and the staff heart-broken. I have had experience as a Catechist. It was clear that the moment for further questioning was not yet." But next day supplies had to be taken through if the column was not to be rationless; for Weston it was "the day of my life." With frantic labor, porters carrying 75 lbs. each, and a total of two and a half hours sleep in two days, the rations reached the front, and the oxcarts were sent home; they were now redundant, and the road was unsuitable for wheeled traffic. But Weston's heroic carriers took over a naval three-pounder gun on a clumsy home-made chassis, which they dragged for two days in addition to their loads. An African witness told of his alarm when the Bishop fell trying to stop the gun going down a slope. Finally, "it was a very cheerful and grateful crowd that entered Dar-es-Salaam at the double with the gun rattling over the roads. The very rattle was welcome, telling of sand left behind and mud passed."(14)

They worked for a fortnight in Dar es Salaam, rather as they had in Tanga. Their camp was a little way out: "the Lord Bishop loved the souls of him men and knew their weakness; and so he was ever unwilling to camp very close to a town." He was also intensely busy with pastoral work, hospital visiting, and even "helping officers with native languages and difficulties" - shauris, as they are called, which perplex many Europeans in Africa, and at which he must have been brilliant! Next, he and Johnstone left with a few hundred porters for the Southern port of Mikindani, taken in September 1916, as were Dar es Salaam, Lindi and Kilwa. Thence they marched over a hundred miles up country to Masasi, a UMCA station which Weston rejoiced to find still intact, its church being used as a hospital. (It was to be amid the bitter fighting a year later.) They returned via Sudi and Lindi to Kilwa Kisiwani, where Richardson joined them; they worked hard unloading troops and stores, and finally, as Weston was taking porters to the Rufiji, he was seized by a high fever. He was put on a boat for Zanzibar, where he refused to land without his men. So he returned to Dar es Salaam, and gathered the Zanzibar men for their return home; "those who were not of Zanzibar cried for the Lord Bishop, so that there was great lamentation," wrote an African witness.(15)

Meticulous military efficiency was combined with inspired Christian leadership. "All the men obeyed every word of the Lord Bishop without question," said the same witness, "not because they were afraid or because they were forced, but because the Lord Bishop treated them as a father does his children. There were troubles, but they were few in number." Johnstone said that the discipline was "the most rigid I have known. When once he decided a thing was possible....he spared no one, himself included." The only theft which seems to have occurred resulted in a more severe beating "than I should have imposed. I am sure, however, that he was right, for such a thing never happened again." He ceased for a time to seem like a churchman and became a soldier; "I knew he hated it all, but I am sure he felt that, by doing his work, he was setting a guide to others who were to follow." A medical officer's report on the men who returned to Zanzibar says: "It was very pleasant to see in what good condition they were. This was due to the great care that the bishop had taken of his men. He had seen that they were properly treated, and this, I regret to say, was not always the case."(16)

In telling transport officials at Korogwe and Bagamoyo his opinion of oversized loads, Weston had the immense advantage of knowing what men could carry in such a climate, for how long, and what food and rest they needed.

The Zanzibar CC seems originally to have been engaged for July and August 1916, with September added later. The three mission officers served without cost to the military; Weston agreed that Baker and Richardson could continue to serve after the end of their engagement, provided that they were "properly commissioned and put on paylists like military officers." Later he complained privately to Watkins that General Ewart (DAAQMG) accused him of wrongfully withdrawing the laymen. "It seems to me a very painful suggestion that my provision of a staff for Z.C.C. free of all charge to the military, and my readiness to help with column carriers apart from Z.C.C. should be taken by G.H.Q. as a basis for a claim for the permanent services of my staff after Z.C.C. ceases to exist." General Headquarters' side of this is not known, but if the Bishop was right, then they had behaved in a most ungrateful and insulting manner; he thanked Watkins warmly for "your kindness to me at all times," and

Watkins' preservation of this letter implies strong sympathy with Weston at the gaucheness of their military superiors. Weston's mental exhaustion can be read in this distressful letter: "it just spoils all the pleasure we have had, and creates a barrier against pleasant memories of our work." (Maybe Johnstone had been wrong in thinking that he had "hated it all.") The cordial relations between Weston and Watkins shown by this letter are evidence of long talks in Dar es Salaam about Weston's practical experience of carriers on the march. Bishop Weston's views would have given Watkins a battery of powerful arguments to use in the struggle to improve working conditions.(17)

THE KIKUYU MISSION VOLUNTEERS

The KMV played a part out of all proportion to their small numbers or the short time that they served; this book has already been enriched by the recollections of a fair number of them. John Arthur's matchless description of the dumping system has preceded Major Lyon's sombre tale, and Bishop Weston's account of the convoy system.

Ni guteithania tuguteithania - "it's our bit we are doing" - was a frequent comment by members of the KMV, who, like the ZCC, included a high proportion of literates.(18) It was based on the pre-war conference movement; missionaries like Barlow, Philp and Chadwick had championed African rights before the NLC, and the KMV was to be a great practical demonstration of African welfare in adverse conditions.(19) John Arthur, one of the founders of the "Kikuyu ideal" and leader of the KMV, was able to combine a growing concern with African rights and an ability to cooperate with government, his relations with Ainsworth and Watkins being very good. He could be critical of excessive use of power, as when he wrote of a District Commissioner of Meru as "a little Czar known by the natives as Kangangi, the small man who is always on the move.... feared by all the people around. He had however from the Government point of view done extraordinarily good work."(20) Athlete, rugger player and mountain climber, Arthur was an outspoken man of strong opinions, a doctor and a Presbyterian minister.

When war began, the Scots mission was at first concerned to keep the work going, like the CMS. Barlow reported that some Africans wanted to fight for the British, but shared the general view that the war was irrelevant to East Africa, whose fate would be settled in Europe. He also hoped that, if the war slowed down economic progress, mission pupils might return "into closer contact with their own people, and cause them to think more of the advancement of God's kingdom." The war gave an opportunity for Christians to repent of their self-indulgence and failure to respond to God's call in time of peace. In 1916 a Carrier Hospital was opened at Kikuyu for carriers returning from German East Africa; by 30 June, 161 patients had been admitted, eighty-eight of whom were then still in the wards.(21)

The real challenge came in April 1917; in addition to the mass levy, all Europeans had to register and be medically examined unless exempted by the District Committees. Having been passed fit at Fort Hall, the CMS missionary at Kahuhia, Rev. H. D. Hooper, reflected that mission boys would have to serve in the Carrier Corps, unless a special force could be laid on for them. This would have a valuable moral effect on the men and "their heathen neighbours"; there would be a chance of sharing the general hardships. "To government officials and others it would be a striking refutation of the commonly repeated story that mission schools were the refuge of all the able-bodied loafers." Many had sought refuge from conscription with missions, but the levy would end this, and the relative freedom of genuine mission followers from the Carrier Corps.(22)

Hooper was about to consult Archdeacon Hamshere when he heard that Arthur had had a similar idea; Arthur presented it to Ainsworth and Watkins, and received their support. The Native Church Committee at Kikuyu agreed at once when Arthur explained the scheme, worried as they were about the imminence of press-ganging. A large prayer meeting was held, at which arguments similar to Hooper's were put to over a hundred young men. After some practical questions about wages and work, ninety-seven handed in their names, including teachers, hospital boys, masons, carpenters and shamba workers; another fifteen joined next day.(23)

The scheme matured so rapidly that on 1 April about 1,800 carriers gathered at Kikuyu (called Thogoto locally) and remained there a month. They were Church of Scotland, CMS, AIM and the Gospel Missionary Society; there were a hundred AIM people from Machakos, and about half the Kikuyu were from Fort Hall. Captain John Arthur was in command, with Second-Lieutenants Hooper, Barlow and Tait, who was also Church of Scotland. There were seven NCOs, five of whom were British missionaries liable for service: Whibley and Gray Leakey of the CMS, and Clarke, Stephenson and Guilding of the AIM.(24) Silas Kiige, Samwel Ngoci and Ishmaeli from Kahuhia said that Leakey was called Murungaru (straight man), and agreed with Nathaniel Mahingu, from Limuru, that Whibley's nickname was Waitina (Big Bottom).(25)

There were three different grades of headmen in the KMV: over a hundred men, over fifty and over twenty-five. A superior headman of the AIM was Tagi, a literate Maasai who was one of their most trusted evangelists. "There is none his equal in the corps, as he had formerly had military training that fitted him admirably for his present duties....Mutua of Machakos is headman over 100, Mabiewa is headman over 50, and a number more of our leading natives are headmen."(26) Samwel Ngoci of Kahuhia was an overseer, perhaps a headman over twenty-five.

During the month at Kikuyu there were troubles, desertions, and "hard work with the boys," as Arthur noted. "Discipline coming in. Companies formed. Police and prison. Latrines. Guards to station etc." Medical checks and probably the dysentery vaccines were given at Nairobi Depot. They were inspected by Charles Bowring (Acting Governor) and Ainsworth (with the rather tepid comment: "quite a good show"!), also by the District Commissioner and chiefs, including Kinyanjui. There was a united service of Communion on Sunday 6 May, and next Saturday they arrived at Mazeras - mile 11/6 from Mombasa - 1,656 strong after the desertions.(27)

Mazeras was "a most lovely camp"; it was cool and the rains seemed to be over. Being on the Mombasa water main, Arthur hoped it would be healthy. Ainsworth also approved the drainage, water and firewood supply, but three men were down with smallpox. Arthur was less enthusiastic by 12 May, when heavy rain was falling, and the clay subsoil probably causing drainage problems. They had to make a permanent camp for 6,000 carriers before they left.(28)

It was a challenge to train and discipline the men. Acclimatization would take up to three months, often with many deaths, but despite Arthur's fears they lost only three men: one from dysentery, and two from tetanus or meningitis. Arthur ordered anti-tetanus serum for all, because though they had had no "injection abscess" despite hundreds of injections, he thought that the deaths could have been due to tetanus from quinine injections. There were hundreds of men down with influenza, malaria, dysentery and smallpox, so that the losses were very small. Each man had five grains of quinine a day, and Arthur's orderlies revaccinated the force under his supervision: "the boys must learn to treat, and be trained." Hygiene was very strict, and the problems of black cotton soil, clay, thick grass, malaria and climatic lassitude overcome. The original large bandas were burnt, and smaller ones built to catch the wind. Grass was cleared, latrines dug, incinerators built. Arthur hoped that it would all help, not only on campaign but at home afterwards, in cleaner villages and better personal hygiene. Discipline included a little kibokoing; Kaniaru remembered that "anyone who disobeyed was whipped." Arthur was pastor, doctor and commanding officer; he met the request of a dying man for baptism. Three men took three days to write up the register, lists of separation allowances and pay advances; home payments seem to have been peculiar to the KMV. After a month's intense care, discipline and hard work, over 1,600 men from the highlands were acclimatized with only three deaths.(29)

The carriers did not like Mazeras. Tagi's is the only known written evidence: "At Mazeras there were a great many mosquitoes, and it was very, very hot. Many of the boys were sick with malaria fever." The local Duruma said: "Oh, you have come to a bad place here, and in the Company that came before you very, very many died, and we think before you leave that many of you will die." Due to bad water and intense heat "I experienced violent diarrhoea," said Wangoto. "We were attacked by dysentery (Murimu wa Kuhara Gatema)," said Kinuthia. "Then we saw many flies, which could make the grass lie down."(30)

Originally General Headquarters intended to send the KMV to Lindi; in fact they were about to embark at Kilindini, when they were ordered back to Mazeras. The change of plan may well have been due to political representations that the KMV should go somewhere healthier, and the new idea was the Dodoma-Iringa line; Nathanial Mahingu spoke as if the change was generally understood to be for health reasons. Tagi had heard that it was hot at Lindi, with "very many mosquitoes, and very, very many of the Kikuyu people who went there died." Barlow, Hooper and three NCOs went to Lindi, presumably to help with the build-up for the coming offensive. Arthur was much relieved at the change of plan. "Had we gone, as was first intended, to the coast regions and on column work, our casualties must have far exceeded [the final 5.5 percent]," but his 50 percent was probably an exaggeration.(31)

They were next to go to Mombo, on the Tanga Railway, via Voi, and march via Handeni to Morogoro, but owing to a shortage of rolling stock they finally went by sea to Dar es Salaam. Again Arthur was relieved, "as they say we would have lost half our strength on the cross-country march." The united Communion Service on the last Sunday at Mazeras was attended by 105 Africans, which suggests how few converts there were in the force. They sent ninety-six sick back to Voi from Mazeras, and ninety more from Mombasa. They were accompanied on the ss Montrose by 400 men of the African Native Medical Corps, "very neat and clean, but we have nothing to be ashamed of." Putties and caps would, thought Arthur, have improved the appearance of the KMV; he had earlier had a "fight with supplies over boys' food and soap," of which they had not enough. They disembarked at Dar es Salaam on 8 July; Arthur saw Watkins and Hill, collected small arms, soap, maps and other necessaries.(32)

Barlow and the others from Lindi rejoined them at Dodoma; Bowring had secured Hoskins' agreement that in future the KMV should be kept together, perhaps after pressure by the missions. There were now 1,499 men: ninety headmen, nineteen hospital orderlies and 1,390 carriers. They left for Iringa in three detachments to support the Belgian column. Arthur was resolved to carry their sick with them, having had to leave eighty-four at Dodoma. They passed through cooler, healthier country with "attractive beech-like forests," and reached Iringa on 27 July.(33)

Arthur praised the arrangements for sick carriers, especially Major Roberts' work in the Iringa Carrier Hospital. "His treatment of his black patients could not be excelled in any mission hospital; he has amassed a large quantity of statistical material that ought to prove of great value." The hospital was beautifully built of local materials and spotlessly clean. Roberts' assistant was a Methodist lay preacher from Johannesburg, "a most excellent Sergt. Major Dales." Arthur praised the important unpaid work of Roman Catholic Fathers and Sisters, since the beginning of the war, in evacuating sick carriers. Carrier hospitals, and convalescent camps in the East Africa Protectorate, all aimed to send them home as quickly as possible, "the best form of treatment that can be given."(34) Success was evidently meeting the devoted efforts to improve the carriers' lot. But the KMV were working on a line, instead of in column, in healthy country, and in an area from which war had receded. They never saw real horrors as did Colonel Beazley: "in rains along Rufiji saw one so-called porter hospital with no doctor, containing 100 wretched savages lying in mud, vomit and worse, suffering from fever, dysentery, pneumonia, and several corpses among the living."(35)

The KMV base at Muhanga was a Roman Catholic mission station, filthy because of the number of men passing through. Arthur did not blame the officer in charge, Lieutenant Butcher, UMCA, who had no spare labor. They had arrived 1,158 strong, and were joined during August by 193 sick from Iringa and 250 replacements, of whom 100 were Mwimbi from Embu District.(36) Some of the men sent back to Voi from Mazeras also came, one of whom was Josiah Munyaka Kivanguli, later an AIM pastor at Kangundu, Machakos District; he had been a dispenser, and had continued to work at Voi after the others left for Mombo and the march to Morogoro.(37)

Of the 150 men who left Mombo, only thirty-seven reached Muhanga, led by a Thogoto mission headman named Benjamin; they included some Nyanza men. Theirs was a grim tale. At Mombo some of their medical orderlies were commandeered, but arrived at

Muhanga on 10 September. Benjamin was appointed to lead the safari, "which showed what some of the Europeans thought of him." At Handeni their jembes (hoes) were taken from them, and at Morogoro their knives. At Dodoma a doctor certified twenty-three as unfit; all but one were then kibokoed, as were some eighty others, not KMV. "From Dodoma to Iringa they had a rotten time"; Benjamin kept his men well up so that they suffered less than the others. "If any boys were found lagging when they got up, the Sarg. would slash them across the face or breast"; even a lad who fell behind as he was sick; many got the kiboko for trifling reasons. When the safari reached Iringa, "very large numbers were at once put in hospital there as the result. Of 117 boys who left Dodoma for us only 50 got to Muhanga." Josphat Njoroge was not with this safari, but was probably one of those whom Arthur had had to leave behind at Dodoma, where "once....we were whipped when we claimed to be sick, and ordered to carry the goods." Benjamin brought fifty men, including some Roman Catholics from Nyanza who had missed them at Mazeras; Arthur found only four of them fit. "This sort of thing I am afraid is not uncommon. The chief authorities never hear about it as there is no one to take the boy's side or listen to his story." Roberts confirmed that ordinary carriers tended to be brutally treated. Arthur spent 1 September with a "ghastly" sick parade until noon, and "writing DML re ill-treatment of Benjamin's safari."(38)

Such blatant barbarity on an important line of communication bears out Arthur's opinion that brutality was not uncommon. Between them, Arthur and Roberts could have produced enough medical evidence to justify the charges which Watkins would have been eager to bring. One can only hope that the white men whose cruelty had incapacitated over a hundred carriers got the punishment they deserved, for breaking standing orders against what was euphemistically called "wastage of labour."

While they supported the Belgian advance on Mahenge, the KMV were mostly at Muhanga Mission, with an overspill at the next camp, Boma Mzinga, where Hooper was in charge. He had ordinary CC men "from Fort Hall, Nyeri, Embu and Ndia and strangest of all from Wimbi." One of the latter recognised Daudi, a KMV headman, and a teacher who had worked in Wimbi. "Thus at last the second purpose of our K.M.V. scheme is now an accomplished fact, namely, direct evangelistic work among the non-mission Kikuyu porters of the ordinary carrier corps."(39)

Muhanga camp was condemned, and a new one was finished on 12 November. There had been thirteen deaths and hundreds of sick since they had come, which was nothing to ordinary carrier wastage, nor to what they would have suffered in the Lindi hinterland. For the first month it was very wet, sickness high, and not enough labor for adequate latrines. There were, however, only forty-three cases of dysentery, 160 of chest infections, and 378 of malaria, no doubt mostly contracted at Mazeras; their health benefited from a football field they constructed, and frequent games.(40)

This ecumenical experiment was inevitably attended by some friction. This is implied by a diary entry: "Good talk with Hooper. Things going quite well now and getting on well with others." But 18 October was "a worrying day trying to reconcile factions etc"; also Barlow had to go home because of his wife's health. Arthur's decision to make Hooper second in command may not have pleased Tait, but reduced the Church of Scotland preponderance. The AIM had no commissioned officer, and there was some trouble between one of their NCOs and Tait. Whereas 26 October was "rather a worrying day," what with the condemnation of the camp and friction between Tait and Clarke (AIM), the morrow was "a great day": Tait had been "brooding on something said weeks ago," and Arthur arranged talks between him, Clarke and Stephenson which cleared the air.(41) These troubles were a microcosm of the greater question of the Mission Federation; Arthur had always before him the "vision of Kikuyu" as he called it, and his own buoyant faith to sustain him.

Arthur saw the KMV experience like this. First, missionaries and followers were enriched by their fellowship and "wandering in the wilderness." Secondly, their experiences – army life, discipline, hygiene, other people of all races, the sea, a new country, organisation – all would train leadership in the future African Church. Thirdly, this end would be helped by the monthly united Communion, evangelism both in the KMV and among the attached personnel, and by discussing traditional life and customs. Finally, all they had done, learned and undergone was evidence of God's preserving care.(42)

This was also strongly felt by Tagi. They had gone away amid the doubts of their neighbours: "God has not power to care for His children, for they have trouble just as we do." But they rejoiced, confident that God would lead them out and bring them back. Their obvious well-being and happiness, as when they marched singing through Iringa, impressed all who saw them. When they returned, their neighbours said: "Surely your God is a God of power, and He has cared for you and returned you to us safely." So sure were the heathen relations of many of the KMV of their deaths, that their property was divided up, and their safe return caused much embarrassment!(43)

"When the Wagikuyu heard that the missionaries were going," said Nathanial Mahingu, "and missionaries don't fight, very many of us agreed to go," including many not of the Church. "We were well looked after – even the nurses were ours; we had come with them from Thogoto. And Dr. Arthur was a nurse too! The government had said that we must never be taken to a place where there was fighting. It would rather we die of disease than from being shot....I wish you saw how people were as fat as hippos when they were coming home." The Kahuhia men said that ordinary carriers were liable to be badly treated; the KMV had no problems, because they were under missionaries. Though the KMV had a favored status, their morale was very high, what with religious enthusiasm and dedicated leadership. Mahingu mentioned the weekly prayer meetings, and others spoke of hymn-singing. "We only sang Christian songs," said Mwova Kataka, "when it was allowed or during prayer time."

They worried little about death; comparatively few suffered it, but also their faith gave them strength to bear it when it came. They did not share the horror of Reri at the idea of a dead man's spirit being unable to find rest far from his home and clan. Both Luo and Kikuyu tended to say, like the gun carrier Atonga, that there was little time to attend to the dead properly, and that the living were too concerned with their own predicament to worry much about the spirits of the dead. This was the opinion of Kinyanjui wa Mukura,

Mahingu's friend who was with the regular CC, and must have seen grim things on the Rufiji: "Once your companion died you were gripped with fear for the rest of your time there," much as Reri felt. But Kinyanjui also quoted the Kikuyu proverb Mundu wa itimu ndari miarage, "once a man is born he can die anywhere," a more carefree philosophy than Reri's.(44) The KMV attitude was summed up by the Kahuhia men: "we felt worried because of leaving our dead in a strange country, but for their spirits we didn't worry because we were Christians."

The opportunists who had joined the KMV to avoid the regular levy had to attend prayer meetings just the same; Kaniaru said, "religion was mostly learned in the war." For some pagans perhaps it was just the formalities, but others may have been genuinely converted. Morning prayers were impossible after they had left Mazeras, but "every morning, shortly after the bugle goes at 5.50, may be heard rising from the huts all over the camp, the sound of the morning hymn." Kaniaru was one of the buglers. They would gather for prayer and Scripture reading during the day whenever possible; after sundown the superior headmen took evening prayers and hymns with an address. The few Roman Catholics repeated Latin prayers and told their beads. The Sunday service was that of the Federation; at Muhanga "there is no such thing as denominations, but a united band of Christ's followers worshipping Him as their one King and Lord."(45)

> Missionaries and boys have had to live together under trying conditions, and under very critical conditions [wrote Hooper]. The ideas of the Kikuyu Conference have been subjected to a long and enforced trial....we meet together unitedly from time to time, and....a return to the merely friendly relations....before the war must spell retrogression for the native Kikuyu mission volunteer.(46)

A feeling of peace came over Arthur, as they waited for news of the closing of the line, and burned the old hospital and the Kaiser in effigy. There was a "wonderful day" of fellowship with Hooper and Whibley, when he also had a long talk with Muthandi, a chief's son with two vexing problems. His girl friend had gone wrong, and was also of a clan into which his clan were forbidden to marry. Having overcome family objections to that, he felt that he must forgive her. The other problem was that, though only the second son, he might unwillingly have to become chief one day. Arthur pointed out the influence for good which a Christian chief might have. It was an unforgettable experience, talking and praying with Muthandi by the light of the burning hospital. They then reached perilous subjects: one was demonstrative behaviour between husband and wife in public, like the Europeans; boys should be circumcised, but girls not at all, they agreed.(47)

Here were roots of future conflicts between Kikuyu traditionalists and the missionaries and their converts. Josphat Njoroge said that Arthur had broached this delicate subject at Mazeras, and "had told us to stop the circumcision of girls when we went home. We didn't like that." Elijah Kaara, clerk at Nairobi Depot, said that one reason for letting men "disappear" at Kariakor was that many had not been circumcised, and it was necessary to prevent them going to the war until they had been. This rather contradicts his own very unlikely story that a circumcision ceremony was held at Mazeras; it is mentioned by no one who was there. European signs of public affection between husband and wife were thought very improper; Matu had been horrified to see Sasi, the Tumutumu missionary (perhaps A. R. Barlow) embracing his wife.(48) Perhaps the "sojourn in the wilderness," and the thought given to such problems, may have contributed to cultural clashes as well as to spiritual awakening.

Josphat Njoroge avoided people of other tribes, but the Kahuhia men Kiige, Ngoci and Ishmaeli "used to go visiting in the other camps. We came to know each other very well, when we learned how to speak Swahili, and we even visited native homes in Tanganyika." They found that "the Wagogo had similar customs to the Kikuyu, [but] they used dogs as part of dowry price....Secondly, the Wagogo knew God, but in their methods of worship they used foodstuffs, while the Kikuyu used animals for sacrifice." Silas Kiige, who was about ninety years old and was commended by his friends for his excellent memory, showed us his fine hardwood staff, which he had cut at Muhanga and which was still one of his most prized possessions.

They heard on 21 November that the line was closing. An order to relay some stores back from Kaswaga, in the Kilombero lowlands, was rescinded to Arthur's relief, "as it would have meant 10% deaths probably." After heavy work returning stores down the line, they reached Dodoma. On 13 December, while hunting for water at Mwitihira, Arthur met Dr. Clive Irvine, Royal Army Medical Corps, who later founded and ran the Church of Scotland hospital at Chogoria, on Mount Kenya. From Morogoro 2,248 men marched to Korogwe, whence they returned to Nairobi by train via Voi.(49)

OTHER MISSION INVOLVEMENT

The mission contribution to the forces was limited by shortage of staff. Some were chaplains, like Chadwick and Macgregor of the CMS. Chadwick was with the column which advanced from Mwanza to Tabora in 1916, and was horrified by the behaviour of Congolese carriers. This bears out other evidence about Belgian indiscipline, and confirms what Arthur was told by a Boer intelligence agent, Coetzee, who was furious at the seizure by Belgian askari of the women and foodstuffs of the Wabonga "after all the good work they have done for us."(50)

Chadwick described an affair which shows how hard it was to prove charges of brutality. A Muganda, Nasanairi Mukasa, alleged that a sick friend, Samusoni, had died after being severely beaten at Mikesse. Watkins told Chadwick to investigate, but Mukasa now altered both the time and place of the outrage. Angry at having had a two-day journey for nothing, Chadwick accused Mukasa of lying. The Europeans whom Mukasa had accused wanted him punished, but Watkins forbade it, as Mukasa would now say that he was being beaten for accusing a European.(51) Race relations were already a matter for delicate handling.

Apart from the ZCC and the KMV, perhaps the main contribution by the missions was their running of the convalescent camps, a key part of Ainsworth's repatriation scheme which saved the lives of many thousands of sick carriers. The Mombasa camp seems to have been staffed both by CMS and by members of the Italian Roman Catholic mission, detailed by Bishop Perlo. Earlier, the Alsatian Holy Ghost Mission had regretfully had to decline, owing to shortage of staff; for the first year of the war some had been interned as German nationals, like their famous compatriot Albert Schweitzer. The Voi camp was run by AIM, assisted by some of the Bishop Perlo's people; the Rev. A.F. Waechter was in charge, relieved as necessary by the Rev. Johnstone. The Italians also worked in Nairobi where the Rev. A. Hamilton and his sister were in charge. Assistance was given at Kisumu by the Mill Hill Fathers Bergmans and McCormack, later by Dr. A. A. Bond of the Friends, Kaimosi.(52)

There was other work among servicemen by the International Committee of Young Men's Christian Associations (coloured men's department), New York. They were concerned about thousands of Christians serving in the war in East Africa, without pastoral care and exposed to Islamic influence; the fear that carriers or askari might be converted to Islam was also voiced officially. Eight Negro secretaries were sent, who visited hospitals, organised athletics, and ran education classes, with lantern slides on the Bible and industry. They first had to persuade the Africans that athletics was not a form of labor, but finally this strange innovation grew popular, helping to replace the dull monotony of the camps with interest and enthusiasm. As to education, both men and officers were interested, and opportunities seized. Men would spend two to three hours over a slate or the alphabet after a long day working in the sun, and some could show their natural ability by proving able to learn the alphabet, write their names and read a little after four weeks. The secretaries were much encouraged by the help and support given by officers, both with classes and games; three missionaries who saw this work offered to do permanent war work for the YMCA.(53)

Bishop Willis of Uganda found a remarkable instance of Christian influence on men who were not baptised. They were Nyanza men somewhere in German East Africa who had learned the Lord's Prayer from a convert at home, but who were in no sort of contact with any mission now. "We are here," they said, "many miles from our own country and our own people. We are dying like flies, and none of us knows whether we shall ever again see our homes. On every side the door is closed and the only door open to us is the door of prayer to God."(54) Arthur had hoped for evangelistic opportunities, but here was a purely African initiative at work, showing that the African side of the church could bear witness without European assistance. The same had happened, in a different way, among African Christians who were steadfast under German brutality. Here we can only allude to the question: how far did the European missionaries encourage independent action by Africans, and devolve authority? The answer is, not much, probably, till after World War II.(55)

The impact of the war on the missions and converts, on Africans in general and on the East Africa Protectorate in particular, remains to be considered. The Kikuyu movement had made the KMV possible, and would bear still more fruit. But what was most significant about the KMV, and probably also the ZCC, was the feeling of guteithania among them; to have "done their bit" gave them a great feeling of pride and achievement. What would be done for them in return?

NOTES

1. Quoted by Wangoto, interview at Kirogo, Muranga District, 21 Feb. 1970.

2. Philp, New Day, 27-29; R. Macpherson, The Presbyterian Church in Kenya (Nairobi: Presbyterian Church of East Africa, 1970), 49-50.

3. S. Sehoza, A Year in Chains (London: UMCA, 1919) - a UMCA convert; I am grateful to Archbishop L. J. Beecher for lending his copies of the Proceedings of the C.M.S. 1914-1917; Frank Weston, The Black Slaves of Prussia (Zanzibar, 1917), 8-9, 17-18.

4. KNA, 43/915, "Outrages in Vanga District"; PRO, CAB 45/31, Drought to Joelson, 17 Nov. 1938.

5. H. Maynard Smith, Frank, Bishop of Zanzibar (London: SPCK, 1926), 186.

6. Ibid., 203-205.

7. Ibid., 191-192; Central Africa, 1917, 27-28.

8. Smith, Frank, 192-193.

9. Central Africa, 1917, 27.

10. Ibid., 28-32.

11. PRO, CAB 45/34, notes 22 July 1932.

12. PRO, CAB 45/30, Anderson to Col. Sec. Nairobi, 11 March 1938; Central Africa, 1917, 31-32.

13. Central Africa, 1917, 28-32.

14. Ibid., 28-32; Smith, Frank, 197.

15. Smith, Frank, 197; for censorship reasons, Weston could say little about this in Central Africa, 1917, 35-36.

16. Smith, Frank, 199-200.

17. WP, Weston to Watkins (private), 10 Oct. 1916.

18. Kikuyu News, 66 (Feb.-April 1918), 3.

19. NLC, 143-144 (Chadwick), 203-210 (Philp and Barlow).

20. EUL, Gen. 763 Box 2, Arthur Papers, 18 June 1916.

21. Kikuyu News, 52 (Nov.-Dec. 1914), 4-7; 53 (Jan.-Feb. 1915), 18-19; 61 (Oct.-Dec. 1916), article by Dr. Jones.

22. CMS Archives, G3 A5/0 1918, 12: Hooper to Manley (Gen. Sec. CMS), 25 Oct. 1917. For the rest of this chapter all dates are 1917 unless otherwise stated.

23. Kikuyu News, 63 (May to July), 4 April.

24. Ibid., J.W.A.'s letter, 21 May.

25. Interview at Kahuhia, 29 May 1970.

26. Inland Africa, 1, 9 (Sept.), 11-12; I am most grateful to Dr. J. Forbes Munro for copies of the extracts.

27. Arthur Papers, Diary 1 April-8 May; Kikuyu News, 63, Arthur's letter 21 May; Rhodes House Mss. Afr. 379-382, Ainsworth's Diary 16 May.

28. Arthur's letter 21 May, Diary 12 May, Ainsworth's Diary 16 May.

29. Kikuyu News, 64, Arthur's letter 17 June; Papers, Diary 26 June to 3 July.

30. Inland Africa, 2, 7 (July 1918), 12; Dr. A. T. Matson writes that Mazeras was found to be unhealthy in 1905, when the Headquarters of 1st KAR (Nyasa) Reserve Battalion was tentatively based there.

31. Kikuyu News, 64, Arthur's letter 17 June; Papers, Diary 26-27 May, and Kikuyu Mission Annual Report, 1918; Inland Africa, 2 7 (July 1918), 12.

32. Kikuyu News, 64, letter 15 July; Diary 25 June-9 July (all diary quotes are from EUL, Arthur Papers).

33. Letter, 17 June; Diary, 10-27 July.

34. Arthur Papers, Circ. Letter No. 2, Muhanga, 5 Sept.

35. PRO, CAB 45/30, Beazley to Director, 19 Oct. 1937.

36. Circ. Letter No. 2, 5 Sept; Diary, 1-28 Aug.

37. Notes kindly given by Dr. J. Forbes Munro.

38. Circ. Letter No. 2, 5 Sept., 4; Diary, 29 Aug.-1 Sept.

39. Circ. Letter No. 2, 6; diary, 13 Sept.-13 Oct.

40. Diary, 20-24 Aug. and 26 Oct.; Circ. Letter No. 2; Kikuyu News, 65 (Nov. 1917-Jan. 1918), letter 3 Nov.

41. Diary, 4 Sept., 7 Oct. and 18-27 Oct.

42.   Postscript to Diary: "The K.M.V.: Summaries."

43.   Inland Africa, 2, 8 (Aug. 1918), 13-15: "More about God's Presence with the Carrier Corps."

44.   Huxley, Red Strangers, 283-285.

45.   Kikuyu News, 65, letter 5 Oct.

46.   CMS G3 A5/0 1918, Hooper to Manley, 25 Oct.

47.   Arthur Papers, ms. letter 1 Jan. 1918; Diary 30 Nov.

48.   Huxley, Red Strangers, 240-241.

49.   Dairy 21 Nov. 1917-18 Jan. 1918.

50.   I am grateful to Dr. J. M. Lonsdale for telling me of this report, which is in the Milner Papers at Rhodes House; see also Arthur's Diary, 6 Oct. 1917.

51.   WP, Chadwick to Watkins, 30 June 1917.

52.   See Chapter 7 above, n. 111, Ainsworth's repatriation scheme.

53.   Ms, on "The Y.M.C.A. with Native Troops and Military Labourers in East Africa" (n.d.); I am grateful to Dr. K. J. King for kindly lending me his copy. Fendall mentions the YMCA: EAF, 173.

54.   "The Reflections of Bishop Willis 1872-1954" (typescript, RCSL), 90-91; I am grateful to Mr. D. H. Simpson for kindly showing me this document.

55.   M. Louise Pirouet, in JAH, 19, 1 (1978), 117-130, "East African Christians and World War I," thinks not much was done this way.

Chapter 11
After the War

"We started politics because of our land"
                (Kinyanjui wa Mukura, carrier, Kiambu)
"There were no political meetings, so far as I know,
till around the 1950s"
                (Kavai Longe, askari, Machakos)[1]

THE WAR AND PROTEST POLITICS

What had the war to do with political protest? The growth of
European pressures, and changes in African society, have been traced
up to 1914. Pre-war problems - labor, wages, medical conditions -
had all been greatly magnified under wartime conditions.

In 1928 R. W. Hemsted, by now a senior official, felt that the
war had taught Africans "the power of organisation," and that there
was some connection between this and the protest movements.[2] He
did not say that the war caused the protest movements or trained
their leaders. Although the men who went to the war experienced the
power of organisation and had many encounters with new ideas, it
was those at home who were in touch with political developments:
increased settler power, demands for more land, more labor and
Crown Colony status.[3]

The acid test is to see what the young men, educated in mission
schools, literate in Swahili and English, were doing during the war:
Jomo Kenyatta, Harry Thuku, James Beauttah, Josiah Njonjo and his
three colleagues as senior chiefs in Kiambu after the war, Koinange
wa Mbiyu, Philip Karanja, and Waruhiu wa Kungu. Joseph Kang'ethe,
president of the Kikuyu Central Association (KCA) for twenty years,
served as an NCO in the Gun Carrier Section. Philip Karanja was a
headman in charge of 500 carriers with the KMV; several other
Kikuyu leaders also served with that force.[4]

Jonathan Okwirri, as a superior headman at Mombasa Depot for
eighteen months had much better access to the news than most
carriers. After the war he became president of the Young Kavirondo
Association (YKA) and a senior chief. Despite the Nandi land
alienations, which had caused suspicion in Uyoma in 1912, he said,
they had not thought the European a bad man otherwise.
Maltreatment of labor on farms had worried them, but "when the
word began to go around that Kenya was to become a colony, those
of us who had some understanding, at least who could read and write,
[knew that] a colony means a settlement containing foreigners, [and

that] finally the land would fall into the foreigner's hands." Though politics were not discussed at the depot, Okwirri read the Standard, The Leader, the Jauti Luo and various Swahili papers, and foresaw that a Crown Colony would become a Dominion. "Even if the settlers had land in the Rift Valley, and we people in Uyoma still had our land, the land would not be held in our name; it would be held in the name of the Dominion....We didn't have anything particularly in mind, except that all we eventually wanted was that our country should remain our country." These views were given by a man whose lucidity of mind and physical vigor were remarkable for his eighty-six years.

Apart from Okwirri, Kang'ethe and Karatu, most leaders with war experience seem to have been with the KMV, serving only ten months in a very carefully run unit, and enjoying exceptionally good conditions. Most of the KMV came from the politically sensitive district of Kiambu, and included a high proportion of educated men. Two men who were friends and neighbors – Kinyanjui wa Mukura and Nathaniel Mahingu – were involved in politics because of fears for the safety of their land, not because of their war experiences; Kinyanjui saw bad times on the Rufiji as a regular carrier, and Mahingu was with the KMV.

A neighbor of Marius Karatu, Joseph Mundia, was conscripted in 1915, fell ill at Voi, and worked as a cook (his pre-war vocation), first in Indian messes, and later for junior officers near Kilimanjaro. "When I came back my brother was forced to go to the war instead of me. He never came back." Mundia was most definite that the first political leaders were the men who stayed at home, "because they could see how we were being treated....People did not start politics because of what they were being told by those who came from the war, but because of the things which were happening here; girls were being forced to work, and if your sheep or goat would be found by the road, it would be taken," no doubt by the tribal police. He thus rejected any direct link between politics and war service; he was a witness whom we met purely by chance, and gave these interesting views quite spontaneously. Though his war experience was less than that of others, Mundia typifies thousands of men who were much more concerned with developments at home.(5)

The political activities of Marius Karatu were not relevant to his war service either; he agreed with Mundia, Mahingu and Kinyanjui that, as the latter put it, "we started politics because of our land." Karatu did, however, have some discussion with Indians, and they gave him this advice: "When the war is over, Mzungu will take your land. What you will be given afterwards will be identity cards. You will also be mistreated, and some will be detained and taken into exile in some far islands, and perhaps they will never see their people again, like Napoleon and Gandhi."

The Leader would not allow Harry Thuku to go and fight; machine man and compositor, he alone knew "how to print maps and sketches of war positions." James Beauttah's request for war service was also turned down, because of his training as a telephonist. Jomo Kenyatta was in the Public Works Department.(6) Of the four future Kiambu senior chiefs, only Philip Karanja saw war service. Josiah Njonjo was first a compositor on The Leader, then clerk to the Assistant District Commissioner of Ngong, G. Orde-Browne, whom he accompanied on long safaris to the German border. The members of the group in the

Kinyanjui wa Makura and Nathaniel Mahingu
  The Author

Pangani suburb of Nairobi who started the East African Association, including Thuku, Abdullah Tairara, Job Muchuchu and Jesse Kariuki, seem not to had served in the war either.(7) In Nyanza, political colleagues of Jonathan Okwirri such as Simon Nyende and Joel Omino seem to have remained in civilian life.(8)

Men with enough education to be clerks either worked at home, like Raphael Osodo as chief's clerk in Bunyala, or Elijah Kaara, who served in the Carrier Corps first as a clerk at Nairobi Depot, then as a storeman in German East Africa. Literate Africans tended, in other words, to be in reserved occupations, remaining nearer to events at home. Nairobi was a better school for a future politician than Dodoma, Lindi, the Rufiji, or even Dar es Salaam. Men at the front or on the lines of communication must have been almost entirely isolated from events at home. But telegraphists, clerks and typesetters, men who could read vernacular and English newspapers, were well briefed about settler ambitions. Any of them could have discussed the War Council, labor demands or the Native Registration Ordinance, either with each other or with Indians or Europeans.

Harry Thuku says plainly: "I read many of the articles that the settlers wrote to The Leader (the paper was strongly in favour of the white settlers), and when I saw something there about the treatment of Africans, it entered into my head and lay quiet there until later on." He also began meeting Koinange wa Mbiyu in 1916, and the two held frequent discussions in Thuku's room in Pangani. "I saw he was quite fearless. He was very much opposed to what had happened with Kikuyu land," particularly his own.(9)

The war had increased settler power through the Committees of Supply, the War Council, and certain Ordinances and Commissions. The Native Followers Recruitment Ordinance of 1915 met their demands for compulsory labor, and the Native Registration Ordinance of 1916 introduced the kipande or identity token, though it was only enacted in 1919. Though the kipande became a major grievance, we have seen that it was vital in running the Carrier Corps.(10) The demand for Crown Colony status, which worried Okwirri, was voiced in The Leader, and was a principal objective of the Land Settlement and Economic Commissions, which began work in 1917 with settler majorities. The former recommended a scheme for European soldier settlement, demanding a labor force of 200,000 for Kiambu alone, which its District Commissioner, G.A.S. Northcote, opposed because the existing, and inadequate, labor force was only 20,000; he and Ainsworth were the only officials.(11) Ainsworth told the Economic Commission, as he had the Native Labour Commission, that the reserves should be inviolate and labor voluntary; carrier recruiting had taken all available men, and only 50 percent were really fit for hard work.(12)

Settler colours were nailed to the mast in the usual uninhibited fashion, especially in Grogan's notorious speech at the dinner of welcome given for Sir Edward Northey in February 1919. All this confirmed the worst fears of any African who could read the press, and also of many who could not. After the Northey dinner, Northcote noted the marked effects produced by the report of the Land Settlement Commission, which "formed a staple topic of conversation at European tables." (Perhaps, even at that early date, some servants knew more English than was good for them.) The Christians under

Koinange conferred with pagan headmen and met the Chief Native
Commissioner; the Kikuyu would certainly organise against any
attempt to reduce the reserves.(13)

Grogan had asked Northey if he was another "telephone girl"
between Nairobi and London. Northey showed that he was not. He
was prompt to bring in Crown Colony status, the kipande, and
compulsory labor for sixty days a year. The soldier settlement scheme
was also introduced, and the Indian community was told the European
interests were paramount. It is, however, fairly certain that much of
this would have happened whoever was governor. Dual administration,
also recommended before the war, was set up, giving Europeans their
own resident magistrates   Provincial Commissioners were now called
Senior Commissioners, and were under the Chief Native Commissioner.
Ainsworth was the first incumbent, but soon retired, in some distress
at the way things were going, and was succeeded by Watkins in an
acting capacity.(14)

The response to these changes was the great baraza at Dagoretti
on 24 June 1921, a significant date in African political history. A
joint memorandum was presented by the Kikuyu Association of chiefs
led by Kinyanjui wa Gatherimu, and by the Young Kikuyu Association,
led by Harry Thuku and formed expressly for the baraza. Their
complaints were summarised as follows:

> When we went to do war work we were told by His Excellency
> the Governor that we should be rewarded. But is our reward to
> have our tax raised and to have registration papers given us and
> for our ownership in land to be called into question; to be told
> today that we are to receive title deeds and tomorrow for it to
> appear that we are not to receive them?

The memorandum was translated by A. R. Barlow, who also
interpreted; Watkins was present as acting Chief Native
Commissioner.(15) Though respectfully stated, there were five
grievances. First, African servicemen had no gratuity, but Europeans
were granted land in Kiambu; there was a widespread
misunderstanding that they should have received gratutities as well as
balances on discharge, which has persisted into recent times.(16)
Secondly, there was the kipande. Thirdly, hut tax had gone up from
Rs.5 to Rs.10, as had poll tax. Fourthly, the rupee was replaced by
the shilling in 1920, "but many people tried to give Africans one
shilling for one rupee," which had been 1s.4d, but was raised to 2s.
Lastly, wages were cut by a third.(17)

Harry Thuku clothed the subconscious feelings of his followers
with articulate grievances, which is the basic achievement of leaders
of protest movements against colonial rule. This is clear from the
testimony of his followers. At Kahuhia they said: "Political activities
in our district were caused by the question of land alienation, and of
the kipande which was the reward we were given for our services:
was it the only reward they could give us after serving them in the
war? But land discontent started in Kiambu and then spread to the
rest of Kikuyuland." The echo from Dagoretti is very clear. Did
Thuku himself think of this very effective argument against the
kipande, or someone else? Even his revolutionary decision to send the
memorandum to Britain may have been suggested by his Indian
advisers, though Thuku himself rejected the idea.(18)

After Thuku's arrest and deportation, his followers formed the Kikuyu Central Association. "Even to this day we belong to KCA," said Nathaniel Mahingu. "Know this, things were started by Harry Thuku." In Nyeri Elijah Kaara had been a KCA organiser, and showed us a sheaf of papers which were about arrangements for the visit of Kenyatta to Britain; "the Europeans got land; all we got was the kipande."

Similar developments were taking place in Central Nyanza, were mission education was in advance of that in Kikuyuland. In 1921 the Young Kavirondo Association was founded by Jonathan Okwirri, Benjamin Owuor, Simon Nyende and others. The epithet "Young" came from the Young Buganda Association which together with the Ganda newspaper published in Kenya, Sekanyolya, was an inspiration to the Kenyan movements. The editor of Sekanyolya was Daudi Basudde, who was telegraphist at Maseno till he was succeeded by James Beauttah.(19) The YKA presented a memorandum to Northey in 1922, similar to the Kikuyu one. They protested against indiscriminate forced labor and the kipande. They demanded higher wages and title deeds, called "tiddly-dee" by men unsure of their meaning, but seeing them as an ultimate safeguard of their land. They also wanted taxes reduced, or abolished for women, and Protectorate status restored.(20)

The Nyanza movement was less militant than that in Kiambu, because there was no threat to the land. The YKA became the Kavirondo Taxpayers' Welfare Association, guided by Archdeacon Owen. Jonathan Okwirri explained the difference between YKA and Piny Owacho (sometimes thought of as an alternative name). Piny Owacho means "the people have said"; it was they who were demanding changes, and was thus "a sort of protection so that no single person could be made a scapegoat."

In both Kiambu and Central Nyanza the post-war protests can be traced to the growth of settler power before and during the war. The Young Kavirondo resolutions omit that invidious comparison between the treatment of African servicemen and European settlers which is the only direct link between the Dagoretti memorandum and the war. Literacy in English and Swahili, not war experience, was the passport to leadership. Politics in Kenya grew out of European pressures on African society, which had caused some response before the war, though undoubtedly the war increased them.

POST-WAR LIFE AND ATTITUDES

Africans were disinclined to work for the settlers. Wartime deaths, exhaustion, influenza and famine kept the labor supply down. The Kikuyu called the influenza kimiri. In Nyanza, the famine was called obando in the north, kanga in the south; obando means maize, which was supplied for relief, and was unfamiliar to many people whose staple diet was still matama. The askari kanga were the new uniformed tribal police who were then beginning to replace the less formal retainers; kanga also refers to their maroon jerseys. So the famine is remembered both for a new food crop, and for improved administrative methods.++ The famine was less acute in Ukambani, though Muumbi Mulei, medical orderly, said that many died of a

++ I am indebted to Aloysius Ongutu for kindly giving me these details.

disease called isuku brought back by servicemen. There was too much work to be done at home to make wage labor attractive, with neglected shambas to cultivate, and other heavy tasks undone for lack of manpower. Nguka Nyaoke said: "Conditions forced me to stay at home, and not to go to work for a European farmer or any other employer. My elder brother, who had remained at home, had died, so that only my father was in the house. I had to remain at home and keep him company. Later, however, I became an askari of my chief." Okech Atonga also stayed at home, though he worked for a year on the railway extension to Uganda. Otochi Onduko settled at home and tried to forget the war, in which thirty of his friends had died.

In Machakos District, men returned to the old life as far as they could; of the men who were interviewed, only Nzioki Wambua, KAR, said he had gone out to work, as a policeman. Kavai Longe, also KAR, said: "I became a teacher, and I taught for twenty years. I also had my business here. I did not work for any European apart from the Catholic missionary who employed me as a teacher....there were no political meetings, so far as I know, until around the 1950s." His neighbours Mwova Kataka and William Nthenge farmed; Mwova, a KMV, also did some preaching for the AIM. Mulei Nguyo described the purification rites on his return, with a feast of beer, thick porridge and a slaughtered ox; old customs and dances were what they had longed for. Muindi Kathuli, a syce, said that his father sacrificed a goat on his return, also for purification; he himself paid for an ox out of his wages and gave a feast.(21) Umoa Mbatha cultivated his shamba and herded cattle; he also resumed the traditional trade with the Kikuyu in gourds and arrows, in whose use and making the Kamba were acknowledged experts. Nguku Mulwa also went on farming "because there were no more raids from the Maasai. They had been beaten once and for all." Perhaps that was more significant than the Europeans' horrible war.

So there was little prospect of labor from Ukambani. Most of the returned carriers donned blankets again; Nguku Mulwa and his friends still favored them. Some kept their military shorts, which became a nuisance: "the return of khaki-clad carriers opened the door to the gravest malpractices," because the retainers of headmen and nzamas (tribal elders) tended to use service clothing as their sole badge of office. There had been bribery to avoid recruitment, and "the returned Carriers and KAR have lost a great deal of any respect which they held for the Elders, and their attitude to Europeans is frequently not what could be desired."(22) In Kitui, H. R. Montgomery said that repatriated carriers were reluctant to go out to work again after their experiences, though treatment had been as good as the hardships allowed. They had gone because they had to, without patriotic feelings, and "the fact that they had given no trouble should be placed to their credit." Now they were opposed to an attempt to get them to work on the railway, and from their point of view, "I can quite understand it."(23)

Montgomery was very sympathetic, but like some of his colleagues and even some missionaries, like Arthur and the Bishops of Mombasa and Uganda, thought that compulsion was perhaps inevitable under post-war circumstances: hence Northey's Labour Circular No. 1, issued over Ainsworth's reluctant name, and its equally reluctant acceptance by the Bishops and Arthur. "We believe that ideally all labour should be voluntary. We recognise that at present this is impossible" and that some pressure was needed to secure an adequate labor supply. Frank Weston absolutely opposed any compulsion whatsoever.(24)

Administrative officers praised the people as a whole for their acceptance of recruiting. In Ukamba, the Provincial Commissioner hoped "that the loyalty shown by the native population at a time of exceptional difficulty....will long be remembered in its favour." It was unfortunate that such dangerous and unattractive work gave so many men their first experience away from home, and he doubted whether much good would come of it.(25) In Nyanza, Ainsworth's aim to treat labor as an asset was to be developed with medical missions, industrial education, and a labor department to protect and distribute labor.(26) Nyanza was still the main labor source: in 1918 nearly 24,000 left the province to work, another 3,000 registering for work in Nyanza. The MLB, which closed down in April 1919, took 869, probably for depot work. Next year 38,700 went out, though the famine had made many unfit, which "cannot be cavilled at," commented the Provincial Commissioner, considering what the province had suffered from famine, influenza, and heavy mortality in the war.(27)

As well as standing up for their people, officers resented settler accusations that they were indifferent to labor needs. They had, after all, borne the brunt of the distasteful wartime recruiting. In 1917 the District Commissioner of Fort Hall had expressed their dilemma and that of the headmen with some heat. Since veiled compulsion had to be used, was every headman to be deposed for every act of petty tyranny? They would only be succeeded by others whose lethargy would lead to further attacks on government by "our scurrilous press."(28) A district officer who was too zealous in preventing labor abuses in a white district was likely to be sent to a less salubrious one; Norman Leys was transferred to Nyasaland because of his outspokenness as a government doctor.(29) Such things cannot have passed unnoticed by Africans.

So the only signs of political unrest after the war were in Central Nyanza, where protest was very moderate, and in Kiambu, where Northcote described the African attitude as insubordinate:

> The fundamental cause is the awakening of the native doubtless owing to what he learned during the war....The native expects the European to act as his master and superior, is puzzled and takes advantage when the European does not so act, but submits willingly when he does. In fact the former system of Bluff, founded upon the obvious difference between White and Black, has broken down and we must in future deal with the native on legal lines....In exactly the same way the Bluff of Headmanship in the native reserves has been called by the native.

Labor recruiting was already straining relations between chiefs and people when war broke out. Demands for carriers were fulfilled at an even greater cost in harmony, and government showed its sense of obligation by issuing medals to those who had been most conspicuous in supporting the war effort: Kinyanjui wa Gatherimu, Mumia, Wambugu wa Mathangani, Mwirigo wa Irimu and Ogada Ondiek were prominent on the list. The Provincial Commissioner for Kenia, H.R.

Tate, commented on the change of attitude in many young men after their war experiences affecting the administration and the tribal authorities.(30)

Of course Africans resented being torn from their homes to serve in a war which did not concern them. "This was not a fair war, because we fought without a cause and, worse still, we lost more men than the whites in our army," said Odandayo Agweli, one of this Nyala askari; the other, Asembo Odera, said that their chiefs should have refused to recruit: "It would have been better to let the white men fight themselves without the Africans because we were quite innocent. And what is more, the white man refused to let us have tribal war." But in Bunyala the main post-war concern, according to Raphael Osodo, was to get rid of Chief Kadimu, of the Wanga clan, who had been imposed on them.

Dr. Philp recalled the cheerfulness with which they accepted their lot, from the moment that they entered the wire cage at Karatina during the mass levy: how the fact of a solemn-faced youth "would suddenly light up, and with a yell of delight he would jump to join his comrades in the Carrier gang."(31)   In the field, as C. W. Hobley explains, they might learn much about themselves as compared with Europeans, especially if the latter were the shenzi Bwanas found among the new officers sent out to the new KAR battalions:

> They saw Europeans shot down and even bayoneted by enemy black soldiers, they realised that very few Europeans were crack shots, they noted the inferior marching capacity of the white man, his inability to find his way about the bush without a native guide, and in some cases they even saw that the courage of the white man was not greater than that of the black.(32)

When Mitole, a post near Kilwa, was attacked, an MLB captain and other whites narrowly escaped court martial for shirking their duty. "It is the duty of all white men, especially when serving with natives, to show the utmost gallantry and calm in face of danger."(33)

THE EUROPEAN REACTION

Bishop Willis recalled one day, in Nairobi, when a KAR battalion marched by, a colonel standing by him exclaimed: "I take off my hat to these men; they do not know what fear means; they have won the war for us in East Africa."(34)   Twenty years after the war Lord Cranworth, a prominent settler, wrote of the carriers: "It was not their quarrel, nor were they of fighting stock, yet they made overwhelming sacrifices in the common cause ... I have always thought that a more generous recognition of their immense services might have been forthcoming." No admirer of the Kikuyu, Cranworth thought that they had, nevertheless, suffered most in the war; they had been invaluable as carriers, and "raised little difficulty in coming to a strange country and undertaking work intensely distasteful and dangerous." Of the Nyanza carriers he wrote: "To many whose general recollection of the period will be one of mingled squalor, hunger weariness or fever, the invincible good

humour of the Kavirondo will remain as a bright spot."(35) These
lines are well known; they could apply to any carriers:

> Oh! the Lindi road was dusty
> And the Lindi road was long,
> But the chap w'at did the hardest graft,
> And the chap w'at did most wrong,
> Was the Kavirondo porter, with 'is Kavirondo song.
> It was "Porter, njo hapa!" (Come here!)
> It was "Omera, hya! Git!"
> And Omera didn't grumble,
> He simply did his bit.(36)

War memorials were set up in 1927 in Nairobi, Mombasa and Dar es
Salaam. Trubutes were published in the Mombasa Times to the
Intelligence Scouts, Arab Rifles, KAR and Carrier Corps. A typical
instance was of a Nyanza ammunition carrier, who held his load
steady with one hand up to the firing line, his other having been
shattered.(37) Everyone agreed that the campaign would have been
impossible without the wapagazi (carriers); other examples of their
bravery are worth adding. At Jasin a porter was rewarded for taking
a dead askari's place in the line; a Nyanza porter brought up
ammunition where it was most needed, coolly carrying a box on his
head where the bullets were thickest.(38)

Sir Philip Mitchell praises the African warrant officers who
"taught us our business, tactfully and sensibly, so that they were
respected and obeyed"; they were the superiors of war-time officers
like himself.(39) A KAR officer wrote of the porters that they took
the same risks as the fighting men, without the same power to
defend themselves, and toiled along patiently day after day, carrying
seldom less than sixty pounds. He concluded, like Watkins in his
advice to MLC officers, that Africans could be led anywhere, but
never driven.(40)

Many a soldier settler in Kenya must have learned this; the war
may have taught Africans and Europeans to be more tolerant of
each other. But despite this genuine admiration, settlers could still
press for compulsory labor, lower wages and the opening of the
reserves to settlement. The Europeans were unanimous that it was
unjust of the War Office and Treasury to withhold the unpaid
balances from payment into tribal funds; but would some of them
have been so decided if they, and not the Imperial Treasury, had
been asked to pay?

The sufferings of Africans in the war made it clear that their
welfare must be improved. The missions had been urging government
to do so before the war; so had many of its officers. In 1917 Dr.
Philp was appalled by the rejection rate among mass levy recruits;
he condemned as totally inadequate the provision of medical services
in reserves. Ainsworth and Watkins agreed with him on both counts;
a plea for widespread improvements was made in 1917 by the
Provincial Commissioner of Nyanza, but to Ainsworth's regret a
scheme for more effective government aid to medical mission work
was turned down in 1923.(41)

Officials in Nairobi and London had feared a movement towards
Islam or "Ethiopian" forms of Christianity among servicemen. But
nothing like John Chilembwe's uprising in Nyasaland occurred. In

addition to the protest movements led by mission-educated men,
there were rising numbers of converts in the Protestant churches by
1918; Arthur was greatly encouraged by the spiritual results of the
KMV experience. The membership of the Church of Scotland
increased from 742 in 1921 to 2,647 in 1926; Dr. Clive Irvine
considered this a time of great spiritual growth. For the CMS, Mr.
Njonjo thought that this movement towards the church was partly
due to disillusionment with government after the recruiting and
subsequent suffering of carriers.(42)

A celebrated Kenya institution which may be called an indirect
memorial to the Carrier Corps came about in this way. After
Thuku's arrest in 1922, the KCA began to oppose the education work
of the Alliance of Protestant Missions. The Alliance began to think
of improved schooling as a means of training future leaders. After
the Devonshire Declaration of 1923 had ruled that African interests
were paramount in Kenya the settlers advocated technical education.
But the Alliance were able to use the unspent balance of £5,600
from the War Relief Fund to start work on a medical college at
Kikuyu. A grant of £10,000 by a Nairobi businessman resulted in its
completion in 1926 as the Alliance High School, one of the most
famous schools in English-speaking Africa.(43)

Government was another source of improvement. As acting Chief
Native Commissioner, Watkins used his experience to improve labor
conditions. In his report he had written that any successful
undertaking proves its honesty by "its ability to profit by its errors
... Judged by this standard it may surely be contended that the
Military Labour Corps has no need to hide its head."(44) All this
expert knowledte was put to use with civil labor management;
paragraph 19 of the MLB Handbook was issued in the Official
Gazette, verbatim, as "Instructions for the Care of Labour by
Government Departments."(45)

Improvement was regrettably slow, as conditions on the Nyeri and
Uasin Gishu railway extensions showed; a death rate of 8.3 percent
would have been thought excessive in wartime.(46) These, and similar
medical and dietary problems, were discussed in the Kenya Medical
Journal, founded in 1924. The concern of the Ormsby Gore
Commission with labor conditions was noted; "they have left it
largely to us to work out our own salvation." A discussion on
African diet, was introduced by Dr. C. J. Wilson at a meeting of the
Kenya branch of the British Medical Association, attended by
Watkins; Wilson pointed out that Kenya was still fifteen years behind
Southern Africa in labor rationing.(47)

The military authorities accepted Watkins' verdict on the MLC.
Major-General G. J. Giffard, Inspector-General of the KAR and West
African Frontier Force, pointed out that in a future war large
numbers of military followers of all kinds would be needed. He
proposed quite simply to base any future MLC squarely on the
foundations described in the Watkins Report and the MLB Handbook:
pay, food, fingerprints, statistics, medical services. All that the
Carrier Corps staff had fought for was vindicated.(48)

In 1939 a new MLC and Pioneer Corps were formed on these lines;
the large number of recruits had the same rations and treatment as
white troops. James Beauttah encouraged men to join, and there was
no compulsion. Chief Njonjo and chiefs from Tanganyika and Uganda

went with Mr. S. H. Fazan to inspect African forces in the Middle East, and were well satisfied with what they saw; men could remit wages home, and the forces' mail system was good.(49) But the equality experienced in the war clashed with the color bar at home; the servicemen were more educated than their fathers, and were probably more discontented afterwards.(50)

The war drastically and painfully widened African experience of the world, but also taught pleasanter and more useful things. A Kenya farmer, in a West African market during World War II, spoke Swahili from force of habit, and was answered by an ex-carrier who had been with the Nigerian Brigade in East Africa.(51) Thousands of Africans learned about white civilisation before World War I, earning wages in Nairobi, Mombasa, Dar es Salaam or Salisbury. In Kenya, the political effects of European rule predate the Great War; the protests after it were primarily against settler ambitions.

NOTES

1. Notes kindly given by Fred Katule.

2. KNA, PC/CP1/1/2, "A Short History of the Kikuyu Province," 1928.

3. See above, Chapter 2.

4. Rosberg and Nottingham, Mau Mau, 27, 31-32.

5. Interview near Limuru, October 1969.

6. Thuku, Autobiography, 14-15; George Delf, Jomo Kenyatta (London, 1961), 35.

7. Interview with Josiah Njonjo, 12 Nov. 1970; Rosberg and Nottingham, Mau Mau, 25-26.

8. K. M. Okwaro-Kojwang', "Origins and Establishment of the Kavirondo Taxpayers' Welfare Association," 111-128, in B. G. McIntosh, (ed.) NGANO (Nairobi: EAPH, 1969).

9. Thuku, Autobiography, 14-16.

10. See above Chapter 4, "Political Undercurrents and the Impact of War" and Chapter 7, "Government, Settlers and Recruiting."

11. Leader, "The Crown Colonies," 7 Nov. 1916; Land Settlement Commission (Nairobi, 1919); Ainsworth's evidence, 10, and Northcote's, 11-12.

12. Economic Commission (Nairobi, 1919), 31-36, evidence of Ainsworth, attack on him, 19; PRO, CO 533/210.

13. W. McGregor Ross, Kenya from Within (London: Allen & Unwin, 1927), 19; EAS 15 Feb. 1919; KNA PC/CP4/2/2, Kiambu AR 1918-1919.

14. Cmd. 873 of 1920 for compulsory labor; CO 533/140/40352 for pre-war forebodings about dual administration.

15. Ross, Kenya, 224-227; Thuku, Autobiography, 18-22; Rosberg and Nottingham, Mau Mau, 36-44.

16. KNA, PC/CP4/1/1, Kenia AR 1917-1918, discontent at Nyeri over wages among returning carriers.

17. KNA, DC/FH6/1, "History of Fort Hall," 25; Rosberg and Nottingham, Mau Mau, 41-47; Ross, Kenya, 199-216 (currency) and 217-224 (wage cut).

18. Kenneth J. King, "Harry Thuku," 163-165 in Kenya Historical Biographies, K.J. King and Ahmed Salim, (Nairobi: EAPH, 1971).

19. Okwaro Kojwang', "KTWA" (NGANO), 120-122.

20. Ibid., 115-116; Mr. Fazan recalls requests for "tiddley dee" in 1921 (notes to author, June 1971).

21. Interview at Ithamboni, Machakos, 3 Oct. 1970 (Kathuli).

22. KNA, DC/MKS/1/1/10, Machakos AR 1918-1919.

23. KNA, DC/MKS/1/1/10, Machakos AR 1917-1918.

24. Cmd. 873 of 1920 gives Labour Circular No. 1 and the "Bishops' Memorandum"; Frank Weston, The Serfs of Great Britain (London, 1920), 12; Cmd. 1509 of 1920, cancelling the Circular.

25. KNA, PC/CP4/2/2, Ukamba AR 1917-1918.

26. KNA, PC/NZA/1/13, Nyanza AR 1917-1918.

27. KNA, PC/NZA/1/15, Nyanza AR 1919-1920.

28. KNA, PC/CP6/3/1, "Emigration from the Reserves 1917."

29. Ross, Kenya, 280, refers to three transfers including that of Leys: Norman Leys, Kenya (London: 4th ed., Cass, 1973), 152, mentions a district officer who shot himself after such a transfer.

30. KNA, PC/CP4/2/2, Kiambu AR 1918-1919; PRO, CO/533/179/23156, "Medals for Chiefs and Headmen," and Chapter 7 above, n.90; KNA, PC/CP4/1/1, Kenia AR 1917-1918.

31. Kikuyu News, 66 Feb.-April 1918), 8-10; see 146-147 above.

32. C. W. Hobley, Bantu Beliefs and Magic (London: Witherby, 2d. ed., 1938), 287.

33. WP, AAQMG Hanforce to Officer Commanding No. 1 Column, 14 June 1917.

34. "The Reflections of Bishop Willis 1872-1954" (typescript, RCSL), 159; I am most grateful to Mr. D. H. Simpson for showing me this document.

35. Lord Cranworth, Kenya Chronicles (London: Macmillan, 1939), 216-217; his Profit and Sport in East Africa (London: Macmillan, 1919), 75-76 (Kikuyu) and 46-47 (Nyanza); his views on Africans were much modified by the war.

36. F. H. Goldsmith, John Ainsworth (London: Macmillan, 1955), 96; there are interesting details of the psychological effects on members of different tribes in Clayton and Savage, Labour in Kenya, 88-89.

37. TNA, Secr. 23428, "Askari Statue Dar es Salaam" (RPA, War F/1/3 i).

38. East Africa, 7 April 1927, 884: "Msigire," "Old Days and War Days," 5, "Tales of the Wapagazi."

39. Mitchell, Afterthoughts, 46.

40. W. Lloyd Jones, K.A.R. (London: Arrowsmith, 1926), 147-151.

41. KNA, PC/CP4/1/1, Appendix 1 to Kenia AR 1917-1918, and PC/NZA/1/13, Nyanza AR 1917-1918; Economic Commission, Philp on 140-142; NLC, Philp on 17; EUL, Arthur Papers, Tate to Sec. Ch. of S. Kikuyu, 15 June 1917, and to Arthur, 8 Dec. 1922; letters Ainsworth to Arthur, especially 28 April 1923.

42. PRO, refs. CO 533, 1917-1918, especially 196/40812; on Ethiopianism, etc.; KNA, DC/KBU/1/12, Kiambu AR 1918-1919, meeting of CNC, Christians and pagans; Arthur's remarks in PC/CP4/2/2, Ukamba AR 1917-1918; Macpherson, Presbyterian Church in Kenya, 77; conversation with Mr. Njonjo and Dr. Irvine.

43. Cmd. 1922 of 1923, Indians in Kenya (Devon. Decl.); B. E. Kipkorir, "The Alliance High School and the Origins of the Kenya African Elite" (Ph.D. thesis, Cambridge, 1969), 142-156, by courtesy of the author.

44. WR. para. 131.

45. OG, 1921, 184-186; see Chapter 9 above, n. 64.

46. Ross, Kenya, 249-250; Hill, Permanent Way. I, 410-422.

47. KMJ, I, 10 (1925), editorial; II, 4 & 5 (1925).

48. PRO, CAB 45/29, "The Organisation of Labour in a Campaign in Tropical Africa."

49. Conversations with Messrs. Beauttah, Njonjo and Fazan.

50. KNA, DC/NN/6/1/1, "An African Soldier Speaks," by RSM Robert S. Kakembo, 7th KAR and Army Education Corps (Kampala, 1944).

51. Anecdote by Mr. Jack Best, Herefordshire, Feb. 1979.

Chapter 12
The Carrier Corps in Kenyan History

> "I think things happened the way they did because
> the world was still asleep. We Africans were still
> powerless and had to fight for the strong man,
> who we believed was fighting for wealth"
>   (Nguka Nyaoke, stretcher bearer)

An accepted aim of Imperial policy, should war come, was the conquest of German East Africa by Indian troops; but though they proved very costly in transport during the Uganda Mutiny, with fearful mortality among porters, the grim warning was ignored by the War Office. In 1914 there was no real organisation for such a campaign, whose advisability was doubted by many officers from Lord Kitchener downwards. Yet for political reasons it went ahead.

The Carrier Corps was started in 1914 by a few East Africa Protectorate and Uganda district officers, whose governments provided porters. But neither the governments nor the carrier officers had sufficient control over the porters, whose management was constantly interfered with by combatant officers. The General Staff showed little appreciation of the administrative problems, sympathy with the porters or understanding of the fact that African troops were superior to Indians or Europeans in bush warfare. From 1916, the MLB staff could hardly keep pace with the expanding military operations, burgeoning numbers of carriers or lengthening lines of communication. The quartermastering and medical services were as good as the hard-pressed staff could provide. Unsuitable food and the impossibility of cooking mealie meal properly on the march or in action caused very many to die of intestinal diseases; rice proved to be the final answer for all African personnel. The achievement of the MLB staff was a brilliant feat of improvisation, one of the greatest achievements of its kind, perhaps, in Imperial history. The War Office was mainly to blame for the mortality, and then refused to pay unclaimed balances to the tribes of missing men. But it finally accepted the whole structure of the MLC as a basis for military labor in a future war.

The post-war protest movements were due to settler pressure, not to the war. By 1914 the Kikuyu were already afraid for their land, and even in Nyanza the threat was sensed; in both areas a generation was emerging from the mission schools, literate in Swahili and English. They were able to understand the implications of settler demands for land, labor and Crown Colony status, which became more insistent as the war brought enhanced power to the settlers. The Kikuyu political leaders had mostly spent the war years in or near Nairobi, though some had served for less than a year with the KMV. Educated Africans usually worked as clerks, telegraphists, compositors or in other skilled occupations; any who were in the Carrier Corps for a long time were likely to be headmen, or clerks at depots, or hospital dressers.

Though the war was not a training ground for the new leaders, it taught men self-reliance, new techniques, and the fact that Africans were often physically superior to Europeans. Resentment was not really a cause of protest, but Africans learned to see that white power depended on chiefs, against whom the Kikuyu militants demonstrated quite as much as they did against Europeans. But in other districts servicemen generally returned to the old life: subsistence farming, trade, dancing.

Most Europeans felt a much greater concern for African welfare, being much better informed about diet, medical needs and housing. The recruiting had shown an alarmingly high rate of unfitness to work. Wartime experience was put to good use in the peacetime management of labor. Real admiration for African courage and endurance did not, however, prevent demands for more stringent labor policies. It is likely, however, that the war experience led to better conditions on farms, and better relationships.

The history of the Carrier Corps may be most important as a story. People were interested in sagas before history became an academic science; legend is still a source from which people have gained courage and counsel from the deeds of their ancestors, or from those of others. To the African people today, the achievement of the Carrier Corps were the achievements of their fathers, with all the sorrow, suffering and glory.

The wapagazi and askari showed great courage, but also much shrewd understanding of this fearful war, and why the Europeans fought each other. Old men talked by the hour of what they saw, where they went and what they did. Their reminiscences, together with written accounts, bring vivid pictures to mind: of reeking black mud and blinding red dust, of long columns of sweating, overloaded carriers, of sudden ambushes by the hidden enemy, of panicking porters dropping their loads and fleeing, of night assaults and the abandonment of half-cooked meals.

Also, one can see ammunition carriers or stretcher bearers trudging fatalistically up to and back from the firing line, indifferent to danger, or perhaps even courting death; "the whistling of the bullets could be heard in the air: 'Siuu! Siuu!'" recalled Nguku Mulwa. The story of the carriers is primarily for their descendants. Something of it is told here, with the assistance of survivors, most of whom have probably by now joined that great army of African soldiers and followers who went far from their homes, to a war which was no concern of theirs.

Appendix 1
East Africa and Uganda Protectorates: Military Labor Recruitment Statistics

Statistics for the four East Africa Protectorate provinces concerned are from provincial and district reports, the latter being preferred if differences arise. For instance, in Ukamba, district reports omit rejects and deserters, who are included in provincial totals. Where figures are lacking, calculations (c) have usually proved possible from the data given. In Nyanza (1914-1915) the provincial total of 21,925 for the Carrier Corps seems too high, when 6,000 also worked for the military within the province, and another 4,000 went to Turkana. In Machakos, figures in district reports are preferred to those given in political records for 1914-1920, which are used by Savage and Munro, JAH, VII, 2 (1966), 323, 338.

NYANZA	Central	North	South	Lumbwa	Nandi	Totals
1914-15	4,572	4,372	8,917	78	230	18,169
1915-16	8,888	7,459	6,822	719	296	24,184
1916-17	5,604	6,469	9,558	269	–	21,900
1917-18	8,922	10,036	8,758	68	–	27,784
Totals	27,986	28,336	34,055	1,134	526	92,037

KENIA	Nyeri	Fort Hall	Meru	Embu	Totals
1914-15	1,868c	296c	500	2,023c	4,687c
1915-16	2,774	2,021	2,904	2,542c	10,241c
1916-17	3,671	2,296	216	2,535c	8,718c
1917-18	5,980	4,098	3,854	5,304	19,236
Totals	14,293c	8,711c	7,474	12,404c	42,882c

Embu includes the Chuka sub-district; the returns for the province are incomplete, but can be improvised.

UKAMBA	Machakos	Kitui	Kiambu	Nairobi	Totals
1914-15	516	(- omitted	by PC	1917-1918)	516
1915-16	2,117	3,064	2,599	747	8,527
1916-17	3,900	3,885	2,359	832	10,976
1917-18	5,076	3,470	2,552	1,345	12,443
Totals	11,609	10,419	7,510	2,924	32,462
Rejects(DC)	-1,120	-2,436	(included	by PC)	-3,556
Final Totals	10,489	7,983	7,510	2,924	28,906

SEYIDIE	Mombasa	Taita	Vanga	Malindi	Nyika	Totals
1914-15	?	300	–	289	667c	1,256c
1915-16	952	exempt	264	639	433c	2,288c
1916-17	1,763	"	482	62c	1,163	3,470c
1917-18	2,175	2,648	473	251c	2,256	7,803c
Totals	4,890	2,948	1,219	1,241	4,519	14,817c

The grand total is about 179,000 carriers, mostly longer in service than the Uganda men, two thirds of whom were probably short-service porters for the Belgian advance.

There are no comparable statistics for Uganda; see pages 84-89 above; notes 61 and 73 give the sources for these statistics - also Watkins Report, Appendix 1, Tables 2 and 6 (b). See Table 3 (a) and (b) of this book, also JAH, 19, 1 (1978), 101-116, for manpower statistics.

	Carriers	Gun Carriers	Medical Staff	Totals	Deaths	%
EACC, 1914-15	3,576	?	?	3,576	854	23
UTC Carr. Sec.	38,944	114	993	40.051	1,701	4
"Carbels"	8,429	?	?	8,429	1,191	14.4
Others	1,000			1,000	?	
"Job" Porters	120,000	(for Belgians)		120,000	???	
MLB, 1917	10,947	449	540	11,936	1,315	10.7
Totals	182,896	563	1,533	184,992	???	

(Compare the East Africa Protectorate total of 178,642)

Appendix 2
Labor for the 1917 Campaign

Estimates of labor needed for the General Staff Plan (25 Feb. 1917) were as follows: (W.P., Secret File)

Memorandum A: first- and second-line transport

	Mouths	lbs. food daily	Porters
Iringa Force (3 battns.)	4,685	9,370	10,568
Rufiji Force (Nig. Brig.)	4,534	9,066	10,568
Kilwa Force (7 battns.)	16,851	33,702	13,236
Lindi Force (4½ battns.)	10,374	20,748	8,385
Reserve Column (4 battns.)			7,540
Maximum requirement of porters			50,297

To place 5,000 lbs. 100 miles needed 2,590 porters
        8,500 lbs.   "   "   "   4,420   "
        9,100 lbs.   "   "   "   4,732   "

Memorandum B: Subsidiary estimates

Iringa Force	3,244	(The Iringa Force had to transfer
Rufiji Force	2,500	744 men to General Northey; 9,300
Kilwa Force	1,800	were for lines of communication:
Lindi Force	2,500	posts, road corps, Kilwa Tramway)
	10,044	extra followers were needed

Memorandum C estimated that yet another 55,765 would be needed for first line, general labor with units and in the rear, totalling 116,106 followers; this was still not enough because of the commitment to supply the Belgians, the shortage of Portuguese East Africa recruits, the high reject rate in the East Africa Protectorate and Uganda, the increased allowance for a KAR battalion from 744 to 1,266 porters, and the extra demand for labor on roads, in ports, hospitals, docks and so on in the rear.

    The numbers actually raised were about 120,000, of whom 67,799 were from the East Africa Protectorate, 11,936 from Uganda, about 30,000 from German East Africa, 9,804 from West Africa, and 776 stevedores from Seychelles. It is not surprising that the 160,000 wanted by General Headquarters were not available.

Appendix 3
Unpaid Wages due to Missing Carriers

1. On 31 March 1922:

	Number of men	Amount owed
Kenya Colony	13,748	£ 66,788 18s 0d
Tanganyika Territory	27,535	£ 94,093 6s 4d
Mafia Island	24	£ 187 6s 6d
Zanzibar Protectorate	325	£ 1,273 16s 7d
Uganda Protectorate	780	£ 2,780 7s 3d
Totals	42,407	£165,123 14s 8d

Source: NAU/SMP 5317; War F/1/3.

2. On 30 October 1925:

		(to nearest £)
Kenya Colony	11,622	£ 52,599
Tanganyika Territory	26,733	£ 89,406
Mafia Island	24	£ 187
Zanzibar Protectorate	621	£ 7,350
Uganda Protectorate	855	£ 3,345
Totals	39,855	£152,887

This shows some progress in meeting claims in Kenya and Tanganyika, but an increase in the numbers unaccounted for in the other three. It all illustrates the much greater mortality suffered by the men of Kenya and Tanganyika; the fact that so many men from the latter were not traced does not bear out the suggestion in the Watkins Report, Appendix 1, Table 7, that many German East Africa deserters may have reached home.

3. On 31 August 1930

Kenya Colony	10,301	£ 49,234
Tanganyika Territory	27,422	£ 90,470
Mafia Island	24	£ 187
Zanzibar Protectorate	621	£ 7,350
Uganda Protectorate	855	£ 3,345
Totals	39,223	£150,586

Source for 2. and 3.: PRO, CO 822/34/26018.

Appendix 4
Examples of Improvements in Rations

31 December 1914   1¼ lb. flour (banana, mealie, wimbi or matama), or rice for rice eaters. ¼ lb. beans. ½ lb. meat, or 1 lb. beans if meat not available. "Arabs, Somali and Swahili Headmen to draw rations at scale for African Troops."

13 July 1915   2 oz. per week of tobacco or snuff "at the discretion of the Senior Carrier Corps Officer at each post." Also for UTC Carriers, 14 June 1916.

Train Rations   On 29 February 1916: 1 lb. dates, ½ lb. powa (parboiled rice). On 22 August 1917: ½ lb. tinned meat, ½ lb. biscuits instead of dates, ½ lb. biscuits instead of powa.

6 October 1916   Additional rations – 2 oz. potatoes, plantains, bananas or sweet potatoes, 2 oz. jaggery or goor (sugars), 2 oz. sim sim oil (or 2 green coconuts weekly).

24 January 1917   Seychelles contingent to have ¼ lb. bread or flour.

17 October 1917   All East African Troops, followers and porters to draw the following rations in future. 8oz. fresh meat, 10 oz. mealie meal, 10 oz. rice, 4 oz. beans, 2 oz. goor, 2 oz. ghee or cooking oil, ½ oz. salt, 6 oz. vegetables (potatoes, onions, sweet potatoes, mohogo or bananas). 1 piece soap per man, 2 oz. tobacco per man per week. 1 lb. dates twice weekly instead of 10 oz. rice and 4 oz. mealie meal. 2 coconuts weekly instead of oils at coast towns. Instead of fresh meat, 2 oz. beans, 1 oz. ghee and 2 oz. goor. In the field ½ lb. preserved meat (or 1 lb. dates or groundnuts) and 1 lb. biscuits to be substituted "if troops are unable to cook."

Sources: WR, Appendix 3, Table 1, and MLB Handbook.

Appendix 5
Causes of Death

A. Causes of death in the UTC Carrier Section, 1915 to 1916 - a force of 32,896 men.

1.	Dysentery and diarrhoea	338
2.	Cerebro-spinal meningitis	319
3.	Pneumonia and bronchitis	157
4.	Malaria	25
5.	Smallpox	11
6.	Killed in action	7
7.	All others	79
	Unknown	331
	Missing, presumed dead	290
	Total	1,557

Source: NAU/SMP 4290, statement no. 4; RPA, War F/1/2.

B. Causes of death between April and November 1917 inclusive, among porters from the East Africa Protectorate, Uganda and German East Africa.

		April	May	June	July	Aug.	Nov.
1.	Dysentery	500	590	1,315	1,170	940	400
2.	Pneumonia	170	255	415	270	255	220
3.	Malaria	75	115	390	280	210	140
4.	Cerebro-spinal meningitis	45	55	85	145	105	65

The death rate was highest when the Carrier Corps was at its greatest strength. the subsequent decline in mortality was probably due to improved administration, as numbers remained high - 110,000 in October and November, when operations were also exceptionally severe.

Source: WR, Appendix 1, Table 3, numbers in the field at various periods; Appendix 2, Graphs 3 and 4, which are only in the PRO copy, CO 533/216/4603.

Select Bibliography and Sources

DOCUMENTARY SOURCES

Official Records

Kenya National Archives

Seyidie Province 1914 to 1918.
16/49 1 and 2, Provincial and District Annual Reports; 37/577, "Porters for the Military," 1-6 (1914-1919) and A-E (district records for 1917) a unique source.
38/579-643, civil and military labor.
43/914-46/1074, files about the Carrier Corps and the military situation in Vanga, Nyika and Taita districts.
The district files are valuable, especially DC/TTA/1-3, with the DC's war diary.

Nyanza Province 1914 to 1918.
PC/NZA/1/10-13, Provincial Annual Reports, the main source for Carrier statistics, are impeccably kept. District reports and records are equally valuable.

Kenia Province 1914 to 1918.
The transfer of Kiambu to the new Kikuyu Province in 1920 has caused some overlapping with Ukamba Province.
PC/CP1/1-9 are political record books covering all Kenia and Ukamba districts except Nyeri, 1901-1926.
PC/CP4/1/1, Kenia Province Annual Reports, 1914-1921.
PC/CP4/2/1-2, Ukamba Province Annual Reports, 1906-1921.
DC/NYI/1/2, Nyeri District Annual Reports, 1913-1931.
DC/NYI/3/1 & 5, PC/CP2/1, Nyeri political records.
DC/FH4/3, political records 1912-1920, DC/FH6/1, History of Fort Hall 1888-1944, and PC/CP6/3/1, "Emigration from Reserves 1917."
DC/MRU/1/1, Meru District Annual Reports, 1912-1924.
DC/EBU/3/2, Embu District political records, 1917-1958.

DC/KBU/1/5-14, Kiambu District and Dagoretti Sub-District Annual Reports, 1913-1921; DC/KBU/3/3-13 & 25, political records.

Ukamba Province is under DC/MKS where not covered by the PC/CP series; DC/MKS/1/1-6, Provincial and District Annual Reports; DC/MKS/4/1-6, Machakos District political records, 1911-1920.

Central Government Library
"Report by Lieutenant-Colonel O. F. Watkins, C.B.E., D.S.O., Director of Military Labour to the B.E.A. Expeditionary Force, on the period from August 4th, 1914 to September 15th, 1919" - the Watkins Report, two copies of the typescript, the third being in the PRO, London.
Lieutenant-Colonel H.C.E. Barnes, Director of Military Audit, "Report on War Expenditure, British East Africa 1916-1917."

University of Nairobi, Department of History, Research Project Archives

Dr. Brian G. McIntosh collected copies of secretariat minute papers at Entebbe and Dar es Salaam, which are a vital source. War F/1/2 contains Entebbe papers, especially NAU/SMP 4290, "Uganda Transport Corps, medical and statistical matters," with other files on wages and unclaimed balances. War F/1/3 includes TNA, Secretariat W1/U 19351, "Unclaimed Wages (in respect of War Service) due to Natives," with a copy of Kenya Government Despatch No. 83, of 7 February 1931, giving the full history of the Porters' Claim. I am in fact indebted to the History Department for all materials from Entebbe and Dar es Salaam, and all quotations from these archives are acknowledged accordingly.

Public Record Office, London

The EAP and Kenya are covered by CO 533, vols. 140-216, which illustrate official attitudes in Nairobi and London to the war and to the Carrier Corps, especially vital because of the burning of the Nairobi Secretariat records in 1938. Vol. 216 contains the most complete copy of the Watkins Report, with full appendices and graphs; also the official government statistics on Followers in /7624. The original copy of Despatch No. 83, with minutes by Nairobi and Colonial Office officials, is in CO 822/34/26018.

Uganda. The story of the dispute over the mass levy of 1917 is in CO 586, vols. 85, 86 and 88; a copy of H. R. Wallis' Handbook of Uganda (2d ed.), with manpower statistics, is in vol. 90.

The King's African Rifles, being under Colonial Office control, are covered by series CO 534.

Cabinet Papers include the materials for the unpublished second volume of the Official History: CAB 44, 3-10, and CAB 45, 6-74: a vital source.

EAP Executive and Legislative Council, series CO 544.

Private and Non-Official Records

The Watkins Papers

These are the property of his daughter, Mrs. E.J.F. Knowles, and are destined for Rhodes House, Oxford. Their value for the Carrier Corps is inestimable.

Rhodes House, Oxford

The Ainsworth Papers (Mss. Afr. 379-382) include his diary written in 1917, while he was Military Commissioner for Labour.

Edinburgh University Library

GEN. Box 764 contains the J. W. Arthur Papers, covering the life and work of the Kikuyu Mission Volunteers.

The Royal Commonwealth Society Library, London

The H. B. Thomas Papers include the only copy of the Military Labour Bureau Handbook known to the author, and other valuable items bearing on the war, especially Standing Orders and Regulations for the Forces in British East Africa 1915.

"The Reflections of Bishop Willis 1872-1954."

Church Missionary Society, Library and Archives

G3 A5/0 1918 contains a letter from the Rev. H. D. Hooper to G. T. Manley, General Secretary, 25 October 1918, about the Kikuyu Mission Volunteers.

PUBLISHED SOURCES

Official

Printed in Nairobi

The Military Labour Bureau Handbook (2d ed. 1917); Standing Orders and Regulations for the Forces in British East Africa 1915.
Evidence and reports of the Native Labour Commission, 192-13, the Land Settlement Commission, 1919, and the Economic Commission, 1919.

Printed in London

The only Parliamentary papers which are relevant are those which went towards meeting the "Porters' Claim": Cmd. 4556 of 1934, Report of the Kenya Land Commission, and Cmd. 4580 of 1934, Kenya Land Commission: Summary of Conclusions reached by His Majesty's Government.

Periodicals

Newspapers and Magazines

Central Africa (UMCA, London).
The East African Standard.
Inland Africa (African Inland Mission).
Kikuyu News (Church of Scotland, Kikuyu).
The Leader of British East Africa.

Journal articles

Journal of African History
Hodges, G. W. T., "African Manpower Statistics for the British
    Forces in East Africa, 1914-1918," 19, 1 (1978).
Killingray, David, "Repercussions of World War 1 in the Gold Coast,"
    19, 1 (1978).
Ogot, Bethwell A., "British Administration in the Central Nyanza
    District of Kenya, 1900-60," 4, 2 (1963).
Page, Melvin E., "The War of thangata: Nyasaland and the East
    African Campaign, 1914-1918," 19, 1 (1978).
Pirouet, M. Louise, "East African Christians and World War I", 19, 1
    (1978).
Savage, Donald C., and J. Forbes Munro, "Carrier Corps Recruitment
    in the British East Africa Protectorate 1914-1918," 7, 2 (1966).
Tignor, Robert L., "The Maasai Warriors; pattern maintenance and
    violence in colonial Kenya," JAH, 13, 2 (1972).

Journal of Hygiene
Kauntze, W. H., "A Polyvalent Vaccine in the Treatment of Bacillary
    Dysentery in East Africa" (Pt. 1 of MD thesis), 18, 4 (1920).

Kenya Medical Journal
Kauntze, W. H., "A Polyvalent Vaccine in the Treatment of Bacillary
    Dysentery in East Africa" (Pt. 2 of MD thesis), 3, 12 (1926-7).
Wilson, C.J., introducing a discussion on "Native Diets" at a meeting
    of the Kenya Branch of the British Medical Association, 2, 5
    (1925).
--------. "Native Diets: a Lesson from Rhodesia," 2, 12 (1926).

Rhodes-Livingstone Journal
Shepperson, George, "The Military History of British Central Africa,"
    26 (1960).

Tanganyika Notes and Records
Taute, M., "Medical Treatment on the German Side," 8 (1939).

Unpublished Doctoral Theses

Cashmore, T. H. R., "Studies in District Administration in the East
    Africa Protectorate" (Ph.D. thesis, Cambridge, 1966).
Kipkorir, B. E., "The Alliance High School and the Origins of the
    Kenya African Elite" (Ph.D. thesis, Cambridge, 1969).

BOOKS

Armstrong, H. C., Grey Steel: J. C. Smuts, A Study in Arrogance (London: Barker-Methuen, 1937)

Austin, H. A., With MacDonald to Uganda (London: Edward Arnold, 1903).

Barra, G., 1,000 Kikuyu Proverbs (London: Macmillan, 2d ed., 1960).

Blixen, Karen, Out of Africa (London: Putnam, 1937).

Bovill, E. W., The Golden Trade of the Moors (London: Oxford University Press, 1968).

Brett Young, Francis, Marching on Tanga (London: Collins, 1917).

Buchanan, Angus, Three Years of War in East Africa (London: John Murray, 1920).

Bulpett, C. W. L., ed., John Boyes, King of the Wa-Kikuyu (London: Methuen, 1911).

Campbell, W. W., East Africa by Motor Lorry (London: John Murray, 1928).

Clayton, Anthony, and Donald C. Savage, Government and Labour in Kenya, 1895-1963 (London: Frank Cass, 1974).

Clifford, Hugh, The Gold Coast Regiment in the East African Campaign (London: John Murray, 1920).

Clyde, D. F., History of the Medical Services of Tanganyika (Dar es Salaam: Government Press, 1962).

Cook, Albert, Uganda Memories (Kampala: Uganda Society, 1945).

Cranworth, Lord, Kenya Chronicles (London: Macmillan, 1919).
----------. Profit and Sport in British East Africa (London: Macmillan, 1919).

Delf, George, Jomo Kenyatta (London: Victor Gollancz, 1961).

Dolbey, R. V., Sketches of the East African Campaign (London: John Murray, 1918).

Downes, W. D., With the Nigerians in German East Africa (London: Methuen, 1919).

Dundas, C., African Crossroads (London: Macmillan, 1955).

Fendall, C. P., The East African Force, 1915-1919 (London: H. F. & G. Witherby, 1921).

Ford, John, The Role of Trypanosomiasis in African Ecology (Oxford: Clarendon Press, 1971).

Gardner, Brian, German East: The Story of the First World War in East Africa (London: Cassell, 1963).

Goldsmith, F. H., John Ainsworth, Pioneer Kenya Administrator 1864-1946 (London: Macmillan, 1955).

Hancock, W. K., Smuts: The Sanguine Years, 1870-1919 (Cambridge: Cambridge University Press, 1962).

Harlow, V., E. M. Chilver, and A. Smith, ed., History of East Africa, vol. 2,(Oxford:Clarendon Press, 1965).

Hill, M. F., Permanent Way: The Story of the Kenya and Uganda Railway (Nairobi: East African Railways and Harbours, 2d ed., 1961).

----------. Permanent Way Volume II: The Story of the Tanganyika Railways (Nairobi: East Africa Railways and Harbours, 1957).

Hobley, C. W., Bantu Beliefs and Magic (London: H. F. & G. Witherby, 2d ed., 1938).

----------. Ethnology of the Akamba and Other East African Tribes (Cambridge: University Press, 1910).

----------. Kenya from Chartered Company to Crown Colony (London: Frank Cass, 2d ed., 1970).

Hordern, Charles, History of the Great War: Military Operations, East Africa, vol. 1 (London: His Majesty's Stationery Office, 1941), August 1914 to September 1916.

Howarth, Anthony, Kenyatta: A Photographic Biography (Nairobi: East African Publishing House, 1967).

Hoyt, Edwin P., Jr., The Germans Who Never Lost (London: Leslie Frewin, 1968).

Huxley, Elspeth, Red Strangers (London: Chatto and Windus, 1939).

----------. White Man's Country: Lord Delamere and the Making of Kenya (London: Chatto and Windus, 2d ed., 1968), vol. 2.

Iliffe, John, Tanganyika under German Rule 1905-1912 (London: Cambridge University Press, 1969).

Jones, W. Lloyd, K.A.R. (London: Arrowsmith, 1926).

Keane, G. J., and D. G. Tomblings, The African Native Medical Corps in the East African Campaign (London: Richard Clay & Sons, 1921).

Kenyatta, J., My People of Kikuyu (Nairobi: Oxford University Press, 1966).

King, K. J., and Ahmed Salim, eds., Kenya Historical Biographies (Nairobi: East African Publishing House, 1971).

Lawrence, T. E., Seven Pillars of Wisdom (London: Jonathan Cape, 1935).

Leys, Norman, Kenya (London: Frank Cass, 4th ed. 1973).

Lindblom, Gerhard, The Akamba (Uppsala: J. A. Lundell, 1920).

Lucas, Charles, The Empire at War, vol. 4 (London: Oxford University Press, 1924).

McIntosh, B. G., ed., NGANO (Nairobi: East African Publishing House, 1969).

Macpherson, R., The Presbyterian Church in Kenya (Nairobi: Presbyterian Church of East Africa, 1970).

Magnus, Philip, Kitchener: Portrait of an Imperialist (London: John Murray, 1958).

Matson, A. T., Nandi Resistance to British Rule 1890-1906, vol. 1 (Nairobi: East African Publishing House, 1972).

Meinertzhagen, R., Army Diary 1896-1926 (Edinburgh, Oliver and Boyd, 1960).

----------. Kenya Diary 1902-1906 (Edinburgh: Oliver and Boyd, 1957).

Miller, Charles, Battle for the Bundu (London: Macdonald and Jane's, 1974).

Mitchell, Philip, African Afterthoughts (London: Hutchinson, 1954).

Mosley, Leonard, Duel for Kilimanjaro (London: Weidenfeld and Nicholson, 1963).

Moyse-Bartlett, H., The King's African Rifles: A Study in the Military History of East and Central Africa, 1890-1945 (Aldershot: Gale and Polden, 1956).

Mungeam, G. H., British Rule in Kenya 1895-1912 (Oxford: Clarendon Press, 1966).

Murray, S. S., A Handbook of Nyasaland (Zomba: Government Printer, 1922).

Ogot, Bethwell A., ed., Hadith 3 (Nairobi: East African Publishing House, 1971).

Perham, Margery, Ten Africans (London: Faber and Faber, 1936).

Phillips, C. F., Uganda Volunteers and the War (Kampala: A. D. Cameron, 1917).

Philp, H. R. A., God and the African in Kenya (London: Marshall, Morgan and Scott, n.d.).

----------. A New Day in Kenya (London: World Dominion Press, 1936).

Reitz, D., Trekking On (London: Faber and Faber, 1933).

Rosberg, Carl G., and John Nottingham, The Myth of "Mau Mau": Nationalism in Kenya (Nairobi: East African Publishing House, 1966).

Roscoe, John, The Baganda (London: Macmillan, 1911).

Ross, W. McGregor, Kenya from Within: A Short Political History (London: George Allen and Unwin, 1927).

Routledge, W. and K., With a Prehistoric People: the Akikuyu of British East Africa (London: Edward Arnold, 1910).

Sandford, G. R., An Administrative and Political History of the Masai Reserve (London: Waterlow and Sons, 1919).

Sehoza, S., A Year in Chains (London: Universities' Mission to Central Africa, 1919).

Shepperson, George, and Thomas Price, Independent African: John Chilembwe and the Origins, Setting and Significance of the Nyasaland Native Rising 1915 (Edinburgh: Edinburgh University Press, 1958).

Smith, H. Maynard, Frank, Bishop of Zanzibar (London: Society for the Propagation of Christian Knowledge, 1926).

Thomas, H. B., The Nile Quest: Speke Centenary Celebrations 1962 (Kampala: East African Literature Bureau, 1962).

Thuku, Harry, with Kenneth King, An Autobiography (Nairobi: Oxford University Press, 1970).

von Lettow-Vorbeck, Paul, My Reminiscences of East Africa (London: Hurst and Blackett, 1920).

Were, Gideon S., A History of the Abaluyia of Western Kenya (Nairobi: East African Publishing House, 1967).

Weston, Frank, The Black Slaves of Prussia (Zanzibar: Universities' Mission to Central Africa, 1917).

----------. The Serfs of Great Britain (London: Universities' Mission to Central Africa, 1920).

Wilson, C. J., The Story of the East African Mounted Rifles (Nairobi: East African Standard, 1938).

Unpublished Typescript
Lonsdale, J. M., "A Political History of Western Kenya."

ORAL SOURCES

Nyanza Province

Central Nyanza District

Bunyala
Raphael Simigini Osodo, 75, chief's clerk, interview 4 July 1970, kindly interpreted by his grandson Felix Osodo (who also provided notes), with Fred Ojiambo.

Asembo Odera, 80, askari in 4 (Uganda) KAR, and Odandayo Mukhenye Agweli, 72, askari in 4 KAR, notes kindly given by Felix Osodo.

Uyoma
Jonathan Okwirri, 86, Senior Chief, superior headman in Carrier Corps, interviews 4 and 5 July 1970, kindly interpreted by his grandson Aloysius Ongutu.

South Nyanza District

Suna
Daniel Orenda, 93, carrier, and Nguka Nyaoke, 85, carrier and stretcher bearer, notes kindly given by Moses Oyugi.

Kisii
Otochi Onduko, age – grade Nyong'atita, carried machine gun ammunition, notes kindly given by John Makori.

Homa Bay
Yohanna Ojwang', 69, carrier; Lazaro Maende, 72, carrier; and William Adiang, 70, askari, notes kindly given by Vitalis Ojode.

Okech Atonga, 78, machine gun carrier, notes kindly given by Richard Siaga, 26 August 1970.

Kenia Province

Meru District

Nyambene Division, Akithii Location
M'Laibuni wa Baikwamba, 80, askari; M'Kon'gu wa M'Maitai, 85, NFD carrier, and M'Nkuraru wa M'Twamwari, age unknown, askari, notes kindly given by Zakayo Munene, 5, 6 and 12 Sept. 1969.

M'Inoti wa Tirikamu, 75, postal carrier on Kajiado-Longido road, and Muthanya wa Muiri, 75+, askari (both of Kaaria age-grade), notes kindly given by Gervase Mutua.

Nyeri District

Mihoti, South Tetu
Kamau Kagimbi, Njaramba age-grade, 1913, askari; and Elijah Kaara, Mbauni (Pound) or Mbia (Rats) age-grade, 1914, clerk at Nairobi Carrier Depot, later storeman, notes kindly given by Njagi Gakunju, who, with James Kuruga, kindly assisted at an interview on 7 November 1970.
Macharia Gacuca, 70, houseboy; Wanjira Gichuhi, 80, and Kang'au Mugambi, 90, the first two from Nyeri, notes kindly given by James Kuruga, on interview at Thomson's Falls.

Fort Hall (Muranga) District

Kabati Market
Interview with Gitombo Muri, cook; Ng'ethe Kamau, ox driver; Mwaura Nganga, askari, and Wabunya Kahindo, who escaped the levy - all of the Njaranga age-grade, kindly conducted by Njagi Gakunju and Dick Waweru, with Albert Muthee and Laurence Narains, 25 November 1970.

Maragwa
Interview on 21 February 1970, with James Beauttah, telegraphist and political leader, in English.

Kirogo
Interview on 21 February 1970 with wa Ngoto and Kihara Wahagi, both KMV, kindly conducted by James Gatune and Geoffrey Maina; Mrs. Gillian Hodges and Canon George Barnard attended both interviews.

Kahuhia Church
Interview on 29 May 1970 with five KMV men: Silas Kiige, Murigi age grade Canon Nathaniel Gachina, Kihiu Muiri age-grade, Ishmaeli, Makanga age-grade: Domenico, Murigi age-grade, and Samwel Ngoci, Njaramba age-grade, Dick Waweru and James Kuruga kindly conducted the interview and translated the tape. Canon Barnard Christopher Hayman (author's cousin) were present.

Ukamba Province

Kiambu District - Kabete/Dagoretti area

Interviews with Marius Ng'ang'a Karatu, 35, hospital dresser; Kinyanjui wa Mukura, 84, Nyarigi age-grade, carrier, and Nathaniel Mahingu, about 85, KMV, kindly conducted by Peter Kinyanjui, son of K. wa Mukura; the tapes were translated by Ngureh Mwaniki and Njagi Gakunju who, with Danson Mukuria Kimani and Geoffrey Maina, were also good enough to conduct further talks with Kinyanjui and Marius Karatu on 8 November 1969. Mrs. Hodges was at the first interviews in June 1969.

Other interviews on 8 November 1969, also kindly conducted by Ngureh, Njagi, Danson and Geoffrey, were with Joseph Mundia, Mbauni age-grade, cook; and Leah Nyamuiru Karuga, Ndungu age-grade, Ngureh's grandmother.

Interview on 10 May 1970 at Ngecha with Kinuthia,Kamande age-grade, Gachuguma wa Kanyoko, Kanyutu age-grade, Kaniaru, Kihiu Muiri age-grade, (Mbauni); and Kang'ethe wa Nyaruchi, all KMV: also an askari, Kihu Muiri age-grade, name omitted; it was kindly conducted and translated by Luciano Njonjo and Njagi Gakunju.

Interview at Gibichiku Farm, Kabete, 12 November 1970, with Josiah Njonjo, District Commissioner's clerk, later Senior Chief, in English.

Notes on Josphat Muranga Njoroge, KMV, kindly given by Danson Kimani; notes on Ngugi, machine gun porter, kindly given by Laurence Gitao. Both were of the Kihiu Muiri age-grade.

Machakos District

Muthetheni

Interviews on 14 June 1969 with Umoa Mbatha, about 85, carrier headman; Muasya Maitha, 90, ammunition carrier; and Nguku Mulwa, 85, syce and mule driver, kindly conducted by Raphael Thyaka, who also gave notes on Nzioki Wambua, 80, askari; Mrs. Hodges attended the interviews. The tapes were kindly translated by Ezekiel Musau and Philip Mwalali.

Kiu

Interview with William Kwinga Nthenge, 85, stretcher bearer, and Mwova Kataka, 85, KMV, in December 1969, kindly conducted by Fred Katule and John Mang'oka; Canon Barnard was present. Fred also kindly gave notes on the two, also on Kimumo Kitui, 81, stretcher bearer, later askari, and Kavai Longe, 75, askari.

Kilungu

Interviews with Mulovi Kivandi, 86, excused service; Musembi Kiindu, 80, machine gun ammunition carrier; and Muindi Kathuli, 80, carrier and mule driver, on 3 October 1970, kindly conducted by Ezekiel Musau, grandson of Mulovi; having also given notes on his great uncle, Mbwika Kivandi, 83, askari.

Kiteta

Mulei Nguyo, 85, askari and storekeeper; Mutiso Kanzivei, 90, carrier; and Muindi Ngaui, 86, carrier headman, notes kindly given by Philip Mwalali, who also helped with the Kilungu interviews.

Mukaa

Muumbi Mulei, 81, messenger and mobile clinic orderly; Silvano Mutiso Mwoloi, 75, medical orderly; and Nduma Muti, 79, carrier headman, noted kindly given by John Mang'oka.

Dr. J. Forbes Munro kindly gave me notes on interviews with the following: at Iveti, Josepth Muinde (askari)and Makau Nzibu (carrier); in Kilungu, Moses Kyele (carrier); at Kangundu, Josiah Munyaka Kivangule (KMV), retired AIM pastor; and at Machakos, Joseph Munyao (clerk).

Seyidie Province

Nyika District

Kaloleni, Giriama

Interview on 26 January 1970 with Mwanyula Bikatana, over 90, ammunition carrier with the German forces, kindly conducted by Matthias Mwagonah and Christopher Katana (his great-nephew); Simeon Mkalla and Crispin Yongo kindly translated the tape.

Note: A better method of interviewing proved to be having a running translation made by the interpreter; thus no subsequent translation was needed, and closer attention could be paid to the evidence as it was given. The author repeats his gratitude to all who helped with this oral work, as witnesses, companions or translators; their contribution to the book has been of enormous value.

Glossary

Unless otherwise stated, the words are in Swahili.

askari	soldier, policeman or other uniformed African.
bakhsheesh	(originally Persian) gratuity, tip, bribe.
banda	hut.
baraza	meeting, for discussion or to hear orders.
bijanjalo	(Luganda) a kind of bean; see maharagwe.
boma	cattle pen, fort, administrative headquarters.
bwana	master, hence white man.
chumvi	salt.
desturi	custom, habit.
duka	shop, store.
ghee	Indian clarified butter.
goor, jaggery	Indian sugars.
groundnut	peanut.
isuku	(Kamba), a sickness, probably dysentery.
jembe	large, heavy hoe.
jumbe	chief, headman.
Kabaka	King of Buganda
kanga	(Luo) tribal policeman, the maroon colour of his jersey.
Katikiro	Prime Minister of Buganda.
kiboko	hippopotamus, or a whip made from its hide.
kipande	"piece" of anything, hence identity token.
lakh	100,000 rupees (Indian).

Lukiko	Parliament of Buganda.
magari	a woollen shirt issued to carrier headmen.
maharagwe	a bean blamed for diarrhoea; see bijanjalo.
mahindi	Indian corn, maize, mealie meal.
maji	water.
matama	sorghum millet.
matoke	(Luganda) cooking banana, plantain.
mhinde	the most suitable bean for carrier rations.
mnyapara	headman.
mohogo	cassava root, commonly grown as a famine crop.
moran	warrior among Maasai and related tribes.
mpagazi	pl. wapagazi, porter, carrier.
mpokya	another kind of bean, suitable for rations.
mwanake	pl. anake, Kamba young man of warrier age.
mzee	pl. wazee, old man, elder, old person.
mzungu	pl. wazungu, Europeans, white people.
ndege	bird, airplane.
ngombe	pl. wangombe, ox, cow, cattle, oxen.
nyama	wild animal, hence meat.
nzama	Kamba council.
obando, bando	(Luo), maize.
panga	bush knife, like the matchet of West Africa, or the machete of Central America.
posho	food, rations, hence (wrongly) mealie meal.
powa	parboiled rice.
risasi	bullet.
safari	trading or hunting expedition, hence journey.
shamba	cultivated land, garden, small farm.
shauri	an affair, hence problem, lawsuit, quarrel.
shenzi	untidy, uncivilised, used of a mongrel dog, hence generally used as a derogatory epithet.
sim sim	(Indian) sesame oil.
syce	(Indian) groom, hence mule driver.
tengatenga	(Nyasaland) porter, carrier.
ugali	porridge, of mealie meal, wimbi or matama.
uji	thin porridge or gruel.
wimbi	bulrush or finger millet.

Index

ABOUT THE AUTHOR

GEOFFREY HODGES is Assistant Master at John Beddoes School, Presteigne, Wales. He read History at Cambridge University and taught in Zambia and Kenya. He has written for the *Journal of African History*.